Pragmatic Conservatism

Robert J. Lacey

Pragmatic Conservatism

Edmund Burke and His American Heirs

Robert J. Lacey
Iona College
New Rochelle, New York, USA

ISBN 978-1-349-94903-8 (hardcover)   ISBN 978-1-137-59295-8 (eBook)
ISBN 978-1-349-95824-5 (softcover)
DOI 10.1057/978-1-137-59295-8

Library of Congress Control Number: 2016947815

Cover illustration: © Юлия Давиденко / Alamy Stock Photo

Printed on acid-free paper

This Palgrave Macmillan imprint is published by Springer Nature
The registered company is Nature America Inc. New York

For Abraham

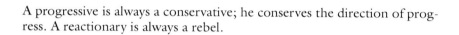

A progressive is always a conservative; he conserves the direction of progress. A reactionary is always a rebel.

—G. K. Chesterton, 1909

Acknowledgments

The idea for this book did not fully come together until I was given the opportunity to co-teach the Sophomore Honors Humanities Seminar at Iona College in the spring of 2012. My colleague Aaron Rosenfeld, from whom I have learned a great deal over the last few years, suggested that I lecture on Edmund Burke. After I took his advice, what started out as an exegesis of the political writings of Peter Viereck grew into something a bit more ambitious. The fruitful discussions in our seminar inspired me to broaden the scope of my project into a study of an underappreciated and misunderstood tradition in conservative political thought. I owe a debt of gratitude to Aaron and the fantastic students we have had the privilege to teach.

I thank my former research assistant, Kate Roberts, who exhibited remarkable attention to detail and organizational skills. I especially appreciate her willingness to spend hours sifting through primary documents at the Rare Book and Manuscript Library at Columbia University. Her efforts proved invaluable to me.

I am grateful to the many people who read parts of the manuscript and offered encouraging words and constructive criticism. The following people deserve special mention: Marcus Aldredge, Carl Bogus, Marc Carbonneau, Gregory Collins, Mary Hagerty, Melody Herr, Jonathan Keller, Josh Klein, Cathy Lavery, David Leitch, Josh Leon, Daniel Lorge, Drew Maciag, Jerome Mileur, Seán Molloy, Claes Ryn, Lisa Szefel, Ralph Whitehead, and Alan Wolfe.

I reserve my deepest gratitude for Rebecca Root, my wife, without whom I could never have written this book. She read every word of the manuscript and gave both incisive editorial comments and moral support; and on the countless occasions when I disappeared to work in my office or at the library, she took loving care of our son, Abraham, to whom this book is dedicated. Now it is my turn to help Rebecca, a scholar of human rights in Latin America, as she works on her next book.

Finally, I would like to thank the journals *Kritike* and *Anamnesis* for permitting me to reproduce significant portions of articles that they graciously published on their websites. A shorter version of Chap. 6 was originally entitled "Leaving the Stag Hunt: The Conservative Denial of Collective Action Problems" (*Kritike* 5:2). In a somewhat different form, Chap. 5 appeared previously as "'Reverence for the Archetype': The Pragmatic Conservatism of Peter Viereck."

CONTENTS

CHAPTER 1

Introduction

Interest in conservative political thought in the United States has increased dramatically in recent years, yet scholars have not come any closer to reaching a consensus on the subject. This should come as no surprise because the conservative tradition consists of many roots and branches, not all of them fully explored. Several critics have argued that the conservative movement today has betrayed its more mature and responsible ancestry by advocating radical change and ambitious enterprises in the name of supposedly ancient principles.[1] According to this view, movement conservatives strive for reactionary ends by radical means, a return to a mythic past using a scorched earth policy. But these critics fail to provide a full understanding of this more mature and responsible conservative tradition. Other than locating it in the ideas of such luminaries as St. Augustine or Edmund Burke, they have very little to say about the philosophical ideas embodied in this tradition or the thinkers who have made vital contributions to its development.

This book is a study of a lost tradition in modern American political thought that demands recovery. I call it pragmatic conservatism. Its origins can be found in the political thought of Edmund Burke, the eighteenth-century British parliamentarian and man of letters who is widely considered the father of conservatism. While conservatives of many stripes claim to be descendants of Burke, only a select few can rightfully say that they are his legitimate heirs. This is particularly true in the United States, where conservatism has struck an especially radical tone. The false (or illegitimate) descendants of Burke base their lineage on flagrant

© The Author(s) 2016
R.J. Lacey, *Pragmatic Conservatism,*
DOI 10.1057/978-1-137-59295-8_1

misinterpretations of—or sheer ignorance about—his ideas. This book aims to set the record straight by presenting a comprehensive exegesis of Burke's political thought and then showing how three twentieth-century American thinkers who are not generally recognized as conservatives—Walter Lippmann, Reinhold Niebuhr, and Peter Viereck—have carried on the Burkean tradition and adapted it to the modern age.

Based on their observations and reading of history, pragmatic conservatives believe in the sinful nature of human beings and, as a result, uphold time-honored and -tested traditions that have proven effective at restraining our darkest impulses. At the same time, they welcome incremental reform, departing from the way things have been done if the evidence suggests it is necessary. Mindful that no one can know anything for certain, pragmatic conservatives caution against making absolute truth claims, especially those on which either bold social plans are built or apologies for the status quo are made. Instead, they heed the provisional truths constructed by their forebears in response to concrete problems and then embodied in the form of tradition, but only so long as they also stand the test of contemporary experience. They rest their final hopes in political, intellectual, and cultural elites, who have the immense responsibility of making sure that this fragile edifice of wayward human beings, flexible traditions, and provisional truths does not collapse into a heap of chaos and relativism.

In the spirit of Edmund Burke, pragmatic conservatives seek a middle way between the extremes that we face in the modern world, a synthesis of seemingly irreconcilable opposites, including relativism and absolutism, individualism and collectivism, atomistic diversity and organic unity, freedom and order, revolution and the status quo, and rule of the many (democracy) and rule of the few (authoritarianism). Their conservatism is not an ideology or a creed but a philosophical temperament informed by a deep appreciation for the virtues of balance and proportion and a penchant for moderation, deliberation, and gradual change. In their search for a middle way in our dynamic age, pragmatic conservatives always prefer to rely on observed experiences and facts rather than abstract theories and assertions of absolute truth. They hope to devise practical solutions to modern problems by drawing on the available empirical evidence but without abandoning all principles in the name of expediency.

Knowing that politics is an inherently tragic arena, pragmatic conservatives acknowledge the difficult trade-offs involved whenever a decision must be made. What sounds great in theory may be disastrous in practice, and what produces satisfactory results on the whole may undermine those values that give life meaning. The final hope of pragmatic conservatives is to strike a delicate balance, a less than ideal compromise, in a world that defies perfect solutions. For this reason, they eschew simple formulas. The ideas commonly associated with conservatism today—small government, low taxes, absolute property rights, unabashed militarism, and so on—make little sense to them, for they know that these ideas often do not agree with the realities of our complex and ever-changing world.

PRAGMATIC CONSERVATISM: A BURKEAN INHERITANCE

Pragmatic conservatism rests on several core ideas inherited from Edmund Burke. With varying degrees of emphasis, pragmatic conservatives share similar beliefs about human nature, tradition, change, truth, and elites. What follows is a more detailed discussion of these core ideas and how they come together to form a coherent and nuanced political philosophy.

According to pragmatic conservatives, human beings are sinful creatures by nature, prone to selfish and aggressive behavior if left to their own devices, and there is little hope that people can transcend their given nature, no matter how much effort societies devote to educating and rehabilitating them. "History consists, for the greater part, of the miseries brought upon the world by pride, ambition, avarice, revenge, lust, sedition, hypocrisy, ungoverned zeal, and all the train of disorderly appetites," said Burke, and these "vices" are "permanent."[2] So, rather than trying to transform people, societies must focus on curbing and channeling their more destructive tendencies.

The best way to counteract or restrain these impulses, say pragmatic conservatives, is to foster a reverence for tradition, which embodies the collective experience and wisdom of our ancestors. "Tradition may be defined as an extension of the franchise. Tradition means giving a vote to the most obscure of all classes, our ancestors. It is the democracy of the dead," said G. K. Chesterton, the English writer who greatly admired Burke. "Democracy tells us not to neglect a good man's opinion, even if he is our groom; tradition asks us not to neglect a good man's opinion, even if he is our father."[3] While it does not discount the opinions and experiences of the living, tradition demands special deference toward our ancestors, whose best practices have worked quite well for many generations, and thus have stood the test of time. One can think of tradition as a collective habit, ways of acting that become so engrained in people that they adhere to them automatically, ritualistically. Serving as a corrective to our natural instincts, this ritualized behavior promotes social stability and predictability.

Revering and obeying tradition does not mean that people should stop thinking altogether. Following custom is not the same as acting slavishly, and it is never advisable to view the past through rose-colored glasses. If a time-tested way of doing things ceases to fulfill its intended purpose and begins to produce undesired outcomes, we must be willing to modify tradition. By temperament, pragmatic conservatives are reformers who recognize the inevitability of change, which they are willing to instigate themselves when the evidence suggests it is necessary. They recognize that the preservation of those traditions that still serve us well—indeed, the preservation of society as a whole—requires flexibility, a willingness to evolve and reform. As Burke put it, "A state without the means of some change is without the means of its conservation. Without such means it might even risque the loss of that part of the constitution which it wished the most religiously to preserve."[4] But pragmatic conservatives insist that we proceed cautiously and incrementally, minimizing the disruption to any other traditions, lest our impetuous attempts to make improvements undermine social stability. Forever mindful that the best intentions can still produce the worst outcomes, they welcome evolution, but never revolution.

We can never be sure of what might happen as a result of our reform efforts, according to pragmatic conservatives, because we can never see the truth clearly. They recognize the fallibility of human knowledge and reason and, as a result, consider all truth claims provisional. Absolute truth *does* exist independently of human experience, in their view, but it remains elusive and inaccessible to us, just beyond the grasp of our understanding. If we catch a glimpse of it, we do so indirectly through the prism of our concrete experiences. Thus it is wise to start from the premise of epistemological humility: we can never know anything for sure. But despite the doubt that hangs over us, we still have the capacity to arrive at tentative truths inductively. On the basis of empirical observations made in the past and present—"on the basis of sure experience"—we can make general truth claims.[5]

Over time, we reify, or make concrete, those truth claims in the form of laws, traditions, and customs, which we must be prepared to modify as new and relevant information becomes available. It is important to stress that, for pragmatic conservatives, the pool of experiences from which we can draw is not limited to the present day. In fact, the experiences of our ancestors matter just as much as those of our contemporaries—perhaps more so because they managed to fashion time-tested truths out of what they endured. Truth, then, is not an immutable product of abstract reasoning or logic, nor is it the preserve of a venerable sage or a vocal multitude. It emerges from the lessons of the past, grows out of the patterns of history. From our ancestors, we inherit traditions and habits that, when reconciled with contemporary experiences, usually serve humanity well. Burke said: "The individual is foolish; the multitude, for the moment, is foolish, when they act without deliberation; but the species is wise, and when time is given to it, as a species, it almost always acts right."[6] In other words, the acquisition of wisdom in this world requires an ongoing dialogue not only with each other but also with our ancestors.

Because it is based on the dynamic world of concrete experience, the epistemology of pragmatic conservatives appears to open the door to relativism and historicism. But, as it happens, they never question the existence of universal truths—truths that remain the same no matter the time or place. They merely insist that such truths cannot be easily deduced through the use of logic or reason and, instead, must be derived painstakingly from a wide range of observed and documented experiences. We arrive at the universal by searching for patterns in the particulars. According to Burke, "the laws of morality are the same every where" but can only be arrived at by examining the "substance" of empirical reality.[7]

Despite their universalism, pragmatic conservatives understand that their epistemological modesty can easily degenerate into crass relativism (or nihilism), producing a crisis of authority in which it becomes increasingly difficult to discriminate between truth and falsehood, fact and fiction, right and wrong. For this reason, they champion elitism as a bulwark against the erosion of belief in truth. Indeed, they defend political, social, and intellectual hierarchies because they do not believe that everyone has an equal amount of knowledge and wisdom or that the average person can go through life without guidance from his betters. But it is crucial to note that their elitism stems neither from a desire to protect the privileges of the rich and powerful at the expense of the poor and downtrodden nor from a shallow contentment with the status quo. They believe that elites, who ideally are among the best and the brightest, have an obligation to serve as trustees of the people and to safeguard those traditions—or reified truths— on which social harmony depends. When accused of adhering to the desires of the nobility and the rich, Burke reminded his peers in Parliament that his defense of a natural aristocracy did not belie the fact that he would always take his "fate with the poor, and low, and feeble."[8] Ultimately, elites must have a strong sense of *noblesse oblige* and harness their privilege and talents for the good of others.

Although pragmatic conservatives believe in serving their fellow human beings, their tragic view of the human condition tempers their ambitions. The law of unintended consequences makes them wary of any enterprise designed to improve people's lives. When such an undertaking actually produces satisfactory results, pragmatic conservatives must still accept the fact that there are no panaceas to the many problems that humanity faces and that even the most Herculean efforts can never do more than mitigate the suffering that so many people must endure. That said, pragmatic conservatives never succumb to hopelessness. They refuse to shrink from their duty and use their tragic sensibility as an excuse to do nothing when action is needed. They know that doing nothing is just another form of action that can have its own unintended consequences.

Because there is no escaping the fact that we must act, the pragmatic conservative rejects the libertarian view that government should always err on the side of inaction and remain limited in size and scope. It has become conventional wisdom that the conservative prefers small government and only makes an exception to this rule in those matters related to national defense and military preparedness. But pragmatic conservatives consider it unwise to make any absolutist claims about the role and form of government because such assertions are based on abstract theories that may not agree with empirical reality. Burke said, "I reprobate no form of government merely upon abstract principles."[9] As it happens, people construct governments in response to concrete problems which arise in a certain time and place. A political structure that did a fine job of solving problems in the nineteenth century may prove disastrous today. Understanding that context matters, pragmatic conservatives cannot embrace any theoretical blueprints detailing the structure and functions of government. In their view, the best government does not conform to a particular theoretical model but rather delivers what people need. As Burke put it, "Government is a contrivance of human wisdom to provide for human *wants*."[10]

Pragmatic conservatives also see liberty as a contextual matter. In their view, the meaning of liberty depends on the circumstances in which people find themselves. But conservatives today ignore context and tend to favor a negative conception of liberty which John Stuart Mill made famous. According to Mill's Harm Principle, freedom means being able to do whatever you want so long as your actions do not infringe on the right of others to do the same.[11] In other words, people should be free of any restraints unless their actions directly harm someone else. This is a negative conception of liberty, involving the absence of restriction or intrusion on one's activity. Put simply, to be free is to be left alone. As any movement conservative would admit, this preference for negative liberty becomes a recipe for small and even ineffectual government. Reluctant to accept such formulas, pragmatic conservatives recognize that freedom often involves more than just removing unwanted restraints. Freedom is a subtle and complex experience that no one should reduce to a simple maxim. It is for this reason that Burke famously said: "Abstract liberty, like other mere abstractions, is not to be found."[12] What one person considers a source of freedom may be seen as a prison by another. Although liberty may mean simply the absence of restraint in certain situations, there are also occasions where leaving people alone may keep them in chains. The fact of the matter is that people often need help unfettering themselves from structural forces (e.g., poverty or racism) that they cannot overcome on their own. In these cases, liberty requires positive action by the government.

Embracing both negative and positive conceptions of liberty, pragmatic conservatives understand that the specifics of the situation dictate whether government should pull back or step in. People have a right to be left alone when they can do something on their own, but they also have a right to government action that ensures equality of opportunity and provides care when they are unable to help themselves. Burke said, "Whatever each man can separately do, without trespassing upon others, he has a right to do for himself; and he has a right to all which society, with all its combination and skill and force, can do in his favour. In this partnership all men have equal rights; but not to equal things."[13] In the Burkean spirit, the pragmatic conservative expects government to play a fairly active role, drawing on "all its combination and skill and force" in order to do what is in people's "favour" when they cannot provide for themselves. Only if it seeks to guarantee substantive equality—or equality of ends—can government be accused of serious overreach.

Because pragmatic conservatives do not accept any absolutist claims about the size, scope, and role of government, preferring instead to keep their options open, they defy ideological labels. It would not be a stretch to suggest that they transcend ideology by rejecting all abstract blueprints and formulas, all righteous crusades that aim to bring about a particular political order. Pragmatic conservatives will inevitably have ideological leanings, left or right, based on what they find to be the most effective policy solutions at the time, but they avoid making permanent commitments to any particular creed. This conservatism is a temperament or a disposition that can co-exist with many different ideologies, allowing one to find common ground and form alliances with what would appear to be odd political bedfellows. For example, while conventional wisdom would suggest that such a meeting of the minds is out of the question, pragmatic conservatives would not rule out the possibility of working with socialists, so long as they were not too militant ideologically. Perhaps more shocking, pragmatic conservatives might even call themselves, say, socialist or liberal. After all, because they rise above ideology, pragmatic conservatives do not assume that their views and those of socialism or liberalism are mutually exclusive. If socialism or liberalism offers solutions that help maintain peace and stability, preserve tradition, and contribute to the general welfare, the pragmatic conservative will not hesitate to embrace it. A perfect example is Prince Clemens Metternich, foreign minister for the Hapsburg Empire from 1809 to 1848, who referred to himself in private letters as a "*socialiste conservateur*" (conservative socialist). Fearing the harmful effects of *laissez faire* on social and political stability, he aligned himself with his socialist contemporaries and called on the state to curb the excesses of capitalism.[14]

Willing to take seriously any reasonable ideas, whether they hail from the left or the right, the pragmatic conservative is prepared to defend all rooted traditions and institutions no matter their ideological origins. For example, President Eisenhower regarded the New Deal, the embodiment of modern liberalism, as established tradition, which a conservative should preserve, fine-tune, and expand when necessary. He thought that a "gradually expanding federal government" was "the price of a rapidly expanding national growth." As a result, he could not abide the radical proposals made by movement conservatives to dismantle the welfare state, calling them "stupid" in a letter to his brother Edgar. "Should any political party attempt to abolish Social Security and eliminate labor laws and farm programs," he wrote, "you would not hear of that party again in our political history."[15] Many intellectuals during the Eisenhower era were making a similar claim: because America had a long and distinguished liberal tradition, the conservative should assume the responsibility of safeguarding it. Stuart Gerry Brown claimed that "*to be an American conservative it is necessary to reassert liberalism.*"[16] Arthur Schlesinger agreed, declaring that any attempts to preserve traditions that were not rooted in the American experience actually betrayed conservatism, giving way to an empty "politics of nostalgia."[17] Thus the Burkean (or pragmatic) conservative in the United States cannot avoid being a liberal.

Although they are often unwilling to admit it, American conservatives today espouse principles that have grown out of the liberal tradition, especially individualism and capitalism. From liberalism, conservatives have inherited the idea that freedom can only be located in the individual and that the state must concern itself with individual freedom before anything else. Conservatives can also thank liberalism for the economic corollary to individualism, the idea that private owners of capital should be able to exchange goods and services in an open marketplace. It is important to note, however, that while conservatives have found much to like in the first principles of liberalism, they have failed to embrace the tradition as it has evolved. When unfettered individualism and capitalism proved untenable by the late nineteenth century, many liberals began to embrace a positive conception of freedom, supporting measures that tamed corporations and other private entities which, even more than government, posed grave threats to individual freedom. American conservatives have rejected their liberal heritage because it would require them to come to terms with how the tradition, adapting to changing times, has found it necessary to create the welfare state and regulate capitalism. While liberalism would compel them to accept a tradition based on the vagaries of concrete experience, today's conservatives would rather cling to an immutable set of absolute principles.

MOVEMENT CONSERVATISM: WITH GOD ON THEIR SIDE

Always viewing the world through an ideological lens, movement conservatives have been unable to come to terms with liberalism. They blame the liberal tradition for promoting relativism, teaching the younger generations that value judgments reflect subjective preferences rather than objective truth. The conservative complaint is as follows: committed to remaining neutral about what constitutes the good life, liberals have abdicated their responsibility to weigh in on important questions about morality and justice. As the world around them surrenders to barbarism, liberals have continued to suspend any judgment lest they impose their beliefs on others. And when they dare to offer an opinion, liberals can only do so on the basis of utility or expediency. Consequently, liberalism gave birth to a world without an authoritative source of truth, making it possible for people with the most power—for example, those with the biggest army or the most money—to define "truth" in accordance with their interests. Though its intentions have been benign, say movement conservatives, liberalism opened the door to a totalitarian nightmare where force becomes the final arbiter of truth, where might makes right.[18]

Most disturbing to movement conservatives is the fact that liberalism has reigned supreme in American intellectual life. In 1950, Lionel Trilling famously declared that "Liberalism is not only the dominant, but even the sole, intellectual tradition" in the United States, a sentiment that was echoed by Louis Hartz, Daniel Bell, and others.[19] Because the major questions of political philosophy had been answered, Bell argued, we had reached "the end of ideology"—a time when the West could focus on making minor adjustments to its liberal democratic institutions and capitalist economy while working to contain communism abroad. For liberals, politics had become an arena where experts could sort out various technical issues, making sure that the state delivered services to the people equitably and efficiently and curbed the excesses of the free market without compromising economic growth. Gone were the days of passionate commitment to great political ideas and moral truths. This was an unfortunate turn of events for conservatives, who believed that the political and moral softness of liberalism imperiled Western civilization. While liberals lacked the courage of their convictions, conservatives were certain of the need to wage an epic battle against the forces of evil.[20]

Emerging in the early 1950s as a reaction against this hegemonic liberal order, movement conservatism comprised three groups—religious traditionalists, economic libertarians, and staunch anti-communists—each of which had its own set of concerns. "[A]ppalled by the erosion of values and the emergence of a secular, rootless, mass society," religious traditionalists hoped to instill time-honored virtues, especially of the Christian variety, in the citizenry. Fearing "the threat of the State to private enterprise and individualism," libertarians wanted to limit the role of government to protecting negative freedoms. Many "disillusioned ex-radicals" found themselves so "alarmed by international Communism" that they became fixated on defeating it, regardless of the cost.[21] As many commentators have pointed out, there were obvious tensions between these strains, and it was not clear that they belonged together. For example, while libertarians wanted to foster individual liberty by shrinking the size of government, anti-communists and traditionalists called for a more active and powerful government, either to defeat the red menace or to inculcate virtue and religious values.

Thanks to the "fusionist" strategies of William F. Buckley and his colleagues at *National Review* (especially Frank Meyer), however, movement conservatism managed to coalesce into a unified ideology. The "cement" of anti-communism did more than anything else to make "fusionism" a success.[22] Buckley understood that the fractious elements of conservatism could come together under the banner of anti-communism because it gave them a common fear. Libertarians may have been wary of big government, but they would make an exception when it came to fighting an ideological enemy bent on destroying individualism and property rights. As a result, they joined forces with the anti-communists to support a massive expansion of the national security state. And while religious traditionalists recognized that free markets sometimes contributed to the erosion of those values that Western civilization holds most dear, they saw a far greater threat in communism, which brazenly rejected God, property, and ancestral wisdom. If the welfare state really did lead us down a slippery slope toward communism, the religious traditionalist could see the sense in embracing economic libertarianism at home. In retrospect, it is obvious that the Cold War helped make movement conservatism possible, giving each faction a reason to align with the others.

In the end, movement conservatives were able to set aside their differences and find agreement on several principles: a zeal for individual economic freedom, unfettered markets, and the nearly absolute right to private property; a belief that piety and virtue are important for society but in the end an individual responsibility; a deep-seated hostility toward the state, associating any attempts to promote the general welfare or the common good with communism; and a commitment to defeating unconditionally the Soviet Union, global communism, and communist subversion at home. Their adherence to these principles resulted in a number of radical gestures, including an eagerness to dismantle the New Deal in its entirety, a willingness to make baseless accusations and violate civil liberties in the search for communist subversives at home, and a determination to roll back global communism even if it required endless war and a flagrant disregard for human rights. Unlike their pragmatic counterparts, movement conservatives refuse to be bound by traditions that do not accord with what they know to be right, and they resent anyone who suggests that they should proceed cautiously and heed the wisdom of sages, past and present, before forging ahead with their plans. Theirs is an unyielding ideology, not a political philosophy.

Even though communism ceased to be a threat after the end of the Cold War in the early 1990s, movement conservatives have not gone away. It may well be the case that movement conservatism reached its apotheosis with the presidential election of George W. Bush in 2000. After all, it did not take long for the Bush administration to reveal its ardor for unfettered markets and supply side economics, its yearning for a return to a pre-New Deal era. But its reckless decision to wage an unnecessary war in Iraq underscores more than anything else how far movement conservatism had strayed from Burkean principles.

As even a cursory analysis makes clear, the decision to invade Iraq in 2003 runs contrary to every core idea of pragmatic conservatism. Because pragmatic conservatives believe that people are sinful by nature, they are skeptical of ambitious projects that promise dramatic change for the better. But the architects of the Iraq War assumed that the occupying force could teach Iraqis the virtues of self-governance and transform the country into a thriving liberal democracy. Whereas pragmatic conservatives insist on deference to tradition unless there is a compelling reason not to do so, the administration threw caution to the wind and boldly announced an entirely new foreign policy doctrine that justified preventive war. Instead of proceeding with care and prudence, the Bush administration rushed to war before exhausting all diplomatic options or even building a compelling case. Indeed its justification for war exhibited an utter contempt for the facts and empirical evidence. Without properly verifying its claims, the Bush administration concluded that Iraq had weapons of mass destruction and an active nuclear program. Getting its facts straight hardly seemed to matter because the plan to overthrow an evil regime was plainly a just cause. Finally, rather than relying on a diversity of expert opinions, the administration systematically ignored anyone who expressed doubts about the decision to invade Iraq, including some of the most informed people on the subject. As the country drifted toward war, the administration engaged in shameless populism, gaining support from the American people by exploiting the misinformation, fear, and jingoism that inevitably arise after a national tragedy.

A number of considerations—including human frailty, tradition, prudence, facts, and expert opinion—should have given Bush pause before he plunged the country into war. But the sad truth is that nothing could have dissuaded Bush from his position. He believed God wanted war. When he urged various world leaders to join the Coalition of the Willing at a meeting in early 2003, Bush invoked biblical prophecy to justify the war in a private conversation with Jacques Chirac, France's president at the time. "This confrontation is willed by God, who wants to use this conflict to erase his people's enemies before a New Age begins," Bush said to Chirac.[23] He shared similar sentiments with a Palestinian delegation with which Bush met only a few months after the invasion of Iraq. According to Nabil Shaath, the Palestinian foreign minister at the time, Bush said, "I am driven with a mission from God. God would tell me, 'George, go and fight these terrorists in Afghanistan.' And I did. And then God would tell me, 'George, go and end the tyranny in Iraq.' And I did."[24] With God on his side, Bush had no doubts about the righteousness of his cause. Pragmatic conservatives never enjoy such certainty, for they do not presume to know where God stands.

BURKE AND HIS AMERICAN CHILDREN

Throughout much of American history, conservatives have largely been apologists for the privileged few, such as slaveholders or plutocrats. They have defended socio-economic systems that create (and widen) inequality and bring misery to many.[25] In recent years, movement conservatives have turned the Republican Party into a bastion of extremism that, in its reactionary longing for a return to a fabled past, has proven unwilling to meet many of the challenges of modern life. Only through a narrow ideological lens have movement conservatives viewed such policy issues as poverty, education, health care, financial regulation, and climate change. Regardless of what history and current information can tell us, today's conservatives generally see free markets and straitjacketed government as the solution to every problem. And they only seem to favor unleashing the power of government when enemies at home and abroad allegedly threaten national security.

This book focuses on a conservative tradition that does not accept the premise that God is on its side, that does not claim to have a monopoly on truth or justice. In Chap. 2, I begin with the father of this tradition, Edmund Burke, who fashioned a political philosophy that takes a realistic look at the problems of modern life and searches for sensible ways to deal with them. In Burke's view, the French Revolution bespoke an eroding faith in traditional sources of political and moral authority. While Burke sympathized with those who suffered under the *ancien régime* and acknowledged the need for reforms to address their grievances, he feared what would become of a world in which people rejoiced in indiscriminate iconoclasm and submitted to the ideological whims of charismatic leaders. As the French Revolution made clear, this was a world beset by chaos and bloodshed. Burke's solution was not to offer a model of a just society based on abstract reasoning or to make bold claims about what God wanted people to do. Instead, he called for a humble recognition that easy answers elude us, that we have no hope of addressing contemporary problems if we fail to proceed cautiously and to seek lessons in the past. We must look back before we move haltingly forward.

Burke's pragmatic conservatism was a response to modernity and, as a result, it still has much to teach us today, perhaps even more than it did his readers in the eighteenth and nineteenth centuries. His ideas have proven especially relevant for those who face the dizzying pace of modern life. It is unfortunate that the few thinkers who have kept his political philosophy alive remain underappreciated, especially in the United States. On this side of the pond, the children of Burke have offered an insightful alternative to the ideologically driven conservatism that prevails today. If only to see what conservatism could be, it would behoove us to listen to these neglected voices. In this book, I focus on three pragmatic conservatives who left a mark on American intellectual life in the twentieth century: Walter Lippmann, Reinhold Niebuhr, and Peter Viereck. Like Edmund Burke, these figures were not trained philosophers who viewed politics in abstract or theoretical terms but rather men of letters and public intellectuals who were steeped in the major issues of their times. And like Burke, they stumbled awkwardly into political philosophy when they found it necessary to address contemporary problems from a broader perspective.

In Chap. 3, I focus on the political thought of Walter Lippmann, the renowned columnist and public intellectual who was a prolific commentator on American politics for over a half century. Although he impressed many of his professors at Harvard, including William James, Irving Babbitt, and George Santayana, Lippmann decided to forgo the academic life and make his mark as a journalist. He never gave up the life of the mind, however, for he wrote several notable books that proved his bona fides as a political philosopher. Right out of undergraduate school, he quickly emerged as a progressive luminary whose sympathies often lay with socialist causes. As his opinions on these matters evolved, Lippmann renounced socialism and eventually acquired a reputation as a liberal realist. Despite his many liberal positions on the issues, Lippmann grew to see himself as a Burkean conservative. This chapter examines Lippmann, a liberal by reputation, as an exemplar of pragmatic conservatism who saw radical tendencies in the extremes of both left and right—for example, in the democratic hope of John Dewey and the fundamentalism of William F. Buckley. The central tenets of pragmatic conservatism—including a pessimistic view of human nature, a commitment to tradition balanced with support for needed reforms, a humble recognition that truths are derived from concrete experiences and embodied in tradition, a trust in elites and experts rather than the masses, and a belief in the virtues of moderation and balance—are all on display in his political thought.

In Chap. 4, I discuss Reinhold Niebuhr, the eminent Christian ethicist and theologian, whose teachings about original sin and the frailties of human nature have influenced generations of thinkers, especially those who have found kinship with the realist tradition. Appearing on the cover of *Time* in 1948, he achieved fame for his trenchant criticism of intellectuals who held a utopian faith in the perfectibility of human beings and the inevitability of social progress. He argued that unchecked optimism and ambition, susceptible to corruption by the will-to-power that resides within all of us, can quickly turn into hubris and political overreach. At the same time, Niebuhr qualified his realism with Christian faith. Juxtaposed to the doctrine of original sin, the Christian law of love (or agape) inspires people to transcend their flawed nature and work toward a better and more just world, but without ever forgetting that this noble aim can never be fully realized. Striking a balance between realism and idealism, Niebuhr argued that the inevitability of sin should steer us away from the naïve quest for human perfection but that the law of love should prevent us from resigning ourselves to the evils of this world. Progress is possible, Niebuhr believed, if we remain modest about what we hope to accomplish and attentive to the lessons of experience, both past and present. As a younger man, Niebuhr exhibited an impetuous streak that stemmed from his frustration with injustice. But, like Lippmann, he evolved into a pragmatic conservative and came to recognize the Burkean strain in his political thought. All the while, Niebuhr remained devoted to the cause of social justice, maintaining his support for workers, African-Americans, and other groups that faced the trials of exclusion and oppression.

In Chap. 5, I explore the political ideas of Peter Viereck, the Pulitzer Prize-winning poet and distinguished professor of history at Mt. Holyoke College for over 40 years. A post-war conservative thinker who made a splash as a young man in the 1950s, Viereck quickly became a marginalized figure in the conservative world, especially after expressing his contempt for McCarthyism and *laissez faire* and his support for the New Deal and

Adlai Stevenson. Never having taken to Buckley and the *National Review* crowd, he found allies among the "new conservatives"—including journalist August Heckscher, sociologist Robert Nisbet, political scientist Clinton Rossiter, and others—who considered themselves traditionalists in the Burkean vein. Though an idiosyncratic figure whose ideas never attracted a large following, Viereck presented a powerful, and consciously Burkean, alternative to the conservative orthodoxy formed by Buckley and others in the post-war era. With vivid prose but subtle argumentation, Viereck made the case for a pragmatic conservatism that eschewed ideology and simplistic thinking. While his thought remained unfashionable during his lifetime, it demands a serious hearing today. The fact that Viereck has been largely forgotten, despite some valiant attempts to revive interest in his ideas, shows how far Burkean conservatism has fallen in the United States.

It is high time that someone remedy this gross oversight by calling attention to the pragmatic conservative tradition in American political thought. That is the aim of this book. And as will become clear in Chaps. 6 and 7, a revival of this neglected tradition can throw in stark relief the radicalism of conservative thought and politics today.

NOTES

1. See, for example, Sullivan, *The Conservative Soul*; Tanenhaus, *The Death of Conservatism*; Mattson, *Rebels All!*; and Bogus, *Buckley*.
2. Burke, *Reflections*, 247–248.
3. Chesterton, *Orthodoxy*, 85.
4. Burke, *Reflections*, 106.
5. Burke, *Sublime and Beautiful*, 99.
6. Burke, "Speech on a Motion for a Committee to Inquire into the State of the Representation of the Commons in Parliament" (1782), in *Works*, VII, 95.
7. Burke, "Speech in Opening the Impeachment, Second Day" (1788), in *Writings and Speeches*, VI, 346. For an insightful study of the Burkean idea that the universal and the particular can be reconciled, and that universal truths can exist in a world teeming with diversity and particularity, see Ryn, *A Common Human Ground*.
8. Burke, "Speech on a Bill for the Repeal of the Marriage Act" (1781), in Kramnick, ed., *The Portable Edmund Burke*, 96.
9. Burke, *Reflections*, 228.
10. Ibid., 151.
11. Mill, *On Liberty*, 26–27.

12. Burke, "Resolutions for Conciliation with America" (1775), *Writings and Speeches*, III, 120.
13. Burke, *Reflections*, 149–150.
14. See Viereck, *Conservatism Revisited*, 115–116.
15. Eisenhower quoted in Micklethwait and Wooldridge, *The Right Nation*, 41–42.
16. Stuart Gerry Brown, "Democracy, the New Conservatism, and the Liberal Tradition in America," *Ethics* 66.
17. Schlesinger, "The New Conservatism in America: A Liberal Comment," *Confluence* 2.
18. See Nash, *The Conservative Intellectual Movement in America*, 42–45.
19. Trilling, *The Liberal Imagination*, ix. See also Hartz, *The Liberal Tradition in America*, and Bell, *The End of Ideology*.
20. Nash, *The Conservative Intellectual Movement in America*, 45–55.
21. Ibid., 131.
22. Ibid., 179.
23. Hamilton, "Bush, God, Iraq and Gog," *Counterpunch* (22 May 2009).
24. MacAskill, "George Bush: 'God told me to end the tyranny in Iraq,'" *The Guardian* (7 October 2005).
25. See especially Robin, *The Reactionary Mind*.

CHAPTER 2

Edmund Burke: Pragmatic Conservative

INTRODUCTION

Edmund Burke, known today as the father of conservatism, was considered a liberal reformer in his own time. In fact, he never called himself a conservative and only became associated with the term more than a century after his death. During his many years in the British House of Commons, the renowned Whig fought the arbitrary and oppressive use of power. At the outset of the French Revolution, many of its most ardent supporters hoped Burke would give it his blessing. After all, in the years prior to the revolution, Burke had warmly received many of them—including Thomas Paine, Jean Baptiste Cloots, and Charles DePont—at his home in Beaconsfield. Trusting they could count on his support, each of these men wrote to Burke in 1789 asking him to speak publicly on behalf of popular sovereignty, the guiding principle behind the revolution, and to propose reforms in Great Britain based on the republican model adopted in France. Meanwhile, Comte de Mirabeau, who at one time had also paid a visit to Beaconsfield, stood before the National Assembly quoting long passages from some of Burke's more famous speeches.

The publication of Burke's *Reflections on the Revolution in France* in 1790 came as a complete surprise to these men and many others. His fierce opposition to the revolution seemed to be an aberration, the ravings of a once great politician and man of letters who at the twilight of his career somehow forgot his liberal legacy and became a reactionary. As a Member of Parliament for over 25 years, Burke had fought against tyranny in

© The Author(s) 2016
R.J. Lacey, *Pragmatic Conservatism*,
DOI 10.1057/978-1-137-59295-8_2

America, Ireland, and India, and he had led efforts to reduce the power of the Crown at home. His sympathy for the Americans, in particular, raised their expectations. After all, the American war for independence inspired the French a decade later. It seemed reasonable to conclude that Burke favored republican government and political equality over monarchy and aristocracy. But Paine and other radicals had misread Burke completely.

Although Burke championed many liberal causes such as American freedom over the years, his reasons for doing so were different from those cited by Paine and his comrades. If they had paid careful attention to his positions on the American crisis, the East India Company, and the Protestant Ascendancy in Ireland, they would not have accused the great orator of betraying his liberal principles when he denounced the revolution with such unrelenting vigor. They would have seen that Burke never invoked abstract theories about the rights of man in his defense of the oppressed. He appealed rather to precedent and traditional rights, those time-honored prescriptions that had grown out of concrete experience.

It is my contention that Edmund Burke was a pragmatic politician and thinker. This means that, originally, conservatism was not a rigid or absolutist ideology but rather a more flexible political orientation that eschewed abstract reasoning and found provisional truth in—and guidance from—history. The first conservative believed that safeguarding traditions, customs, and prescriptive rights is the most effective way of restraining the natural tendency of human beings to exercise their will arbitrarily. Elites play a vital role in the preservation process, ensuring that traditions are not only observed but also revered in society as a whole. Exalting traditions in this way, however, does not mean that they are a reflection of immutable truths that must be preserved for all time. Instead, they represent time-tested ways of doing things which deserve reverence only so long as they serve their intended purposes. If they cease to do so, we must welcome reform—cautious and incremental change to these traditions and past practices—in order to address emerging problems. The preservation of those traditions that still serve us well—indeed, the preservation of the social order as a whole—requires thoughtful reform.

As will be stressed throughout this chapter, Burke's theory of knowledge is decidedly pragmatic. He often expressed his contempt for abstract thinking and deductive reasoning. In his view, we arrive at truths inductively, and over time we reify truths that prove useful in our experience through the creation of traditions and customs. His preference for induction over deduction did not make him an apologist for relativism or historicism, of which both hostile and friendly critics have accused him over the years.[1] He always maintained that universal truths can and do exist. The only catch is that universals are derived from particular concrete experiences, not through the use of logic or some other abstract method. What distinguishes Burke from twentieth-century pragmatists, such as William James and John Dewey, is that the pool of experiences from which one should draw is not limited to the present day. For Burke, the experiences of our ancestors matter as much as, or perhaps more than, those of our contemporaries. We ignore the lessons of history at our peril. Burke's belief that we must acquire truths inductively also applies to ethics. It is from the accumulation of knowledge derived from aesthetic experiences that we develop a sense of right and wrong. Moral judgment requires an active imagination, an ability to view situations from the perspective of others, not obedience to doctrines etched in stone. In the end, Burke was neither a relativist nor an absolutist, neither a Romantic nor a rationalist. He believed in absolute truths but doubted the capacity of human beings to perceive them with any clarity. At best, we can view them obliquely through experience, both real and imagined. But they are there, becoming more vivid before our eyes, however imperfectly, in the form of our many laws, traditions, and customs.

"Leave the Americans as they anciently stood"

Edmund Burke distinguished himself as a gifted man of letters early in his career, publishing two well-received books—*A Vindication of Natural Society* (1756) and *A Philosophical Enquiry into the Origin of Our Ideas of the Sublime and the Beautiful* (1757)—while in his twenties. The former was a work of political satire that ironically extolled—but actually eviscerated—the ideas of Viscount Bolingbroke, who argued that man had no need for the doctrines and institutions of the Christian church because of the infallibility of his instincts and natural inclinations. The latter is a philosophical treatise on aesthetics, which Burke began writing during his undergraduate years at Trinity College, Dublin. Among other things, the book reveals Burke's tendencies toward empiricism, undoubtedly influenced by Locke and Hume, and his contention that ethical beliefs are hewn from aesthetic experiences.

By the early 1760s, he gravitated toward a career in politics, becoming an indispensable aide to the Marquis of Rockingham. He entered Parliament in 1765, and he quickly assumed a leadership role within the

Rockingham faction of the Whig Party. His aforementioned reputation as a liberal rested on his opposition to the arbitrary and excessive use of power by the British government in America, Ireland, India, and Great Britain itself. In the first three cases, he accused the government of harmful innovation and disregard for tradition. It imposed unprecedented taxes on the Americans, leading to widespread unrest and demands for independence. It persecuted Catholics in Ireland and, in denying them opportunities to enter elite ranks, severed their ties to stabilizing traditions and institutions. Perhaps most disturbing to Burke, the government empowered the East India Company to act as its proxy in the subcontinent of South Asia, giving company officials free rein to violate local laws and customs in their efforts to enrich themselves through extortion and other exploitative practices. At home, he fought the King's attempts to weaken the independence of Parliament through the use of patronage.[2]

In the end, Burke championed several liberal causes but always for *conservative reasons*. His aim was to preserve the integrity of established traditions and institutions, not to secure the natural rights of those people about whom he was concerned. Most of his contemporaries believed that Burke had ceased to be a liberal when he opposed the revolution in France. Indeed, his reputation as one of the founders, if not *the* founder, of conservative thought rests largely on *Reflections on the Revolution in France*. But his impulse to conserve existed from the beginning of his career. He always saw reform as a means by which existing institutions could be saved. Burke's example shows that liberalism and conservatism do not have to be mutually exclusive categories. One can adopt the methods of the liberal to serve the ends of the conservative.[3]

It should not be overlooked, however, that according to conventional wisdom among Burke scholars in the nineteenth century, Burke was a proto-Benthamite, a liberal who defended reform on utilitarian grounds. The most prominent scholar to make this case was John Morley. He exercised considerable influence over many Burke scholars who came in his wake, although most thought it necessary to qualify Morley's utilitarian reading. They observed certain inconsistencies and tensions in his thought that made it difficult to accept the simple view that Burke was a straight-up utilitarian. Burke's occasional appeal to universal moral laws, for example, did not always square with his stated preference for "expediency" as a guide for action. These scholars found it necessary to offer more nuanced interpretations of Burke's thought. Their efforts typically involved attempts to reconcile the foundationalist and anti-foundationalist claims evident in his speeches and writings. If he was not quite a utilitarian, there were similar philosophical labels that might apply to the eighteenth-century liberal—perhaps empiricist, pragmatist, or positivist.[4]

In the first half of the twentieth century, Burke finally began to emerge as an icon of conservatism. A few thinkers, such as Harvard professor Irving Babbitt, invoked his ideas in their attempt to explain the rise of totalitarianism. Then, after World War II, a burgeoning group of conservative scholars in the United States saw a kindred spirit in Burke, finding inspiration in his virulent opposition to the French Revolution. As they saw it, global communist revolution posed a similar threat, and Burke's writings on the French Revolution helped them sharpen their arguments and explain how the Soviets imperiled Western civilization. Along with Burke, they feared the utter contempt for tradition that animated the revolutionary. Metaphorically, both Jacobins and Bolsheviks wanted to scorch the earth and start anew. The human toll that such an ambitious enterprise would inevitably take did not concern them. Rather than accept the constraints of tradition and past experience, they hoped to graft their theories—their abstract plans for radical change—onto the world. Godless and nihilistic, the revolutionary came to believe that everything was permissible. According to many of these conservative thinkers, Burke responded to the nihilistic Jacobins with a defense of natural law theory, which posits a set of universal moral precepts that transcend human experience and remain the same no matter the time or place. Handed down by God, the natural law remains obscure to us until accessed through reason or Christian revelation.[5]

While it is understandable that post-war conservatives would find fault with how Morley and others portrayed Burke as a utilitarian, they overreached when they turned him into a natural law theorist. Eager to make use of Burke in the struggle against communism, they willfully ignored the overwhelming evidence pointing to his misology—his mistrust of reason. In his writings about the French Revolution and its intellectual ancestors, Burke proved to be one of the most trenchant critics of the Enlightenment. He anticipated many of the arguments made by postmodern thinkers of the late twentieth century, calling attention to the dangers of hyper-rationality. Yet he remained premodern in his insistence that the past can reveal to us, however dimly, venerable truths.

A discussion of Burke's response to the crisis in America can shed light on how misology and traditionalism informed his politics. When Great Britain started imposing taxes on America in 1764, it caught many people by surprise. It was unprecedented and unwelcome, sparking protests and general unrest throughout the colonies. Edmund Burke favored the repeal of the Stamp Act, delivering his inaugural speech in the House of Commons on this very issue in January of 1766. In what appeared to be an auspicious beginning to his parliamentary career, Burke and the Rockingham Whigs were able to repeal the Stamp Act two months later. But they could not convince their peers in Parliament that levying any taxes on the Americans was both unjust and unwise. Anyone could see that new taxes lay just beyond the horizon. Foreshadowing what was to come, the repeal of the Stamp Act included a resolution asserting the sovereign right of Parliament and the Crown to make laws that affect the colonies, including any form of taxation. This was a clear refutation of the rallying cry behind many of the protests in America: "No taxation without representation."

Burke disagreed with the rights claim that taxation required representation, for the colonies belonged to Great Britain, whose Parliament had the power to tax anyone in its dominion. But he was equally dismayed by Parliament's insistence that it had the sovereign right to tax the colonies whenever it wanted. Making such absolutist claims was dangerous, in Burke's view, because it ruled out any consideration of what might be the prudent course of action in a particular set of circumstances. In theory, Parliament had the legal right to do all kinds of things, including the imposition of unwanted taxes on the colonies, but as Burke said to his peers in Parliament, the real "question" was "not whether you have a right to render your people miserable; but whether it is not your interest to make them happy?" Ultimately, said Burke, there is far more wisdom in choosing to "abide by a profitable experience" than a "mischievous theory."[6] For Burke, concrete consequences mattered far more than theoretical rights when making policy decisions.

Burke's aversion to theory and preference for experience is apparent in many of his speeches and writings on the American crisis. Aware that there was no way of arbitrating competing claims about abstract rights, Burke pointed to tradition and custom as a way of finding common ground. "I am not here going into the distinction of rights, nor attempting to mark their boundaries," said Burke to his peers in Parliament not long after the Boston Tea Party. "I do not enter into these metaphysical distinctions; I hate the very sound of them. Leave the Americans as they anciently stood, and these distinctions, born of our unhappy contest, will die along with it." Until 1764, Great Britain was satisfied with the economic advantages brought about by mercantilism, restricting the trade Americans could conduct with other nations. The Americans had no complaints either. Burke continued:

> Be content to bind America by laws of trade: you have always done it. Let this be your reason for binding their trade. Do not burden them by taxes; you were not used to do so from the beginning. Let this be your reason for not taxing. These are the arguments of states and kingdoms. Leave the rest to the schools; for there only may they be discussed with safety. But if, intemperately, unwisely, fatally, you sophisticate and poison the very source of government, by urging subtle deductions, and consequences odious to those you govern, from the unlimited and illimitable nature of supreme sovereignty, you will teach them by these means to call that sovereignty itself into question.[7]

Clearly, the prudent course of action was to adhere to ancient tradition and custom. Discussions of abstract rights have no place in matters of government policy; they should be relegated to the schoolroom, where uncompromising words and logic have no consequences. If Great Britain continued to impose unwanted taxes on America while invoking the right of sovereignty, the result would be further discontent. Even more worrying for Burke was the prospect that the Americans would reject sovereign right in favor of other rights—for example, the right to representation before taxation—that would lead to permanent separation between the mother-land and her colonies. Burke's words proved prophetic. The war for independence began a year after his celebrated speech on American taxation.

Burke earned a reputation as a supporter of the American Revolution, but this was never the case. He sympathized with their plight, and he believed earnestly that Parliament should be conciliatory in its actions toward the Americans in order to prevent revolution. He favored repealing all taxes imposed on them, because they violated traditions dating back to the early seventeenth century. These traditions were so ancient that they had developed into the "chartered right of Englishmen" living abroad. Perhaps more importantly, Burke understood that the Americans had enjoyed over a century of independence from Parliament and the Crown, which shaped their unique character and temperament. The Glorious Revolution had a particularly powerful influence on the American character, infusing a "fierce spirit of liberty" in many Englishmen who immigrated to the New World in the late seventeenth century. It was prudent to take all of these factors into consideration when dealing with the Americans. But Burke rejected the view that the Americans had an absolute right to declare independence on the grounds that they did not enjoy direct and proportionate representation in Parliament. And he certainly did not agree with the famous invocation of inalienable rights penned by Thomas Jefferson. Without question, Burke supported all attempts to defeat the revolution and to restore the status quo in the American colonies. Upholding the British Empire remained his highest priority.

When the Americans successfully won their independence in 1783, Burke wished them well, and he believed that their continued respect for British traditions would help them prosper. He had a high regard for George Washington and the Federalist Party, whose leadership in the early years of the nascent republic created much-needed stability. Again, this did not mean he supported the American Revolution or would support revolutions that erupted elsewhere. Paine and other supporters of the French Revolution got the wrong idea about Burke's earlier sympathies and later good wishes for the Americans, mistaking them as evidence of his support for radical political innovation. A careful reading of his speeches and writings on the American crisis shows that Burke would have no sympathy for the theories that inspired the revolution in France and led to the wholesale rejection of precedent and tradition. Burke dedicated his career to preventing political turmoil and revolution, both at home and in its many colonies. The liberal causes for which he became known—for example, opposing the persecution of Catholics in Ireland and the abuses of power in India—were all intended to promote stability and prosperity by pragmatic means.

Burke believed that the threats to stability and prosperity were many, and as a politician, he understood the need to address their proximate causes. But he believed that the ultimate cause of these threats was the flawed nature of human beings. In Burke's view, this ruled out the possibility of radically transforming society for the better, creating heaven on earth through political means. There were limits to what could be expected of people. To Burke's sober reflections on the realities of human nature we now turn.

"THE TRAIN OF DISORDERLY APPETITES"

As is the case for most conservative thinkers, the Christian doctrine of original sin influenced Burke's view of human nature. In the heart of human beings lie passions and appetites that lead them down a wayward path. Their woes originate in their sinful nature, not in the institutions built by society. "History consists, for the greater part, of the miseries brought upon the world by pride, ambition, avarice, revenge, lust, sedition, hypocrisy, ungoverned zeal, and all the train of disorderly appetites," said Burke. "These vices are the *causes* of those storms." It is fashionable to argue that the "instruments in great public evils"—such as "kings, priests, magistrates, senates, parliaments, national assemblies, judges, and captains"—constitute the actual cause. But nothing could be further from the truth. Eliminating these institutions and offices does not get at the root of the problem. "A certain quantum of power must always exist in the community, in some hands, and under some appellation," he said. "Wise men will apply their remedies to vices, not to names; to the causes of evil which are permanent, not to the occasional organs by which they act, and the transitory modes in which they appear."[8] In Burke's view, altering the structure of social and political institutions does nothing more than change the names of the instruments of evil. Permanent and deep-seated, the sources of evil can always find residence somewhere else—in a different political system, institution, or office. For the source of evil is human nature itself. Within all of us lurk certain traits that make evil and sin possible. The external structures in which we operate will never change that fact. Regardless of the exogenous factors, people tend to be tribalistic, selfish, capricious, power-hungry, and overly ambitious by nature. A combination of some (or all) of these characteristics in most people produces a recipe for social discord.

Anticipating the arguments made by James Madison in Federalist No. 10, Burke argued that human beings have an innate tendency to align themselves with people of similar interests and opinions—to form cliques and factions. The consequences of this tribal instinct are significant: "I admit that people frequently acquire in such confederacies a narrow, bigoted, and proscriptive spirit; that they are apt to sink the idea of the general good in this circumscribed and partial interest." People "make bad citizens" when they focus their efforts on the parochial interests of tribe or party.[9] As people pursue their narrow self-interest, the common good falls by the wayside and social discord intensifies.

The tendency to factionalize may be just a subspecies of our innate selfishness. It is often the case that people form alliances to serve their individual interests. As Burke reminds his readers in *Reflections*, people will most readily reveal their "selfish temper and confined views" when they become free of obligation. Left to their own devices, they will disregard what they owe to their fellow men and to posterity.[10] One of the reasons Burke believed in the importance of tradition (which will be discussed in detail later) is that it restrains the selfish instinct and imposes duties upon all of us.

Given their selfish nature, most people find a life full of responsibilities and hard work onerous. By nature, they are capricious and cavalier to a fault. "The life of adventurers, gamesters, gypsies, beggars, and robbers is not unpleasant. It requires restraint to keep men from falling into that habit." The vicissitudes of such a dissolute life—with its "shifting tides of fear and hope, the flight and pursuit, the peril and escape, the alternate famine and feast of the savage and the thief"—are far more exciting than one of "slow, steady, progressive, unvaried occupation." In the end, most of us find a routine life insufferably "tame, languid, and insipid."[11] This longing for adventure and excitement makes human beings morally unreliable. In a letter to the Chevalier de Rivarol, Burke condemned those philosophers whose "morality has no idea in it of restraint" because they believe in the innate goodness of our passions and appetites. "When their disciples are thus left free and guided only by present feeling they are no longer to be depended upon for good or evil," wrote Burke. "The men who today snatch the worst criminals from justice will murder the most innocent persons tomorrow."[12] Unburdened by restraints of any kind, human beings dwell in a world beyond good and evil. Today they forgive criminals; tomorrow they kill innocents. They follow the fickle desires of the heart without any concern for conventional codes of morality.

Given the chance to follow their hearts, most people will find it impossible to resist the allure of power, especially once they are given a taste of it. "Those who have been once intoxicated with power, and have derived any kind of emolument from it," said Burke, "never can willingly abandon it." Even when they are "distressed" by the possession of power, people "will never look to anything but power for their relief."[13] Power is such an addictive intoxicant that one never wants to relinquish it, even when it makes life more painful for everyone. This is why Burke opposed the excessive concentration of power. Few people could exercise moral restraint while wielding such might. Burke would have agreed with Lord Acton's famous dictum: "Power tends to corrupt and absolute power corrupts absolutely. Great men are almost always bad men."

The lust for power is an example of the overweening ambition that, according to Burke, stirs so many people. It is important to note, however, that Burke saw ambition in largely a positive light earlier in his career. In *A Philosophical Enquiry into the Sublime and Beautiful*, Burke described ambition as a natural corrective to our tendency to learn from and connect with others through the process of imitation. While imitation is vital, perhaps the primary way by which we learn anything and then perfect our mastery of it, people—indeed, humankind as a whole—could not progress without the driving force of ambition. "[I]f men gave themselves up to imitation entirely, and each followed the other, and so on in an eternal circle," said Burke, "it is easy to see that there never could be any improvement amongst them. Men must remain as brutes do, the same at the end that they are at this day, and that they were in the beginning of the world." God gave us ambition to make sure we did not wallow in the mire of complacency. He wanted man to improve by "excelling his fellows in something deemed valuable amongst them."[14]

The problem with ambition is that it can become excessive, as Burke began to acknowledge later in his life, especially after the eruption of the French Revolution. In *A Letter to a Noble Lord*, he wrote apocalyptically about the "thorough-bred metaphysician" who looks upon humanity with the cold and abstract detachment of a scientist. "These philosophers consider men, in their experiments, no more than they do mice in an air pump, or in a recipient of mephitick gas." Guided by a crude Machiavellianism, the metaphysician no longer considers the moral implications of his plans to improve the world. Rationally conceived ends justify even the most horrific means. "It is remarkable," Burke wrote, "that [the thorough-bred metaphysicians] never see any way to their projected good but by the road of some evil." They can do this because ambition stultifies their moral imagination. "Ambition is come upon them suddenly; they are intoxicated with it, and it has rendered them fearless of the danger, which may from thence arise to others or to themselves."[15] Influenced by the events in France, Burke believed that ambitious men represented a danger to the social order. Always "discontented" and "puffed up with personal pride and arrogance," these men "generally despise their own order." They seek distinction and honor by transcending the age into which they were born, blazing a new trail which others will follow. This is why he recommended in *Reflections* that men of ability, no matter how good their intentions may be, should "pass through some sort of probation" on "the road to eminence and power."[16] Without robust checks created by law and tradition, such men may be able to realize their ambitions all too easily.

Informed by a fairly pessimistic view of human nature, Burke had little tolerance for philosophers who largely saw goodness in the heart of man. They seemed to be willfully ignorant of history and current events. But

Burke did not see human beings as complete savages either. He believed that human beings feel pity and sympathy when confronted with the suffering of others. In addition, most people also experience a small measure of delight in these instances, making them eager—even happy—to help those in distress. This may sound perverse, but as Burke points out, a sheer repugnance toward the suffering of others would make people "shun with the greatest care all persons" experiencing pain and misfortune.[17] Inspired by a mixture of pity and delight, people have a natural desire to ease the pain of others.

People not only want to assist others in pain; they also try to avoid suffering themselves. It is natural for people to recoil in the face of the "sublime"—that which inspires terror and fear because of its ability to inflict pain. For this reason, the use of the sublime in politics was an effective way of regulating behavior. "The power which arises from institutions in kings and commanders, has the same connection with terror. Sovereigns are frequently addressed with the title of *dread majesty*," said Burke. And "young persons little acquainted with the world, and who have not been used to approach men in power, are commonly struck with an awe which takes away the free use of their faculties."[18] While nature may make people capricious and power-hungry, they are also quick to obey a terrifying sovereign or god. Indeed, as Burke reiterates many times in the *Sublime and Beautiful*, fear is the most powerful passion that dwells in the heart of man, exceeding even love, lust, or anything else associated with pleasure.[19] The reason is that we feel pain more intensely than we do pleasure. Not surprisingly, the fear of pain convinces most people to be compliant.

Burke also considered it wrong-headed to view human nature as completely fixed. While Burke regarded some innate human traits as "universal," he also maintained that human nature "is modified by local habits and social aptitudes."[20] In his praise for the legislators of ancient republics, Burke credited them for their keen observations of human nature. They understood "the effects of those habits which are communicated by the circumstances of civil life" and were "sensible that the operation of this second nature on the first produced a new combination; and thence arose many diversities amongst men."[21] Here Burke acknowledged that biology is not destiny. Environmental and circumstantial factors shape our habits, becoming so engrained over time that they are "second nature" to us. Because each person internalizes a different set of experiences that define him, society comprises a broad array of people with different tendencies, dispositions, passions, and talents.

Human nature, then, is a complex mixture of biology and social construction, not merely a reflection of immutable instincts. This suggests that Burke's view of human nature is only moderately pessimistic. If instilled with traditions, customs, and mores that curb their baser tendencies, people may be—to paraphrase Abraham Lincoln—touched by the better angels of their nature.

"People will not look forward to posterity, who never look backward to their ancestors"

In a speech before the Young Men's Lyceum of Springfield, Illinois, Lincoln warned his audience of the dangers of radical change at the hands of talented men burning with the desire for fame and glory. They cannot abide a more modest life, toiling in the shadow cast by the great men who came before them. They seek immortality by leaving such a deep impression that future generations will never forget their accomplishments. The problem is that what they do is not nearly as important to them as having left their permanent mark on history. Said Lincoln:

> Towering genius disdains a beaten path. It seeks regions hitherto unexplored. It sees *no distinction* in adding story to story, upon the monuments of fame, erected to the memory of others. It *denies* that it is glory enough to serve under any chief. It *scorns* to tread in the footsteps of *any* predecessor, however illustrious. It thirsts and burns for distinction; and, if possible, it will have it whether at the expense of emancipating slaves, or enslaving freemen. Is it unreasonable then to expect, that some man possessed of the loftiest genius, coupled with ambition sufficient to push it to its utmost stretch, will at some time, spring among us? And when such a one does, it will require the people to be united with each other, attached to the government and laws, and generally intelligent, to successfully frustrate his designs.[22]

This passage captures the chilling amorality of the towering genius. Emancipating slaves or enslaving freemen—either choice is acceptable to him, so long as his immortality is assured. Lincoln understood that only widespread reverence for the law and tradition could effectively restrain such men, whose thirst for distinction made them a threat to both freedom and order.

These words echo Burke's thoughts on the subject perfectly. Burke reacted so violently to the French Revolution because it ran roughshod over nearly every sacred tradition in that country, creating a vacuum in which a horde of towering geniuses would scramble to realize their ambitions and make their loftiest dreams a reality. Years before the Reign of Terror, Burke saw it coming in the wake of so much innovation. In one fell swoop, the revolutionaries dismantled centuries of tradition, taking power away from the monarchy, the aristocracy, and the church. In place of the *ancien régime* they created a republic organized around the untried theories of the philosophers, which did not serve the needs of the people so much as it created chaos. They unleashed the furies, and then came Robespierre and the Guillotine.

One can think of tradition as the collective wisdom of past ages put into practice. It was important for Burke because it serves as a check on the innate desire for pure freedom, teaching us that a meaningful life involves fulfilling our obligations and strengthening our ties to others. Many Enlightenment thinkers, including Locke and Rousseau, described human beings as independent agents who saw civil society as a contract entered only out of necessity. Burke rejected this view. "Society is indeed a contract," said Burke, but not anything like those that "may be dissolved at pleasure," such as a "partnership agreement in a trade of pepper and coffee, calico or tobacco, or some other such low concern." He continued:

> It is to be looked on with other reverence; because it is not a partnership of things subservient only to the gross animal existence of a temporary and perishable nature. It is a partnership in all science; a partnership in all art; a partnership in every virtue, and in all perfection. As the ends of such a partnership cannot be obtained in many generations, it becomes a partnership not only between those who are living, but between those who are living, those who are dead, and those who are to be born. Each contract of each particular state is but a clause in the great primaeval contract in eternal society, linking the lower with higher natures, connecting the visible and invisible world.[23]

This is no mere contract of necessity or expedience serving the short-term interests of the living. It is a sacred partnership linking together generations of people who seek perfection in science, art, and virtue. This is not an enterprise that one generation can complete on its own. Each generation continues the work of its ancestors and then passes it on to posterity.

It is the duty of the living to preserve and uphold tradition not just to show reverence for their forebears but to ensure that the next generation inherits a world worth living in—and for. Those who feel no obligation to the past will not care what happens in the future. "People will not look forward to posterity," said Burke, "who never look backward to their ancestors."[24] Indeed, those who are "unmindful of what they have received from their ancestors, or of what is due to their posterity,...act as if they were the entire masters." Once they consider it "amongst their rights to cut off the entail, or commit waste on the inheritance," they will "leave to those who come after them, a ruin instead of an habitation." Having inherited a "ruin" from their prodigal ancestors, the next generation will be equally selfish and uncaring about the future. Why care for posterity when your own forebears showed so little concern for you? The new motto becomes *Every generation for itself.* Once we cease to uphold tradition, each generation feels free to start anew, changing the state whenever and however it desires. The consequences are dire, for "the whole chain and continuity of the commonwealth would be broken. No one generation could link with the other. Men would become little better than the flies of a summer."[25] If we renounce tradition, we abrogate our obligations toward other men. Once free of all obligations, we lose our humanity.

Perhaps one of the chief benefits of tradition is that it provides guidelines for action to which we do not have to give much thought. When we follow tradition, we can go on auto-pilot. It is not unreasonable to view tradition as a kind of habit—a habit of not just one individual but an entire community. Thoughtlessly conforming to tradition or habit certainly makes life easier, and few would find fault with those who perform trivial tasks mechanically. But when something important arises, many people will insist that only rational thought and logic should guide our behavior. Burke could not disagree more. While tradition comes in many different forms, Burke showed particular interest in two kinds—prescription (or traditional rights) and prejudice (or traditional opinions).

Burke believed that rights grow deeper roots in a society when they are derived not from abstract reason but from ancestors who found a need for them as a way to address practical problems. In other words, rights should stem from the practices and compacts of preceding generations, and over time, they become cherished tradition. The legal term for traditional rights is prescription. Said Burke:

> You will observe, that from Magna Charta to the Declaration of Right, it has been the uniform policy of our constitution to claim and assert our liberties, as entailed inheritance derived to us from our forefathers, and to be transmitted to our posterity; as an estate specially belonging to the people of this kingdom without any reference whatever to any other more general or prior right.[26]

Whereas appeals to a "more general or prior right" are unnecessary and ultimately the "result of a selfish temper," traditional rights are the "result of a profound reflection" on the past. Because we consider "our liberties in the light of an inheritance," they become "noble" and assume "an imposing and majestic aspect." Unlike abstract rights, which are invented out of thin air, prescription "has a pedigree and illustrating ancestors… It has its gallery of portraits; its monumental inscriptions; its records, evidences, and titles."[27] Our forefathers fought for these prescriptive rights long ago, risking their lives in order to make a better world for their fellow men and their descendants. For their valiant efforts, said Burke, these great and noble men deserve our reverence; they should walk among the immortals. Accordingly, he praised the "chartered rights of Englishmen" enshrined in documents such as the Magna Charta and the 1689 Bill of Rights, and he disparaged the abstract and unpedigreed "rights of man" claimed by the likes of Thomas Paine.

Burke's defense of traditional opinions (or prejudice) runs along similar lines. While it is common to equate it with bigotry or intolerance, Burke expressed his unabashed approval of prejudice, which he saw as beliefs inherited from our ancestors and generally accepted by our contemporaries. "[I]nstead of casting away all our old prejudices, we cherish them to a very considerable degree," said Burke, in reference to his fellow Englishmen; "we cherish them because they are prejudices; and the longer they have lasted, and the more generally they have prevailed, the more we cherish them." His beloved Englishmen have little faith in "naked reason" and instead rely on "general prejudices," seeing the "latent wisdom which prevails in them."[28]

Prejudice does not only embody age-old wisdom; it also instills in people the habit of acting on that wisdom. "Prejudice is of ready application in an emergency," said Burke; "it previously engages the mind in a steady course of wisdom and virtue, and does not leave the man hesitating in the moment of decision, skeptical, puzzled, and unresolved. Prejudice renders a man's virtue his habit; and not a series of unconnected acts. Through just prejudice, his duty becomes a part of his nature."[29] Thanks to prejudice, we internalize our moral obligations, making them such an important part of who we are that we will act on them with determination and consistency.

What are these prejudices that Burke held so dear? The following passage gives us a clue: "We fear God; we look up with awe to kings; with affection to parliaments; with duty to magistrates; with reverence to priests; and with respect to nobility."[30] So long as we cherish these prejudices, said Burke, we will act on two principles upon which civilization stands: the spirit of a gentleman (or chivalry) and the spirit of religion (or piety). The former taught honor and loyalty to rank; the latter taught belief in a god who inspired fear and demanded virtue.

In *Reflections*, Burke lamented the decline of chivalry after hearing about the insults endured by the queen of France at the start of the revolution. He described chivalry as "that proud submission, that dignified obedience, that subordination of the heart, which kept alive, even in servitude itself, the spirit of an exalted freedom." He praised it for inculcating people with a respect for hierarchy while at the same time producing a "noble equality" that turned "kings into companions" and commoners into "fellows with kings." "Without force, or opposition," said Burke, "[chivalry] subdued the fierceness of pride and power; it obliged sovereigns to submit to the soft collar of social esteem, compelled stern authority to submit to elegance, and gave a dominating vanquisher of laws, to be subdued by manners." Chivalry created a society where people knew and accepted their place in the class system, making them free of the ambition to exceed their station. By the same token, nobles were expected to be gentle-hearted and generous of spirit in their exercise of power. But with the destruction of the *ancien régime* in France, those "pleasing illusions, which made power gentle, and obedience liberal," were quickly disappearing.[31] For Burke, this was a tragedy of epic proportions.

Equally tragic was the attack on religion leveled by the French revolutionaries. Burke argued that government officials should have faith in God and that the church should be inseparable from the state. Because "they stand in the person of God himself" in their political capacity, officials "should not look to the paltry pelf of the moment, nor to the temporary and transient praise of the vulgar, but to the solid, permanent existence."[32] The best way to safeguard religious prejudices was to follow the British model of unifying church and state. "[The British] do not consider their church establishment as convenient, but as essential to their state; not as a thing heterogeneous and separable; something added for accommodation," said Burke. "They consider it the foundation of their whole constitution, with which, and with every part of which, it holds an indissoluble union. Church and state are ideas inseparable in their minds, and scarcely is the one ever mentioned without mentioning the other."[33] The French sought to replace the church with a civic education that would teach citizens to "identify with an interest more enlarged and public"—that is, to be enlightened. But, according to Burke, such a secular education is "founded in a knowledge of the physical wants of men"—in the vulgarities of corporeal existence—that will only serve to inflame selfish desires.[34] A godless state cannot sustain civic virtue.

It is nearly impossible to overstate the importance of tradition in Burke's political thought. We can think of tradition as a set of guidelines inherited from our most pedigreed ancestors, keeping the fabric of society together by inculcating civic-mindedness, chivalry, and piety among other virtues. And once ingrained as habit, they liberate us from having to deliberate over every idea we embrace and every action we take. While these guidelines are not infallible, they will serve us well more often than not. For tradition is hewn from the experiences of our forebears. Nevertheless, we should be prepared to depart from tradition when circumstances require. As the world around us changes, said Burke, so must we.

"A DISPOSITION TO REFORM"

Burke's fierce opposition to the French Revolution, for which he is best known today, has earned him a reputation in some circles as a stodgy traditionalist, even a reactionary.[35] It did not help his cause when his words sometimes betrayed a cranky resistance to change. At times, Burke seemed to suggest that whenever possible, it was always better to endure the abuses of power and other injustices than to invite further calamity by trying to remedy them. Accept your fate, he seemed to say, and take some comfort in the fact that things could be far worse.

But it should come as no surprise to anyone familiar with his political career that Burke supported many reforms. The mischaracterization of Burke as a reactionary or an arch-conservative stems from a failure to see the crucial distinction that he made between reform and innovation. While he favored reform, he regarded innovation as a grave threat to the social order and to humanity itself. In his view, the Jacobins in France were innovators whose calls for radical change and contempt for tradition laid the groundwork for a hitherto unknown barbarism. He saw himself as the consummate reformer, one who accepted the necessity of change in a dynamic world but who cautioned against relishing it too much.

From the Burkean perspective, reform can be understood as slow, deliberate, and measured change that addresses specific problems while preserving the integrity of existing institutions and traditions as much as possible. Although Burke acknowledged the inevitability and necessity of change, he insisted that it occur incrementally. In his view, reform should be "slow, and in some cases imperceptible," requiring "many years" in some cases before it is completed.[36] For it is the only way that the reformer can implement helpful solutions without doing harm to those traditions that serve us so well. "All we can do, and that human wisdom can do, is to provide that the change shall proceed by insensible degrees," he said. "This has all the benefits which may be in change, without any of the inconveniences of mutation."[37] By adhering to the principle of incrementalism, the reformer can strike a delicate balance between progress and preservation. According to Burke, the ability to find this equilibrium is the mark of a true leader: "A disposition to preserve, and an ability to improve, taken together, would be my standard of a statesman."[38] Unlike the impetuous French, said Burke, the people of England agreed with the notion that tradition and reform are not mutually exclusive.[39]

The English were not the only ones to recognize incrementalism as the key to finding a balance between improvement and tradition. In his never-completed history of the English, Burke recounted a story about Pope Gregory, who took pains to convert heathens to Christianity as gradually as possible. He allowed new converts to continue practicing many pagan ceremonies and rituals, so long as they did not clash with the Christian teachings to which they were being slowly introduced, and instead of destroying their old temples, he converted them into churches. Said Burke:

> Whatever popular customs of heathenism were found to be absolutely not incompatible with Christianity, were retained; and some of them were continued to a very late period. Deer were at a certain season brought into St. Paul's church in London, and laid on the altar; and this custom subsisted until the Reformation. The names of some of the church festivals were, with a similar design, taken from those of the heathen, which had been celebrated at the same time of year.

According to Burke, the Pope considered it prudent to make the transition from paganism to Christianity gradually "in order that the prejudices of the people might not be too rudely shocked by a declared profanation of what they had so long held sacred."[40] While the Pope wanted to save souls, he was also mindful of the fact that traditional opinions and practices do not die easily. Simply forbidding them would have been seen as an act of hostility. He found a workable compromise by allowing people to observe many of their ancient traditions, especially the more innocuous ones, within a broader Christian framework. In the short term, these converts who continued their pagan ways were Christian in name only. But accommodating the old ways as much as possible minimized disruption in people's lives and made them more receptive to Christianity in the long run.

While reform efforts often conflict with the old ways, there are times when they go hand-in-hand. That is to say, reform may be *necessary* to save tradition. "A state without the means of some change is without the means of its conservation," said Burke in *Reflections*. "Without such means it might even risque the loss of that part of the constitution which it wished the most religiously to preserve."[41] Later on in the same text, Burke reiterated this point: "I would not exclude alteration neither; but even when I changed, it should be to preserve."[42] Even if our default is to abide by tradition without questioning it too much, a stubborn refusal to accept change in all circumstances can create a crisis of legitimacy in which people begin to doubt the efficacy of established institutions. Tradition must remain flexible enough to accommodate change, proving itself to be adequately responsive to new problems that arise in a dynamic world. Tradition cannot survive if it becomes too rigid and uncompromising. It must be able to bend so as not to break.

That said, the reformer should only welcome change as a last resort. Only when it becomes evident that working within the existing framework is no longer sustainable should the reformer push for change. The disruption to people's lives requires a compelling reason. Conditions must become unbearable before the reformer sets to work. As Burke put it, "I must bear with infirmities until they fester into crimes."[43] This is because the reformer must never forget that his actions can do great harm. His good intentions notwithstanding, the consequences of his actions could be worse than the miseries he wants to alleviate. "If circumspection and caution are part of wisdom, when we work only upon inanimate matter, surely they become a part of duty too, when the subject of our demolition and construction is not brick and timber, but sentient beings" who could "be rendered miserable" by reform efforts. A profound sense of humility must guide the reformer, who would be well advised to "fear himself" as he sets out to make a better world.[44] Acutely aware of the responsibility weighing upon his shoulders, he would never effect change for trivial reasons.

To the contrary, the proponent of innovation does not wait for infirmities to turn into crimes. He demands immediate and dramatic change, the wholesale rejection of tradition on the grounds that it hinders progress. For the innovator, "it is a sufficient motive to destroy an old scheme of things, because it is an old one. As to the new, they are in no sort of fear with regard to the duration of a building run up in haste," said Burke. "They conceive, very systematically, that all things which give perpetuity are mischievous, and therefore they are at inexpiable war with all establishments."[45] His inclination is to tear down and start anew, even if conditions under the established order are tolerable.

The innovator's contempt for tradition runs so deep that nothing short of its complete destruction will satisfy him. "All the decent drapery of life is to be rudely torn off," said Burke. "All the super-added ideas, furnished from the wardrobe of a moral imagination, which the heart owns, and the understanding ratifies, as necessary to cover the effects of our naked shivering nature, and to raise it to dignity in our own estimation, are to be exploded as a ridiculous, absurd, and antiquated fashion."[46] For Burke, the wardrobe of tradition is necessary to cover the defects of our nature and to recover our humanity. For the innovator, these "super-added ideas" are patently "absurd" adornments that serve to obscure what is at the heart of the established order—hypocrisy, lies, and corruption.

By removing the fineries of tradition, the innovator hopes to disabuse people of those myths that have been used to justify the inequities of the existing power structure. Once disrobed, "a king is but a man; a queen is but a woman." The problem with the iconoclasm of the innovator is that it destroys everything in its path, sparing not even those traditions that bring out the best of humanity. Once kings and queens are exposed as merely men and women, the innovator reaches the logical conclusion that "a woman is but an animal; and an animal not of the highest order. All homage paid to the sex in general as such, and without distinct views, is to be regarded as romance and folly. Regicide, and parricide, and sacrilege, are but fictions of superstition."[47]

Unfortunately, in his rush to expose the lies and superstitions that lie at the heart of the traditional order, the innovator jettisons the good with the bad. He eviscerates those traditions that restrain our darker passions, that instill within us an active moral imagination that fosters compassion and human decency. Almost nothing is forbidden in his barren moral landscape. The "thorough-bred metaphysician" is an exemplary innovator, cold-hearted and determined to slaughter sacred cows. So driven is he to turn his ambitious plans into reality that the costs to his fellow human beings hardly seem to matter. The metaphysicians

> are ready to declare, that they do not think two thousand years too long a period for the good that they pursue. It is remarkable, that they never see any way to their projected good but by the road of some evil. Their imagination is not fatigued with the contemplation of human suffering through the wild waste of centuries added to centuries of misery and desolation. Their humanity is at their horizon—and, like the horizon, it always flies before them. The geometricians, and the chemists, bring, the one from the dry bones of their diagrams, and the other from the soot of their furnaces, dispositions that make them worse than indifferent about those feelings and habitudes, which are the supports of the moral world.[48]

Other human beings become mere abstractions to the metaphysicians, whose eagerness to innovate will never be "fatigued with the contemplation of human suffering." They set out to remake the world in accordance with their blueprints and diagrams, blissfully unconcerned about the concrete consequences of their efforts. They keep those people on whom they perform their experiments at a safe distance, at the margins (or "horizon") of their awareness. As a result, these men have "nothing of the tender parental solicitude which fears to cut up the infant for the sake of an experiment."[49] They see not infants before them but lab mice.

The metaphysicians to whom Burke referred were not hypothetical. In his discussions of the dangers of innovation, he always had the French Revolution in mind. Never one to mince words, Burke condemned the revolutionaries for not only rationalizing but also celebrating their inhumanity as the only way to bring about a better future. "Humanity and compassion are ridiculed as the fruits of superstition and ignorance. Tenderness to individuals is considered as treason to the public," he said. "Amidst assassination, massacre, and confiscation, perpetrated or mediated, they are forming plans for the good order of future society."[50] Burke described the Jacobins as those who were "resolved to destroy the whole frame and fabric of the old societies of the world, and to regenerate them after their fashion."[51] From their perspective, "the will, the wish, the want, the liberty, the toil, the blood of individuals, is as nothing. Individuality is left out of their scheme of government. The state is all in all. Everything is referred to the production of force; afterwards, everything is trusted to the use of it."[52] Never afraid to use the terrifying power of the state to accomplish their goals, the Jacobins turned priceless human beings into expendable commodities. They were willing to sacrifice flesh-and-blood men at the altar of Mankind.

Burke despaired over the government established by the revolutionaries. Because they made a fetish of unrestrained state power, they failed to create a system of checks and balances that promotes moderation and compromise. In the *ancien régime*, the conflict among competing interests made "deliberation a matter not of choice, but of necessity," and also made "change a subject of *compromise*, which naturally begets moderation." This system of multiple factions went a long way toward "preventing the sole evil of harsh, crude, unqualified reformations."[53] Frustrated by the painstakingly slow pace of change in that system, the Jacobins streamlined government, giving the Assembly the power to do whatever it wished. "That Assembly, since the destruction of the orders, has no fundamental law, no strict convention, no respected usage to restrain it," said Burke. "Instead of finding themselves obliged to conform to a fixed constitution, they have a power to make a constitution which shall conform to their designs. Nothing in heaven or upon earth can serve as a control on them."[54] Free of traditional and institutional impediments, the Assembly could exercise power arbitrarily, tyrannize with impunity. And this it did—with unalloyed pleasure.

For Burke, what made the French Revolution so tragic was that it did not have to happen. It was neither necessary nor inevitable. Although far from perfect, the flawed constitution of the *ancien régime* could have been salvaged. "Your constitution, it is true, whilst you were out of possession, suffered waste and dilapidation; but you possessed in some parts the walls, and in all the foundations of a noble and venerable castle," said Burke. "You might have repaired those walls; you might have built on those old foundations. Your constitution was suspended before it was perfected; but you had the elements of a constitution very nearly as good as could be wished."[55] Had the king and queen really been "inexorable and cruel tyrants," who had devised plans for "massacring the National Assembly," one might consider "their captivity just."[56] Or if the situation in France had been as bad as Germany's "at the period when the Hanse-towns were necessitated to confederate against the nobles in defence of their property," then the revolutionaries in France might have been justified in "freeing the world from such a nuisance"—and using extreme measures to do so.[57] But, in Burke's view, conditions in France were never so grim. He could not find "any incorrigible vices in the noblesse of France, or any abuse which could not be removed by a reform very short of abolition."[58]

Writing to his son in September of 1791, a time when he still maintained hope that the monarchy in France could be restored, Burke specified the kinds of reform he had in mind. Most important was the establishment of a "free constitution" that placed limits on monarchical power and abolished arbitrary imprisonment and other abuses. Although he was hardly a champion of the new French republic, Burke understood that there was no hope of going back to the old regime without making serious concessions. He even agreed that a return to the past without reform would be worse than the loathsome present. "For my part, for one, though I make no doubt of preferring the ancient course, or almost any other, to this vile chimera, and sick man's dream of government," said Burke, "I could not actively, or with a good heart and clear conscience, go to the re-establishment of a monarchical despotism in the place of this system of anarchy."[59] If one could refer to only one piece of textual evidence confirming that Burke was not a reactionary, this would be it. He did not have any sentimental attachment to the *ancien régime* or long for some idyllic past. He merely held out hope that France could find a balance between tradition and improvement, between the old and the new.

"To be wrong in theory and right in practice"

Ultimately, Edmund Burke favored moderate reforms based on compromise because of the practical benefits. His emphasis on concrete results instead of abstract principle speaks to a strong pragmatic strain in his thought. Although he believed in absolute truths, Burke did not think that human beings could ever say with certainty that they had discovered them. No matter how much logic and abstract thought we devote to the search, absolute truth will remain elusive, just beyond our grasp. Therefore, we have to settle for provisional truths that can be arrived at inductively through empirical observation. In a world where people are so certain about their truth claims that they do not hesitate to impose them on others, there is wisdom in the humble acknowledgment that no one has a monopoly on the truth. While certainty spurs heedless innovation, humility gives way to cautious reform.

It is important to explore in some detail Burke's epistemology in order to put to rest popular but spurious interpretations of his thought. As mentioned earlier, many Burke scholars have described him as a natural law theorist who believed in the existence of universal truths about politics, which are made available to us through reason or revelation. In their view, everyone is obligated to obey these truths, no matter the time or place. But, as this section will make clear, the textual evidence does not support such a reading. Burke never offered a general theory of truth or knowledge as a professional philosopher would do, but a patient reader can make out a coherent epistemology in his thought.

The simple fact is that Burke had little use for grand philosophical speculation, and he did not trust the bold conclusions often drawn from deductive reasoning. Influenced by empiricists such as Locke and Hume, he believed in induction, gleaning general knowledge from sensory experiences. He argued that "establishments" are the product "of various necessities and expediencies" and "not often constructed after any theory." To the contrary, "theories are rather drawn from them."[60] It is perfectly acceptable—nay, it is preferable—to ignore a theory when it does not work in practice. A theory without practical value is just plain wrong, and we should try to construct a new one anchored in what concrete experience tells us. "It is, I own, not uncommon to be wrong in theory and right in practice; and we are happy it is so," said Burke; "but as it is impossible to avoid an attempt at such reasoning, and equally impossible to prevent its having some influence on our practice, surely it is worth taking some pains to have it just, and founded on the basis of sure experience."[61] We should be wary of any theory derived solely from abstract thought.

Burke considered abstract reasoning especially worthless when applied to the complex affairs of human beings. "I cannot stand forward, and give praise or blame to any human actions, and human concerns, on a simple view of the object, as it stands stripped of every relation, in all the nakedness and solitude of metaphysical abstraction," said Burke. "Circumstances (which with some gentlemen pass for nothing) give in reality to every political principle its distinguishing color, and discriminating effect. The circumstances are what render every civil and political scheme beneficial or noxious to mankind."[62] The problem with imposing principles that are formulated in a vacuum of abstraction is that they may have no relevance to the actual circumstances in which people find themselves. We deem a particular "political scheme" good or just not because it conforms to some abstract principle but because it is observably "beneficial" to society. Only from experience can we construct reliable political principles. And we should not ignore the experiences of other countries, for Burke expressed his wish that France had drawn on the "wise examples" of countries such as Great Britain—which "had kept alive the ancient principles and models of the old common law of Europe"—before it decided to pursue its destructive course.[63]

It is not a stretch to suggest that, for Burke, the practice of politics should follow the standards of an empirical science. "The science of constructing a commonwealth, or renovating it, or reforming it," he said, "is, like every other experimental science, not to be taught a priori."[64] In the realm of politics, there are no inalienable first principles from which one can deduce truths of universal value. As with any other experimental science, politics must begin with concrete experiences and observations from which more general truths can be derived. That there are limits to what we can know from sensory experience should not deter us from empirical research. As Burke said, "A theory founded on experiment and not assumed, is always good for so much as it explains. Our inability to push indefinitely is no argument at all against it."[65] While it is certainly true that theories derived from experiment have explanatory limitations, the alternative is far worse. Indeed, theories founded on idle speculation or assumption have a tendency to overreach by trying to explain everything.

Burke cautioned against this kind of hubris. "If an enquiry thus carefully conducted, should fail at last of discovering the truth, it may answer an end perhaps as useful, in discovering to us the weakness of our own understanding," he said. "If it does not make us knowing, it may make us modest. If it does not preserve us from error, it may at least from the spirit of error, and may make us cautious of pronouncing with positiveness or with haste."[66] We must accept the epistemological limits posed by the human condition. In his study of aesthetics, Burke conceded that it was "impossible" to give a definitive explanation of "why certain affections of the body produce such a distinct emotion of the mind, and no other; or why the body is at all affected by the mind, or the mind by the body." The most that the seeker of truth can do is follow the chain of causes and events. This is an enterprise that certainly provides useful empirical information, but it ultimately leads to a dead end. The big questions and mysteries remain unanswered. "That great chain of causes, which linking one to another even to the throne of God himself, can never be unraveled by any industry of ours," he said. "When we go but one step beyond the immediately sensible qualities of things, we go out of our depth."[67] While Burke did not doubt the existence of God and other enduring truths, he believed it was beyond the capacity of human beings to have any direct contact with them—or to comprehend them with any clarity. At best, we see evidence of God and other truths obliquely, filtered through the haze of our sensory experiences.

Burke provided some examples of how human beings derive general concepts from experience. Arguing that abstract thinking lags behind what story-telling can teach us, Burke said: "Men had always friends and enemies before they knew the exact nature of vice and virtue; they naturally and with their best powers of eloquence, whether in prose or verse, magnified and set off the one; vilified and traduced the other."[68] The implication here is that stories about enemies and friends only later gave rise to more abstract conceptions of vice and virtue. We call those who intend to hurt us "vicious" or "bad." We call those who intend to help us "virtuous" or "good." By offering a brief genealogy of morals in this passage, Burke anticipated arguments put forth by Nietzsche over a century later. He expanded on this theme in another essay, arguing that the difference between truth and falsehood, at least in the world of politics, stems from our concrete experiences with good and evil, respectively. "What in the result is likely to produce evil is politically false; that which is productive of good, politically true."[69] Burke showed his preference for inductive thinking in suggesting that larger political and ethical truths grow out of aesthetic experiences. That which makes us happy is good and thus true.

For Burke, aesthetic experiences could play an important role in the formation of general concepts, particularly those about morality. Much like the Roman poet Horace, who believed that moral choices are largely a matter of taste, Burke saw a direct connection between aesthetics and ethics. "Whatever certainty is to be acquired in morality and the science of life; just the same degree of certainty have we in what relates to them in works of imitation," he said. "Indeed it is for the most part in our skill in manners, and in the observances of time and place, and of decency in general, which is only to be learned in those schools to which Horace recommends us, that what is called Taste by way of distinction, consists."[70] According to Burke, aesthetic taste is a form of judgment that involves three faculties: sensory perception, imagination, and reasoning. Those who develop refined aesthetic tastes by using these faculties will correspondingly heighten their moral sensibility. The most important faculty in the development of morals is imagination. This is because we mainly learn through imitation, said Burke, and one of the benefits of consuming good art is that we learn to imitate the lives of others. In other words, we learn to imagine living in another person's place, seeing things from his unique perspective. It is for this reason that Burke could say in all seriousness that "the theater is a better school of moral sentiments than churches, where the feelings of humanity are thus outraged."[71] Good art stirs the moral imagination more effectively than the most inspired sermon, because it broadens our horizon of possible experiences from which we are able to derive ethical principles, while sermons merely convey the commands of a god who remains forever abstract, remote from the hardships of daily life.

Burke also demonstrated his wariness of abstract thinking in his discussions of government. Revealing his consequentalist colors, Burke said, "To those who say [the British Constitution] is a bad one, I answer, Look to its effects. In all moral machinery, the moral results are its test."[72] Burke also argued that it was impossible to make an abstract argument in favor of a single type of government. Though clearly an enemy of democracy, Burke did not rule out the possibility that this form of government could be useful—even necessary—in circumstances far different from what human beings had hitherto experienced. As a result, he opposed any theories that regarded one form of government as ideal. "I reprobate no form of government merely upon abstract principles. There may be situations in which the purely democratic form will become necessary. There may be some (very few, and very particularly circumstanced) where it would be clearly desirable."[73] In the end, human beings construct governments as a way to address concrete problems. As Burke put it, "Government is a contrivance of human wisdom to provide for human *wants*."[74]

"Government is not made in virtue of natural rights"

Burke most often expressed his distaste for abstract thought in his discussions about liberties and rights. The main problem with abstract (or "pretended") rights is that they are completely divorced from the moral complexities of real life and, as a result, veer toward simplistic extremes. They do not serve us well in practice because they resist compromise, any attempts to find common ground or a middle way. The adherents of abstract rights see compromise as the language of the devil. This is not the case for those who understand rights as Burke did. For Burkeans, abstract rights do not ring true in the inherently tragic world of politics, where we must choose between degrees of imperfection. The actual rights of human beings have tangible rewards.

> The pretended rights of these theorists are all extremes; and in proportion as they are metaphysically true, they are morally and politically false. The rights of men are in a sort of *middle*, incapable of definition, but not impossible to be discerned. The rights of men in governments are their advantages; and these are often in balances between differences of good; in compromises

sometimes between good and evil, and sometimes between evil and evil. Political reason is a computing principle; adding, subtracting, multiplying, and dividing, morally and not metaphysically or mathematically, true moral denominations.[75]

Interestingly, Burke flirted with relativism in this passage, suggesting that "the rights of men in governments" seek an achievable compromise, not conformity with absolute principles. His moral universe had many shades of gray, not a stark choice between black and white, between absolute evil and absolute good. We can locate our rights in the most advantageous options, which produce the least amount of evil in our experience.

"If civil society be made for the advantage of man," said Burke, "all the advantages for which it is made become his right."[76] Once one begins to see rights as serving "the advantage of man," the following conclusion becomes unavoidable: the rights of human beings depend on the circumstances. While the revolutionaries in France saw rights as inalienable liberties to which all people are entitled no matter the circumstances, Burke believed that rights changed with the times and the place. As a result, in addition to liberating people from their bonds, rights may impose certain duties and restraints if they prove advantageous in some concrete way. "In this sense the restraints of men, as well as their liberties, are to be reckoned among their rights," he said. "But as the liberties and the restrictions vary with times and circumstances, and admit of infinite modifications, they cannot be settled upon any abstract rule; and nothing is so foolish as to discuss them upon that principle."[77]

Burke's impatience with abstraction became especially pronounced when he discussed the responsibility of government to address specific problems. He preferred to talk about practical solutions, giving the state the tools to provide for the advantages of men. "The state is to have recruits to its strength and remedies to its distempers. What is the use of discussing a man's abstract right to food or to medicine?" he asked. "The question is upon the method of procuring and administering them. In that deliberation I shall always advise to call in the aid of the farmer and the physician, rather than the professor of metaphysics."[78] This passage does not suggest that Burke ruled out the possibility of recognizing food and medicine as rights. But he clearly believed that these rights have significance only if the state can secure them, demonstrating its ability to feed the hungry and medicate the sick. His focus on finding remedies and implementing them make him sound like something of a policy wonk. That should not surprise us given his strong pragmatic streak. Burke often expressed his preference for concrete criteria (such as "happiness") by which each society can judge its level of freedom. "Abstract liberty, like other mere abstractions, is not to be found," said Burke. "Liberty inheres in some sensible object; and every nation has formed to itself some favorite point, which by way of eminence becomes the criterion of their happiness."[79]

Burke's unrelenting focus on the here and now, his pragmatic belief that we construct rights in accordance with the "wants" and "advantages" of men, suggests that he categorically rejected the existence of absolute rights. This is not entirely true. On several occasions Burke acknowledged the likely existence of absolute rights; he only doubted our capacity to apply them to human affairs. Burke said, "Government is not made in virtue of natural rights, which may and do exist in total independence of it; and exist in much greater clearness, and in a much greater degree of abstract perfection; but their abstract perfection is their practical defect." There are natural rights that exist independently of government and the experience of men, but they have limited practical value. Once applied to human affairs, these natural or "metaphysic rights" enter our lives "like rays of light which pierce into a dense medium" and then are "refracted from their straight line." Because of the "complicated mass of human passions and concerns, the primitive rights of men undergo such a variety of refractions and reflections, that it becomes absurd to talk of them as if they continue in the simplicity of their original direction."[80] In other words, the messiness of real life gets in the way of keeping natural rights in their original simplicity and elegance. These rights may in fact exist in some transcendental realm outside of earthly experience; unfortunately, our flawed nature makes realizing them impossible. We cannot recreate heaven here on earth.

Burke also called into question our ability to comprehend our natural rights with any certainty. He remained skeptical for the simple fact that political thinkers who make absolute claims about our natural rights work under the assumption that there is a difference between nature and society. "The state of civil society, which necessarily generates this aristocracy, is a state of nature; and much more truly so than a savage and incoherent mode of life," he said. "We are as much, at least, in a state of nature in formed manhood, as in immature and helpless infancy."[81] Hoping to identify some incontrovertible truths about human nature, many political thinkers, such as Locke and Rousseau, imagined life for human beings in a so-called state of nature—a world without civil society or government.

But Burke considered this a futile exercise, because no such world has ever existed. As one might expect, their abstract thought experiments led to questionable ideas about "the right of men to act anywhere according to their pleasure, without any moral tie." According to Burke, "no such right exists," because people "are never in a state of *total* independence of each other. It is not the condition of our nature; nor is it conceivable how any man can pursue a considerable course of action without its having some effect upon others."[82] Burke repudiated the liberal assumption that each of us is an autonomous and unencumbered self, neither dependent on nor responsible for other human beings in his community. Rather than imagining people in a state that never existed, he started from the premise, based on empirical evidence, that people are naturally social and interdependent creatures who rely on others for help and are duty-bound to help others in return.

When Burke attacked the East India Company for abusing its power as a colonial administrator working on behalf of the UK, he seemed to contradict himself on the issue of natural rights. He delivered countless speeches on the subject, hoping to persuade his colleagues in Parliament to restrict the power of the Company and to hold its most powerful official, Warren Hastings, criminally responsible for some of its more flagrant abuses. As Governor-General of Bengal, Hastings had allegedly presided over the gross exploitation of the local population. Interestingly, the Company invoked moral relativism to justify some of its more shameful practices. What is not legal or morally acceptable in England, they suggested, may be so in India. In a long speech delivered at the opening of Hastings' impeachment trial, Burke expressed his dismay that the Company "had formed a plan of Geographical morality, by which the duties of men in public and in private situations are not to be governed by their relations to the great Governor of the Universe, or by their relations to men, but by climates, degrees of longitude, parallels not of life but of latitudes." He argued that "the laws of morality are the same every where, and that there is no action which would pass for an act of extortion, of peculation, of bribery, and of oppression in England, that is not an act of extortion, of peculation, of bribery, and of oppression in Europe, Asia, Africa, and all the world over."[83] Scholars who see Burke as a natural law theorist regard his appeal to "the Governor of the Universe" (or God) as especially powerful evidence.

But it is important to note that Burke provided an alternative to God, arguing that the "duties of men" may be governed instead by people's "relations to men." This reference to human relations comports with the pragmatic side of Burke. Then, immediately after the foregoing passage, he added an important caveat that poses a serious challenge to natural law interpretations of his thought. "This I contend for," he said, "not in the technical forms of it, but I contend for it in the substance."[84] The suggestion here is that some universal moral truths—bribery and extortion are bad, for example—do exist, but they stem not from abstract thinking (or "technical forms") but from observations of empirical reality (or "substance"). In other words, bribery is bribery everywhere because its negative effects are universal. Whether one travels to Europe, Asia, Africa, or any other continent, people experience the same consequences of bribery. The same holds for many other immoral acts, including extortion and oppression.

Perhaps more than any other, natural law interpreters of Burke point to another passage from the same speech in which he invoked a higher law in his attack on arbitrary power. "Arbitrary power is a thing which neither any man can hold nor any man can give away. No man can lawfully govern himself by his own will; much less can he be governed by the will of others," he said. "We are all born in subjection, all born equally, high and low, governours and governed, in subjection to one great, immutable, pre-existent law, prior to all our devices, and prior to all our contrivances, paramount to all our ideas, and all our sensations, antecedent to our very existence." Then, in an apparent *coup de grâce* to any pragmatic readings of Burke, he contended that this "great law does not arise from our conventions or compacts" or "from our vain institutions. Every good gift is of God."[85] This passage certainly supports the view that Burke believed in a divine law that pre-exists all human experience. But we already knew that Burke believed in natural laws and rights that exist independently of us. The question was whether we can apprehend those truths, if only dimly, and how we might go about doing so. In other words, this powerful passage does not contradict the argument made earlier about Burke's epistemology: Any greater truths we may come to know must pass through our concrete experiences. Or, put differently, the light of truth only reaches us after it is refracted and distorted through the prism of our material existence. The existence of God and other transcendent truths does not change the fact that we can only know what our senses and faculties allow us to know.

What troubled Burke so greatly about Warren Hastings was the immense God-like power that he wielded as Governor-General of Bengal. Not accountable to any laws or traditions, Hastings possessed an unchecked power that was bound to breed corruption and oppression. According to Burke, this is a universal truth grounded in observations of human nature. Recall the earlier discussion of the intoxicating and destructive allure of power that, in his view, no one can resist. Experience teaches us that human beings cannot handle absolute power responsibly. Only God should have this kind of power. The important point to understand here is that Burke arrived at this universal principle—that no one should be given absolute power—from the humble perspective of a human being who would never claim to have direct access to God or absolute truth. Burke accepted that God and absolute truth exist beyond the horizon of human experience and that no one can escape this circumscribed condition. But he could never agree with the natural law theorist, who claims to have attained knowledge of moral and political truths through abstract reasoning or revelation. Such arrogance resembles that of Rousseau, whom Burke called "the insane Socrates of the National Assembly."[86]

"The species is wise"

In order to avoid the hubris of Rousseau and other thinkers who influenced the French Revolution, said Burke, the science of politics should remain focused on addressing "human wants" and doing what is to the "advantage of man." But it is important to stress that the "human wants" to which Burke refers must include those of our ancestors. We arrive at useful principles by drawing not only on the experiences of today but also on those from the past. The relevance of past experiences in Burke's epistemology should not surprise anyone who is familiar with his reverence for tradition. Recall that Burke considered society a contract, a sacred "partnership not only between those who are living, but between those who are living, those who are dead, and those who are to be born."[87] In other words, the general truths governing our social order—for example, ideas about the structure of government and the rights that it should safeguard—should be obtained from the experience and wisdom of our ancestors as well as our contemporaries.

In Burke's view, the experiences of just one person, or of even an entire generation, can never yield enough information to make definitive political decisions. The whole sweep of history—that is, the experiences of generations past—must be taken into account.

> The science of government being therefore so practical in itself, and intended for such practical purposes, a matter which requires experience, and even

more experience than any person can gain in his whole life, however sagacious and observing he may be, it is with infinite caution that any man ought to venture upon pulling down an edifice which has answered in any tolerable degree for ages the common purposes of society, or on building it up again, without having models and patterns of approved utility before his eyes.[88]

If contemporary experience suggests that we should replace the current structure or policy with something new, we should first remember that "for ages" it served "the common purposes of society." Therefore, we should not ignore why past generations built this seemingly obsolete edifice in the first place. We should respectfully consider the "utility" it once had and how it could be lost if we abandoned it hastily. Before acting rashly, we should remember that the science of politics relies on more knowledge "than any person can gain in his whole life."

In a strange way, Burke subscribed to the idea that crowds have wisdom. He accepted the view that wisdom is not the preserve of the lonely sage locked away in his study or hermitage. But his "crowd" was intergenerational, and the truth emerged slowly over the stretch of many generations. "A nation," he said, "is not an idea only of local extent and individual momentary aggregation, but it is an idea of continuity which extends in time as well as in number and space." The fate of a nation should not be set by the "tumultuary and giddy choice" of a democratic majority; instead, it should involve "a deliberate election of ages and of generations." Burke could not have disagreed more with Thomas Paine's assertion that the living should never be held hostage by the dead. In his view, the dead should get a vote for the simple fact that their experiences and wisdom, though hardly infallible, have something to teach us. Thus, the living should not define a nation of people through choice and force of will. Instead, a nation is

made by the peculiar circumstances, occasions, tempers, dispositions, and moral, civil, and social habitudes of the people, which disclose themselves only in a long space of time. It is a vestment which accommodates itself to the body. Nor is prescription of government formed upon blind, unmeaning prejudices. For man is a most unwise and a most wise being. The individual is foolish; the multitude, for the moment, is foolish, when they act without deliberation; but the species is wise, and when time is given to it, as a species, it almost always acts right.[89]

Out of the concrete circumstances of our ancestors, emerge tempers, dispositions, habits, and traditions that we inherit. To ignore these inheritances would be foolish, because they serve to restrain the worst aspects of our nature, prevent us from acting solely in accordance with will and caprice, and give us much-needed guidance and rules for action. Acting on our own, either as an individual or a group, we will likely make poor decisions and follow the wrong path. Drawing on the experience and wisdom of past ages, we are more likely to do the right thing.

The implication here is that our ancient traditions and laws embody truths. But it is important to note that, because of the occasional need for reform, these reified truths must remain provisional. Tradition, then, is a solid foundation upon which we cautiously build new edifices. This suggests that, despite his pragmatic bent, Burke embraced foundationalism in his belief that we must come to terms with truths that precede our own desires and experiences. The only twist is that the foundational truths to which Burke believed we should defer are concrete and malleable, not abstract and absolute. To their credit, said Burke, the British understood that we do not discover or invent truths on our own so much as we inherit them in some imperfect form. "We know that *we* have made no discoveries," said Burke; "and we think that no discoveries are to be made, in morality; nor many in the great principles of government, nor in the ideas of liberty, which were understood long before we were born, altogether as well as they will be after the grave has heaped its mould upon our presumption."[90]

Adhering to the truths embodied in ancient traditions contains an element of elitism that does not sit well with Burke's democratic critics, for it enfranchises the dead at the expense of the living. In the *Rights of Man*, a direct response to Burke's *Reflections on the Revolution in France*, Thomas Paine wrote, "Every age and generation must be as free to act for itself, *in all cases*, as the ages and generation which preceded it. The vanity and presumption of governing beyond the grave is the most ridiculous and insolent of all tyrannies." When a person dies, his powers and desires die along with him. He is no longer concerned with the affairs of human beings and, therefore, should not have "any authority in directing who shall be its governors, or how its government shall be organized or how administered."[91] Burke disagreed with the idea that each generation should be free to do as it pleases, because he believed it would unleash the selfish desires of the people. People need to be reminded of truths that come before their existence and transcend the pettiness of everyday life.

But who would shoulder the responsibility of preserving our traditions— our reified truths—and ensuring that the people revere them? According to Burke, this is the role of the "true natural aristocracy"—which was such "an essential integrant part of any large body [state] rightly constituted" that it should be entrusted with a disproportionate share of political and social power.[92] Burke believed that natural aristocrats needed to be men of property, education, and good breeding—people who could manage the duties of leadership and governance. Considering the idea of political equality—one person, one vote—abhorrent, Burke found it inconceivable that common people should make their voices heard in the affairs of state. When the chancellor of France said that "all occupations were honourable," implying that everyone was entitled to an equal share in political decision-making, Burke bristled. While there is nothing disgraceful about being a "hair-dresser" or a "tallow-chandler," we should regard them as positions not of honor but of servility. "Such descriptions of men ought not to suffer oppression from the state," said Burke; "but the state suffers oppression, if such as they, either individually or collectively are permitted to rule."[93] In other words, giving political power to the likes of hair-dressers would give way to tyranny.

Not surprisingly, Burke opposed democracy, calling it "the most shameless thing in the world" because it gives to the people as a whole an "absolute and unrestrained" power without the possibility of attributing a commensurate portion of blame to each individual. Each person can contribute his small share to the collective power while hiding behind the veil of anonymity. "The share of infamy that is likely to fall to the lot of each individual in public acts, is small indeed," said Burke. Able to make decisions without the fear of shame or retribution, the people have the power to oppress minorities with impunity. "If I recollect rightly, Aristotle observes, that a democracy has many striking points of resemblance with tyranny. Of this I am certain, that in a democracy, the majority of the citizens is capable of exercising the most cruel oppressions upon the minority," said Burke; and the "oppression of the minority will extend to far greater numbers, and will be carried on with much greater fury, than can almost ever be apprehended from the dominion of the single sceptre."[94] Several decades before Tocqueville made similar arguments, Burke warned his readers of majority tyranny, insisting that by virtue of their strength in numbers, the majority can exceed the cruelty of a king.

For this reason, Burke believed that the natural aristocracy should function as an intermediary between the people and the government. Instead of carrying out the desires of the people with little more judgment than an errand boy, the natural aristocracy should represent their interests. As true representatives of the people, they should act not as mere delegates, who flatter the people by giving them what they want and telling them what they want to hear, but as trustees who do what is best for the people, even if it is unpopular in the short term. When Burke first became the member for Bristol, he told them that he intended to be a representative who used his judgment. While he agreed that the wishes of constituents should hold some sway over representatives, he held that their independence was vital. "But his own unbiased opinion, his mature judgment, his enlightened conscience, he ought not to sacrifice to you, or to any set of men living," said Burke. "Your representative owes you, not his industry only, but his judgment; and he betrays, instead of serving you, if he sacrifices it to your opinion." Burke also rejected the idea that a Member of Parliament had a responsibility to represent parochial interests. "You choose a member, indeed" he said; "but when you have chosen him he is not a member of Bristol, but he is a member of *Parliament*."[95] Always mindful of the effects of policy proposals on the entire country, the representative should act as a "trustee for the *whole*, and not for the parts."[96]

In order to ensure that representatives acted as trustees, Burke opposed any political innovations that would enfranchise more people and remedy the inequality of representation that still existed in Great Britain in the late eighteenth century. Most egregious were the so-called "rotten boroughs"— small parliamentary districts in which a powerful landowner could bribe the handful of voters to select the person he wanted to serve as member. Burke did not want to widen the franchise or establish equal representation, at least not so soon, because he believed that only some four hundred thousand people—men of property, leisure, breeding, and education—could handle the responsibility of suffrage. To expand the franchise to millions of hair-dressers and others of low rank would invite disaster. "It is said, that twenty-four millions ought to prevail over two hundred thousand. True; if the constitution of a kingdom be a problem of arithmetic," said Burke. "This sort of discourse does well enough with the lamp-post for its second; to men who *may* reason calmly, it is ridiculous. The will of the many, and their *interest*, must very often differ; and great will be the difference when they make an evil choice."[97] Expanding the franchise beyond a few hundred thousand might have appeared to be sensible, at least mathematically, but current circumstances made it imprudent to empower the largely ignorant masses, whose desires were not yet compatible with their interests.

Understandably, his theory of representation made Burke vulnerable to accusations of "being a man of aristocratic principles." His elitism notwithstanding, Burke made it clear that he was not a sycophant of the nobility. "I am no friend to aristocracy," he said. "I would rather by far see it resolved into any other form, than lost in that austere and insolent domination."[98] His natural aristocracy included more than those with a title or noble lineage. "You do not imagine," he said, "that I wish to confine power, authority, and distinction to blood, and names, and titles. No, Sir. There is no qualification for government, but virtue and wisdom."[99] In his speech on a bill calling for the repeal of the Marriage Act, Burke claimed that he had "no vulgar admiration" for the nobility, though he appreciated that they served a vital purpose in preserving order and stability. "I hold their order in cold and decent respect," said Burke. "I hold them to be an absolute necessity in the Constitution; but I think they are only good when kept within proper bounds."[100] The nobility had an important role to play because it was presumed that they represented certain virtues, such as honor and duty, on account of their titles and noble lineage. They symbolized virtue and wisdom, even if they did not actually possess it, and their presence served to slow down the pace of change, compelling people to consider the wisdom of their inheritance before forging ahead willy-nilly.[101] But this did not mean that the nobility had the right to exercise arbitrary power, never subject to constitutional checks, or to exclude men of talent like Burke from serving in elite positions.

Burke was even more offended by the suggestion that his notion of natural aristocracy meant "an adherence to the rich and powerful against the poor and weak." He reminded his fellow parliamentarians that he had incurred the wrath of some of his colleagues for not paying sufficient deference to the rich. "When, indeed, the smallest rights of the poorest people in the kingdom are in question," he said, "I would set my face against any act of pride and power countenanced by the highest that are in it; and if it should come to the last extremity, and to a contest of blood—God forbid! God forbid!—my part is taken; I would take my fate with the poor, and low, and feeble."[102] While he did not think the poor and low were capable of self-governance, Burke had great compassion for them. He believed that their grievances could be resolved slowly—indeed, over many generations—by reforms sponsored by representatives who act as trustees. So, he did not oppose political equality because he wanted to protect the privileges of the rich and powerful. Both his political career and writings belie such an interpretation. Unfortunately, Burke's words taken out of context can produce the wrong impression—that he was an apologist for the status quo. Though undoubtedly elitist, he never intended to champion hierarchy for its own sake. Burke only favored class distinctions and inequality in order to preserve traditions and pass reforms that promoted social stability. And, as discussed earlier, he did not rule out the possibility that circumstances may change, making democracy not only acceptable but desirable.[103]

CONCLUSION

The Burke that emerges in these pages sounds very different from what most of us associate with conservatism. Simply put, the father of conservatism is not a conservative by any mainstream definition currently in use. Whereas conservatism today relies on abstract reasoning to arrive at uncompromising and absolutist principles, Burke employed a pragmatic approach whereby provisional principles are derived from concrete experiences. American conservatives in particular have taken "principled" stands that mainly serve the interests of the rich and powerful. As inequality has widened, public education has steadily deteriorated, and millions continue to live without health insurance, conservatives have stubbornly adhered to the principles of small government and negative liberty regardless of the consequences. They pride themselves on standing by their principles, willfully ignoring practical solutions to real-world problems.

What I hope has become clear is that Burkean conservatism has little in common with today's version. His was a strain of conservatism that, if applied today, would lead to a very different set of policy positions. In fact, one can imagine a resurrected Burke aligning himself with the Democrats for their willingness to promote cautious reform, striking a balance between improvement and tradition. While they allow empirical facts to guide their attempts to redress various social ills, they also work within the parameters of a constitutional framework inherited from our forefathers. Ostensibly representing the left, the Democratic Party actually embraces a moderate brand of politics that eschews extremes. This gravitation to the center agrees with Burke's political thought, suggesting that the supposed party of the left in American politics can be understood as conservative in the original sense of the term. The true radicals can be found on the other side of the aisle, where Republicans dream of dismantling the welfare state and restoring what they see as the traditional family. Theirs is a mix of *laissez faire* economic policies and intrusive social policies that does not agree with the world as it stands today. Like the Jacobins whom Burke regarded with so much dread, the right in this country hopes to remake reality in accordance with its abstract principles, no matter what history and experience may teach us. This was not true of Burke's twentieth-century American heirs, who were not often considered conservative by their contemporaries. Never fully embraced by either side of the ideological spectrum, these luminaries showed that Burke's ideas about human nature, tradition, reform, knowledge, ethics, and elites continue to have relevance and applicability in the modern age.

NOTES

1. See, for example, Strauss, *Natural Right and History*, 294–323; and John Morley, *Burke*.
2. See Byrne, *Edmund Burke for Our Time*, 117–153; Lock, *Edmund Burke*; Kirk, *Edmund Burke*, 51–147.
3. See Kirk, *The Conservative Mind*; Kirk, *Edmund Burke*.
4. See Morley, *Burke*; Byrne, *Edmund Burke for Our Time*; Kramnick, *The Rage of Edmund Burke*.
5. See Kramnick, *The Portable Edmund Burke*, ix-xxxix; Byrne, *Edmund Burke for Our Time*.
6. Burke, "Resolutions for Conciliation with America," in *Writings and Speeches*, III, 135 & 152.
7. Burke, "Taxation," in *Writings and Speeches*, II, 458.
8. Burke, *Reflections*, 247–248.
9. Burke, *Thoughts on the Present Discontents*, in *Works*, I, 527. See Kirk, *Edmund Burke*, 81–82.
10. Burke, *Reflections*, 119.
11. Burke, *Letter to a Member of the National Assembly* (1791), in *Works*, IV, 10–11.
12. Burke, "Letter to the Chevalier de Rivarol" (1791). Quoted in Kirk, *The Conservative Mind*, 33.
13. Burke, *Letter to a Member of the National Assembly* (1791), in *Works*, IV, 11.
14. Burke, *Sublime and Beautiful*, 96.
15. Burke, "A Letter to a Noble Lord," in Kramnick, ed., *The Portable Edmund Burke*, 225–226.
16. Burke, *Reflections*, 135, 139–140.
17. Burke, *Sublime and Beautiful*, 92.
18. Burke, *Sublime and Beautiful*, 110.
19. See Burke, *Sublime and Beautiful*, 86 & 101.
20. Burke, *Appeal from the New to the Old Whigs*, in *Works*, IV, 206–207.
21. Burke, *Reflections*, 299–300.

22. Lincoln, "Address to the Young Men's Lyceum of Springfield, Illinois" (January 27, 1838), in *Selected Speeches and Writings*, 19–20.
23. Burke, *Reflections*, 194–195.
24. Ibid., 119.
25. Ibid., 192–193.
26. Ibid., 119.
27. Ibid., 119–121.
28. Ibid., 183.
29. Ibid.
30. Ibid., 182.
31. Ibid., 170–171.
32. Ibid., 189.
33. Ibid., 197–198.
34. Ibid., 256.
35. See especially Robin, *The Reactionary Mind*.
36. Burke, *Reflections*, 280–281.
37. Burke, *Letter to Sir Hercules Langrishe* (1792), in *Works*, IV, 301.
38. Burke, *Reflections*, 267.
39. Ibid., 119–120.
40. Burke, "An Essay towards an Abridgement of the English History," in *Writings and Speeches*, I, 430.
41. Burke, *Reflections*, 106.
42. Ibid., 375.
43. Ibid., 251.
44. Ibid., 280–281.
45. Ibid., 184.
46. Ibid., 171.
47. Ibid.
48. Burke, "A Letter to a Noble Lord," in Kramnick, ed., *The Portable Edmund Burke*, 225–226.
49. Burke, *Reflections*, 277.
50. Ibid., 160–161.
51. Burke, "A Letter to William Smith," in Kramnick, ed., *The Portable Edmund Burke*, 356.
52. Burke, *Second Letter on a Regicide Peace*, in *Works*, V, 375.
53. Burke, *Reflections*, 122.
54. Ibid., 133.
55. Ibid., 121–122.
56. Ibid., 178.
57. Ibid., 240.
58. Ibid., 245–246.
59. Burke, "Letter to Richard Burke" (1791), in William and Bourke, *Correspondence of Burke*, III, 349.

60. Burke, *Reflections*, 285.
61. Burke, *Sublime and Beautiful*, 99.
62. Burke, *Reflections*, 89–90.
63. Ibid., 123–124.
64. Ibid., 152.
65. Burke, *Sublime and Beautiful*, 55.
66. Ibid., 54.
67. Ibid., 159–160.
68. Burke, "Hints for an Essay on the Drama" (1761), in *Writings and Speeches*, I, 557.
69. Burke, "Appeal from the New to the Old Whigs," in *Works*, IV, 169.
70. Burke, *Sublime and Beautiful*, 74.
71. Burke, *Reflections*, 176.
72. Burke, "Speech on a Motion for a Committee to Inquire into the State of the Representation of the Commons in Parliament" (1782), in *Works*, VII, 96.
73. Burke, *Reflections*, 228.
74. Ibid., 151.
75. Ibid., 153.
76. Ibid., 149.
77. Ibid., 151.
78. Ibid., 151–152.
79. Burke, "Resolutions for Conciliation with America" (1775), *Writing and Speeches*, III, 120.
80. Burke, *Reflections*, 150–152.
81. Burke, "Appeal from the New Whigs," *Works*, IV, 175–176.
82. Burke, *First Letter on a Regicide Peace*, in *Works*, V, 321.
83. Burke, "Speech in Opening the Impeachment, Second Day" (1788), in *Writings and Speeches* VI, 346.
84. Ibid.
85. Ibid., 350–351.
86. Burke, *Letter to a Member of the National Assembly* (1791), in *Works*, IV, 26.
87. Burke, *Reflections*, 194–195.
88. Ibid., 152.
89. Burke, "Speech on a Motion for a Committee to Inquire into the State of the Representation of the Commons in Parliament" (1782), in *Works*, VII, 95.
90. Burke, *Reflections*, 182.
91. Paine, *Rights of Man*, in *Collected Writings*.
92. Burke, *Reflections*, 180–181.
93. Ibid., 138.
94. Ibid., 228–229.

95. Burke, "Speech at Mr. Burke's Arrival in Bristol," in Kramnick, ed., *The Portable Edmund Burke*, 156. See Kirk, *Edmund Burke*, 90–91. Having never warmed up to his theory of representation, his Bristol constituents voted him out. They clearly wanted a delegate, not a trustee. In advocating justice for the Irish, Burke went against his anti-Catholic constituents. In supporting free trade with the Irish, he went against the commercial interests of many people in Bristol.

96. Burke, *Reflections*, 303.

97. Ibid., 141.

98. Burke, *Thoughts on the Present Discontents* (1770), in *Works*, I, 458.

99. Burke, *Reflections*, 139.

100. Burke, "Speech on the Repeal of the Marriage Act" (1781), in Kramnick, ed., *The Portable Edmund Burke*, 96.

101. Burke, *Reflections*, 139–140.

102. Burke, "Speech on the Repeal of the Marriage Act" (1781), in Kramnick, ed., *The Portable Edmund Burke*, 96.

103. Burke, *Reflections*, 228–229.

CHAPTER 3

Walter Lippmann: Unlikely Conservative

INTRODUCTION

Unlike most political thinkers, celebrated journalist Walter Lippmann did not toil in obscurity, writing for a small and rarefied audience of scholars. For over 35 years he wrote a syndicated column in which at least three times a week he commented on the events of the day and offered his incisive analysis of problems, both domestic and international. Published in newspapers throughout the country, his column reached an audience of about ten million people, many of whom would not form an opinion on a matter until they had read what Lippmann had to say. And for half a century, including his earlier years as a staff writer for *The New Republic* and then as editorial director of the *New York World*, he had the attention—and sometimes the ear—of policymakers at the highest levels. Even presidents sought his counsel. For his was a voice of reason that tried to make sense of an especially tumultuous time, beginning with those hopeful years before World War I and ending with the darkest period of the Vietnam War.

While his fame rested primarily on his journalistic efforts, Lippmann also made a name for himself as an author of serious books that took a step back from the chaos of current events and engaged the larger questions of political theory. Lippmann regarded these two endeavors—one topical, the other philosophical—as complementary, even symbiotic. His philosophical reflections informed, and drew on, his reportage. "I have lived two lives," said Lippmann at the age of 70. "One of books and one of

© The Author(s) 2016
R.J. Lacey, *Pragmatic Conservatism*,
DOI 10.1057/978-1-137-59295-8_3

newspapers. Each helps the other. The philosophy is the context in which I write my columns. The column is the laboratory or clinic in which I test the philosophy and keep it from becoming too abstract." James Reston said of Lippmann that "while philosophy may be his true love, journalism has been his mistress."[1] Having threatened many times to leave the daily grind of editorial writing for good, Lippmann could never resist the allure of journalism and devote himself exclusively to his true love. Philosophy may have given Lippmann the deeper pleasures of reflecting on the human condition and offering theoretical insights, but journalism connected him to the thrilling world of politics. Remaining loyal to both his true love and his mistress, Lippmann became in his time a first-rate public intellectual whose ideas were penetrating and original yet always lucid and relevant.

Based on what he wrote in his books and columns, Lippmann earned a reputation over the course of his career as a liberal. He contended that the state could be a force for good, improving the lives of those who suffered under the vicissitudes and disruptions of the modern economy, and protecting American interests from nation-states with imperialistic aims. He supported a whole host of liberal reforms in the domestic sphere and cautioned against deploying the military in an effort to pursue unrealistic global ambitions. Without question, his political commitments placed him comfortably within the liberal establishment. At the end of his life, however, Lippmann characterized his intellectual legacy in a surprising way. "I am a conservative," he said in a 1971 interview.

> I think I always have been. But that doesn't mean I'm a conservative who agrees with William Buckley. I hope and trust that I am a conservative who agrees with Edmund Burke. I believe in certain fundamental things in philosophy and constitutional law which are conservative as against the Jacobins.[2]

This might have been a curious statement for many people who followed Lippmann throughout his career. But, as this chapter will make clear, Lippmann's self-assessment was astute—and largely on the money. Only long after his death did Burke become known as the father of conservatism. Lippmann's political thought deserves a similar posthumous reappraisal.

It should be said that much of the scholarship on Lippmann suggests that his ideas suffered from inconsistency, shifting several times over the course of his long career. Perhaps it would be unfair to demand consistency from a journalist who hastily wrote thousands of editorials in reaction to a turbulent world, but Lippmann does not escape this allegation even when his critics focus exclusively on his philosophical works. Indeed, a substantial body of literature makes the claim that Lippmann, though he had flashes of brilliance and left behind a few works of enduring value, was an uneven thinker whose oeuvre does not offer a coherent political theory. Scholars often accuse him of abandoning his pragmatic liberalism and moving toward an absolutist conception of the truth which culminated in his conversion to natural law theory. According to Benjamin Wright, Lippmann expressed "five distinct points of view" over the course of his career as a writer of philosophical books. "The only ties that bind the five sets of premises, kinds of reasoning, and conclusions together," he said, "are the common authorship, Lippmann's engaging style, and his apparent conviction in each book or pair of books that he has discovered and is providing a generalized map of the promised land."[3] This withering comment is decidedly unfair. But even the less biting criticisms of Lippmann overstate the discontinuities in his philosophical work and, as a result, fail to identify what is a fairly cohesive corpus of political ideas, which emerges in his writings just after World War I and comes to fruition in his last major work, *Essays in the Public Philosophy.*

The key to finding coherence in Lippmann's political thought is to take seriously his self-identification with Burkean conservatism. Although he may have exaggerated in claiming that he had always adhered to Burkean conservatism, a close reading of his philosophical works reveals a clear evolution toward this mode of thought. The seeds of his Burkeanism had been planted during his callow years as a socialist and, shortly after, as a progressive. By the early 1920s, when he challenged traditional democratic theory, the seeds had grown into visible buds. A decade and a half later, his Burkeanism came into full bloom with his delineation of a higher law grounded in history and tradition. Underneath what appears to be the many phases of Walter Lippmann's political thought—whether it be socialism, progressivism, democratic elitism, New Deal liberalism, free market liberalism, or natural law conservatism—lies a growing commitment to Burkean principles.

Concerned about the degree to which modern life brought out the worst in human nature, Lippmann increasingly saw adherence to tradition, often embodied in law but just as often in custom, as a way of ensuring social and political stability. As a liberal, Lippmann never relinquished his belief that reforms were necessary to address emerging problems in a dynamic world, though he favored caution and incremental change instead of ambitious attempts to overturn the social order in accordance with abstract principles. His aversion to abstract principles rested on his pragmatic epistemology, the belief that truths were derived from concrete experiences. Even his appeals to a higher law, which he believed all people should heed no matter the time or place, never contravened his pragmatism. For he grounded the higher law in what he called the "ancestral order"—the traditions that emerged out of past experience. In his view, these traditions represented enduring (even universal) truths borne out by the human predicament. Lamenting the fact that the "acids of modernity" had dissolved many of these traditions and left nothing in their place, Lippmann blamed unfettered democracy for undermining the work of elites—including experts, scholars, and political insiders—who sought to draw on the wisdom of the ancestral order in their attempts to solve existing problems. Without the guidance of tradition, said Lippmann, we are left with a false choice between the anarchy of *laissez faire* and the tyranny of collectivism. In the spirit of Burke, Lippmann searched for balance, a middle way in a world beset by extremes.

"The method of freedom"

Like Edmund Burke, Lippmann was known during most of his lifetime as an advocate for liberal or progressive economic policies. He did not hesitate to challenge the prevailing socio-economic order or political establishment, and he directed much of his criticism toward *laissez faire* capitalism and its corollary, a feeble government that failed to address the problems of modern life. Despite the shifts in tone and emphasis throughout his long career, Lippmann never abandoned the liberal cause, which he believed struck a harmonious but delicate balance between the extremes of *laissez faire* and collectivism.

Lippmann actually started his career as a socialist, a sharp critic of progressives, liberals, and other "goo-goo" reformers who, in his view, failed to push for meaningful change, their proposed half-measures amounting to little more than an apology for the status quo. He helped found the Socialist Club at Harvard in his sophomore year, became active in the Intercollegiate Socialist Society, and then freelanced for a number of socialist periodicals in the years immediately after graduation. But Lippmann never became doctrinaire in his commitment to the movement and recoiled from the Marxist call for revolution and a fundamental reordering of society. He gravitated to socialism as a young man simply because he saw it as the most effective way of bringing an end to the social and economic inequities from which so many people suffered. More in agreement with his beliefs were the British Fabians, led by Beatrice and Sidney Webb, who eschewed the utopian thinking of Marxism and anarchism and put forward a realistic reform agenda designed to make improvements in the lives of the poor, the exploited, and the dispossessed. The Fabians believed in a peaceful and incremental path to socialist victory, culminating not in the complete overthrow of the existing political and economic order but rather in the rise of an enlightened administrative state that regulated the uses of property and enabled labor unions to play a greater decision-making role in the workplace.

In his early years as a writer, Lippmann championed the Fabian cause but often showed his ambivalence about the socialist enterprise as a whole. Even while still at Harvard he made it clear that his commitment to socialism was provisional, resting ultimately on its demonstrated utility. "Socialism stands and falls by its fruits in practice," he wrote in April of 1910. "If it can be shown that public enterprise, where tried under democratic conditions, fails to produce a beneficent effect on the health, happiness and general culture of a community, or that private enterprise is more beneficent, then the socialist case collapses. And good riddance to it."[4] Lippmann also betrayed a wariness of the burgeoning administrative state during his socialist phase. "Without any doubt," he wrote, "socialism has within it the germs of that great bureaucratic tyranny which Chesterton and Belloc have named the Servile State."[5] These were hardly sentiments with which many of his fellow socialists would agree or even sympathize.

Lippmann had little use for militant socialists, ideologues who adhered to its tenets without question. Writing for the socialist monthly *International*, Lippmann condemned "simple-minded socialists" who perceived the conflict between labor and capital in Manichean terms—that is, as an epic struggle between good and evil—and he even refused to endorse Eugene V. Debs for the presidency in 1912, even though he was the Socialist Party nominee, because the candidate and his followers proved too radical for Lippmann's tastes. "It is of far more far-reaching importance," he wrote, "that men should become liberal-minded than that they should believe in a radical creed." It is little wonder that the young socialist expressed more interest in the candidacy of Woodrow Wilson.[6]

In his second book, *Drift and Mastery*, Lippmann made a definitive break from socialism, finding common cause with the New Nationalism of Theodore Roosevelt. It certainly made sense: the Fabian socialism with which he had become enamored during his college years—or at least his understanding of it—did not differ all that much from the Rough Rider's policy platform. Now an unabashed progressive, Lippmann called for a "war on poverty" and the creation of "democracy in industry" by strong labor unions. He envisioned a country where big government tamed big business, capitalism thrived but operated within a regulatory framework that enforced fair play, and unionized workers exercised some control over the means of production. Under the banner of progressivism, Lippmann still embraced most of the Fabian policy agenda but without the ideological rigidity, without the militancy that precluded the "liberal-minded" questioning of assumptions.

Throughout the 1920s, Lippmann focused most of his attention on democratic theory and ethics. But when the Great Depression gave Lippmann a reason to revisit questions about political economy, there was little doubt that he remained faithful to liberal ideas. In *The Method of Freedom* (1934), a vigorous defense of the modern liberal state, Lippmann expressed his support for a whole host of government interventions in the economy. He called for laws that punished corporate fraud, regulated industry, broke up monopolies, protected the collective bargaining rights of workers, restricted reckless speculation on Wall Street, and limited other potentially harmful uses of property. In accordance with Keynesian economic principles, he endorsed a countercyclical fiscal policy—that is, lower taxes and increased spending during a downturn and the opposite during an upswing. He also praised measures that tackled the problem of "proletarian insecurity," including a minimum wage and a comprehensive system of social insurance that protected people against accident, sickness, disability, old age, and unemployment. Lippmann even declared that all able-bodied adults, whose dignity rested in large part on "the opportunity to earn and acquire independence," had a "right to work." When people could not find jobs in the private labor market, the government should become the employer of last resort. He concluded that the modern state had an obligation "to insure the weak against the hazards of existence and to restrain the strong from accumulating excessive wealth and power."[7]

Those who accuse Lippmann of inconsistency argue that the publication of *The Good Society* (1937) marks a reversal in his thinking, a clear disavowal of the New Deal and the modern liberal state. According to this conventional narrative, Lippmann had somehow fallen under the spell of Ludwig von Mises and Friedrich Hayek, the arch-wizards of the Austrian school of economics. This account is completely off base. It is certainly true that he made a point of underscoring, perhaps in more ominous tones than ever before, the dangers of collectivism and centralized economic planning in the first half of the book. But this shift in emphasis is understandable in the light of global events at the time, particularly the growing threat of fascism and communism. And one should not overlook the fact that Lippmann had issued similar, if a bit more muted, warnings in *The Method of Freedom* and even in his first book, *A Preface to Politics*, written when he was still a socialist.[8] Furthermore, in the second half of *The Good Society*, Lippmann went on to recommend most of the same policies he had embraced three years earlier, including Keynesian fiscal policy, trustbusting, regulation of businesses and markets, collective bargaining for workers, income redistribution, and a system of social insurance.[9] Despite accusations to the contrary, Lippmann actually reinforced his commitment to liberal values, and he never deviated from this position for the rest of his career. Indeed, he defended the regulatory and welfare state during the Eisenhower years and even championed the Great Society in the 1960s.

Lippmann demonstrated his unwavering support for liberal values most vividly in his devastating criticism of *laissez faire*. Throughout his life, Lippmann maintained that *laissez faire* was a deeply flawed idea that did not agree with the historical record or make any sense in theory. In *The Good Society*, Lippmann pointed out that the "pure doctrine of non-intervention in production and trade has never in fact been practiced anywhere." In his view, the ostensible supporters of *laissez faire* were hypocrites who "wished to impose free capitalism on others and to escape it themselves." He even went so far as to characterize the history of the nineteenth century as "the record of the struggle of various interested groups to carve out for themselves areas in which competition was limited for their own advantage."[10] So, while the captains of industry preached the gospel of *laissez faire*, claiming that the victims of capitalism have no one to blame but themselves, they failed to acknowledge that their own triumphs were due in no small part to favorable government intervention, that they enjoyed a competitive advantage as a result of a tariff, a subsidy, investment in infrastructure, or another form of special treatment for which they lobbied unrelentingly.

Although pure *laissez faire* had always been an historical fiction, the idea actually had revolutionary origins, inspiring policies that liberated capital from the old order and laid the groundwork for the Industrial Revolution. Armed with legitimate grievances, its proponents pushed for the eradication of antiquated laws, institutions, and customs that constrained the uses of capital and stifled economic opportunity and growth. Unfortunately, said Lippmann, an idea that made practical sense in the late eighteenth and early nineteenth centuries morphed into a metaphysical principle. No longer just a prescriptive measure at a certain moment in history, *laissez faire* became for its supporters a universal law grounded in the belief that the right to property precedes the existence of government and civil society. Transcending public affairs and positive law, property rights were "natural" and therefore "beyond human interference" in their view.[11] This meant that any government control of private property, however reasonable and sensible under the circumstances, violated the inalienable rights of the owner. With the advancement of industrialization, this idea became increasingly discordant with reality. In the end, said Lippmann, proponents of *laissez faire*, including Herbert Spencer and others of his ilk, "became apologists for miseries and injustices that were intolerable to the conscience." Theirs was a "philosophy of neglect."[12]

Regarding the apotheosis of *laissez faire* with dismay, Lippmann insisted that property rights do not exist independently of the law. "I suppose that a solitary man cast ashore on an undiscovered island could be said to have freedom without law," he wrote. "But in a community there is no such thing: all freedom, all rights, all property, are sustained by some kind of law." People could only enjoy the right to property when a stable government made its presence felt, validating titles, adjudicating contractual disputes, coining money, and performing other vital functions. "While theorists were talking about laissez-faire, men were buying and selling legal titles to property, were suing for damages," said Lippmann. "In these transactions, by means of which the work of society was carried on, the state was implicated at every point. All these transactions depended upon some kind of law, upon the willingness of the state to enforce certain rights and to protect certain immunities."[13] For this reason, Lippmann concluded that all "rights" are "ultimately a creation of the state and exist only where they are organized by the government."[14]

Lippmann underscored the fact that the absence of government intervention made property insecure. By creating law and order and providing protection, the state establishes the conditions necessary for property ownership. Without the state, property exists only in theory, as an unfulfilled wish or a dashed hope. For a concrete example, Lippmann could have pointed to the looting and extortion that plague failed states. No one is safe in his possessions, let alone in a position to enjoy economic success, when the chaos of statelessness ensues. "Without the implied willingness of the state to intervene with all its power, the rugged individualist who preached laissez-faire would have been utterly helpless," said Lippmann. "[He] may have imagined that in his economic life he was the person that God and his own will had made. But in fact he was a juristic creature of the law that happened to prevail in his own epoch."[15] In calling the "rugged individualist" a "juristic creature," Lippmann struck at the heart of the American myth, the idea that the self is a completely autonomous agent who, with a little pluck and talent, will reach great heights if government just stays out of the way. He dispelled the romantic notion that anyone can enjoy freedom and rights outside a legal framework.

Along the same lines, Lippmann also saw corporations as "legal creatures" to which the state conferred various privileges and immunities. Without the interference of government, said Lippmann, the "rugged individualist" would never have been able to start "a corporation with limited liability and perpetual succession."[16] Quite simply, corporations would not exist at all if the government had not willed them into being and dedicated resources to their protection. Lippmann also decried the personhood status given to corporations by the courts because it was based on a gross misreading of the Fourteenth Amendment and made it far more difficult for the government to "fix the terms on which these legal creatures could do business."[17] Now, rather than a complex property arrangement created by the government, and therefore subject to its regulatory authority, the corporation had magically become a "person" endowed with natural and constitutional rights. From the perspective of *laissez faire*, the corporation was on moral par with the rugged individualist and enjoyed the same rights. But by shining a light on the legal origins of both property and corporations, Lippmann exposed the chimerical thinking behind *laissez faire*.

Lippmann also understood that shattering the myths of rugged individualism and corporate personhood called into question the *laissez faire* claim that it is possible a priori to "define the limits of the jurisdiction of the state."[18] There may be good reasons for placing limits on the power and scope of the state, but no one can draw a definitive line in the sand on the basis of natural rights or any other abstraction. Governments define and grant rights as they see fit, so they get to decide on the limits under which they must operate. Arbitrarily imposing absolute limits could unwisely straitjacket the government. After all, changing circumstances may require unexpected and ad hoc adjustments to the authority of government which will then lead to a recalibration of individual rights. In other words, the fact that rights are legal creations means that they can never be absolute; they must remain qualified and provisional. "The rights of property," said Lippmann, "are a creation of the laws of the state. And since laws can be altered, there are no absolute rights of property."[19]

It should be noted that proponents of *laissez faire* did not just invoke absolute property rights in their arguments. They also built their case on classical economic theory, making the utilitarian argument that unfettered markets generate more wealth for society as a whole because they are more efficient and productive than the alternatives. But, as Lippmann pointed out, this prediction only holds true if certain assumptions are met. Unfortunately, many of these assumptions—including perfect competition, perfect knowledge, and perfectly mobile labor and capital—do not correspond with the real world of economic life. While useful, the classical economic model is necessarily simplistic and limited in its predictive power. Proponents of *laissez faire* went astray when they began to believe that the model was an accurate picture of reality.

According to Lippmann, classical economists seemed to have forgotten that the original intent of the model was not so much to mirror reality but to paint an aspirational picture. "So what the political economists had conceived in their science was not a picture of the world as it is but a picture of the world as it needs to be remade," wrote Lippmann. Classical liberals should have realized that the overly simplistic model was an implicit call for reform, a provocation for government to find ways of refashioning economic reality so that markets could actually function as the theory predicted. "Instead of the classical economics being an apologetic explanation of the existing order, it is, when properly understood, a searching criticism of that order," Lippmann explained. "It is a theoretical measure which reveals how far short of the promise, how unadjusted to the needs of the division of labor, is the actual society in which we live."[20] The model reminded us that economic reality does not measure up to theory, but it also paved the way for reform. Government interventions should try to align the real world as closely as possible with the assumptions of the model. The predictive accuracy of the model depends entirely on the extent to which reform can successfully accomplish this rather daunting task. Unfortunately, for Lippmann, many classical economists still embraced *laissez faire* lest government intervention become a collectivist enterprise that stymied initiative and innovation. Lippmann rejected this false choice and never gave up in his search for a middle way.

In Lippmann's view, the chief aim of liberalism was to chart a course through the narrow straits between collectivism and *laissez faire*, between tyranny and anarchy. Although these hazardous outcomes were commonly seen as opposites, Lippmann believed that they shared far more in common. Both were pernicious, just like Scylla and Charybdis, the monsters that flanked the Strait of Messina in ancient Greek mythology. Both put people at "the mercy of men who can act arbitrarily," said Lippmann. "Indeed, despotism may be defined as the anarchy of lawless rulers, and anarchy as the despotism of lawless crowds."[21] The lawless inspire so much dread because no one can tell what they will do at any given moment or whom they will choose as their next victims. Whether they be kings or warlords, tyrants or mobs, they are beholden to no laws higher than themselves. Either extreme, then, creates abject conditions from which its victims seek deliverance. Indeed, despotism and anarchy amount to the same thing for those unfortunates who must endure them.

Lippmann believed that the liberal tradition had found a way to avoid the hazards of either extreme. In *The Method of Freedom*, Lippmann made a distinction between absolute collectivism (or the directed economy) and free collectivism (or the compensated economy). The former involves centralized economic planning by a totalitarian state that forbids producers and consumers to make their own choices. Government officials make all economic decisions according to "definite national objectives" and regard the citizen as "a conscript" whose life must be "dedicated to the state." Lippmann pointed out that countries at war, even liberal democracies, often resort to absolute collectivism out of military necessity. But, even in times of peace, totalitarian states never relinquish this authority, claiming that various threats to national security necessitate an indefinite militarization of social and economic life. "Under absolute collectivism, be it of the fascist or communist type," said Lippmann, "the government is in fact the master, the citizen a subject and a servant."[22]

The method of free collectivism, on the other hand, preserves private initiative and free choice as much as possible and only authorizes state intervention in the economy for the purpose of counteracting—or compensating for—the failures and abuses of capitalism. In effect, the compensated economy solves what social scientists call collective action problems. In those situations where individual actions lead to "collective disaster," the state must intercede and do what a crowd of individuals fails to do on its own. "It follows that if individuals are to continue to decide when they will buy and sell, spend and save, borrow and lend, expand and contract their enterprises, some kind of compensatory mechanism to redress their liability to error must be set up by public authority," said Lippmann. "It has become necessary to create collective power, to mobilize collective resources, and to work out technical procedures by means of which the modern state can balance, equalize, neutralize, offset, correct the private judgments of masses of individuals." The method of freedom, then, does not intend to enforce conformity with "an official pattern" but rather "to maintain a working, moving equilibrium" in a market economy.[23] In such a system people enjoy considerable latitude, a fairly wide range of freedom, in their private transactions. The state certainly imposes limits on their activities, but not unduly so, and only to preserve the health of the economic order as a whole. In other words, it strikes a necessary balance between individual freedom and the general welfare.

The concept of balance was critical in Lippmann's writing. He saw balance as a necessary middle way, a golden mean that steered clear of extremes. It was the only viable option, for both tyranny and anarchy (or, in their modern forms, collectivism and *laissez faire*) threatened to take away everything human beings hold dear—including freedom, security, order, happiness, even life. But one should not confuse balance with centrism. In his theoretical writings, Lippmann reaffirmed the legitimacy of most New Deal policies and even called for measures that went well beyond what FDR could accomplish. His enthusiasm for the Great Society in the late 1960s speaks to this point. This means that the golden mean—or "the mean between excess and defect"—is not a fixed point on a spectrum. One must not think of it, for example, as the halfway point between excess and deficiency—or, say, between collectivism and *laissez faire*. Impossible to pinpoint precisely in an ever-changing world, its location is a matter of social and historical context.[24] So, what constituted balance for Lippmann made him a mainstream liberal in his own time and might very well place him on the far left in the American political landscape today.

No matter where Lippmann may fall on the ideological spectrum, he championed liberal values largely because he believed they would maintain the balance necessary to conserve that which made life worthwhile. For example, Lippmann supported various measures that would reduce the gap between the haves and have-nots not because it served the cause of social justice but rather because he considered it vital to ensuring social and political tranquility. "It is by the reduction of the extremes and the fostering and the maintenance of a middle condition among its people that a modern state can make itself most solid and serviceable," wrote Lippmann. In order "to preserve an economy run by private transactions but held in balance by collective action," he continued, "it is necessary to take as an avowed object of policy the abolition both of the proletariat and of the plutocracy." Lippmann recognized that many critics would "cry that this is socialism, Marxism, the class war, and confiscation," but he insisted that it was quite the opposite. "It is a policy," he said, "which is frankly and unashamedly middle class in its ideal." Citing Aristotle as an influence, Lippmann argued that a large middle class was the key to maintaining peace and stability. He praised the middle class for resisting the "contagious fevers of huddled and amorphous crowds" and for being rather "bourgeois and dull" and "stubborn and careful." At the same time, they "have hold of the substance of liberty and cling to it," said Lippmann, and "they have self-respect, and of their fate, though it be a small one and private, they are masters."[25] Comfortable and complacent, the middle class have no interest in overturning the system. But they also exhibit a quiet dignity in their readiness to guard their liberties and the property that they have acquired through honest and hard work.

Lippmann supported labor unions for similar reasons. Not only did they help millions of Americans enter the middle class, but they also acted as a countervailing force against capital, making sure that its predatory and exploitive practices were held in check. As Lippmann scholar Barry Riccio put it, Lippmann "took his hat off to the American labor movement for recognizing that a balance of power between capital and labor was an indispensable part of a civilized society."[26] Lippmann feared the alternative to strong unions: a widening gap between the rich and poor followed by revolution and absolute collectivism. Unions carried out a vital function in a system of free collectivism, balancing private initiative with compensatory action by the state. In effect, these measures saved free enterprise and private property from themselves by attenuating their self-destructive tendencies.

The idea of balance informed nearly every aspect of Lippmann's political thought. In his writings on international relations, he argued that maintaining a balance of power—and not seeking an outright victory against ideological enemies—represented the best chance for peace and stability in the global order. And on domestic matters, he increasingly found wisdom in the Founders, whose system of checks and balances was designed not to remove the causes of faction but merely to control its mischievous effects. Given what he saw as the inevitability of faction and conflict, Lippmann did not find hope in blueprints of an ideal society or in abstract notions about truth and justice. Instead, he sought pragmatic solutions that would maintain a working equilibrium between opposing ideas or forces—including chaos and order, liberty and security, *laissez faire* and collectivism, capital and labor, rich and poor. As the following discussion will make clear, his quest for balance was rooted in the central principles of Burkean conservatism.

"Men have been barbarians much longer than they have been civilized"

Throughout most of his career Lippmann had a fairly negative view of human nature. Although he did not see human beings as irrevocably sinful, neither did he place hope in their ability to become paragons of virtue. Even during his early years as a socialist, Lippmann scoffed at the idea that people could achieve perfection. While certainly educable, he argued, people could only accomplish so much given the moral limitations under which they operated.

Reflecting on his youth in his later years, Lippmann admitted that there was a brief time when he naively subscribed to the socialist belief that improvements in material conditions would have a transformative effect on the nature of human beings. "Insofar as we imagined what it would be like," said Lippmann, "we had vague notions that mankind, liberated from want and drudgery, would spend its energies writing poetry, painting pictures, exploring stellar spaces, singing folk songs, dancing with Isadora Duncan in the public square, and producing Ibsen in little theatres." Lippmann and his compatriots seemed to believe that a change in the economic base would liberate human beings from their alienation, eradicating their acquisitive impulses and unleashing a latent desire to create, to explore, to learn. "Those were the days when we believed in Man and forgot there were only men and women, when we believed that all you had to do to save the world was to rearrange the environment."[27]

Lippmann would eventually come to the conclusion that these pie-in-the-sky socialists "overlooked the appetite of mankind for the automobile, the moving picture, the radio, bridge parties, tabloids and the stock market."[28] People naturally craved material goods, entertainment, and titillation; they did not often have an urge to satisfy aesthetic or intellectual impulses. No matter what changes might occur in their material lives, people would not so easily abandon the joys of consumption and passive leisure for the toils of artistic creation and intellectual engagement.

Two of Lippmann's professors at Harvard, Irving Babbitt and Graham Wallas, weakened his faith in human nature. An early admirer of Rousseau, Lippmann learned from Babbitt to question the romantic idea that people were innately good and only deviated from their nature because of the corrupting influences of civilization.[29] The Fabian socialist Graham Wallas taught Lippmann that the underlying assumption of political science, that people made judgments and decisions after a rational consideration of the facts, did not take into account the stark realities of human nature. In truth, said Wallas, people were far more likely to rely on instinct, prejudice, and habit when forming an opinion on a political issue.[30]

Thanks in large part to the influence of his professors, Lippmann would embrace a more clear-headed version of socialism while still an undergraduate. In the spring of 1909, Lippmann delivered an address before the Socialist Club at Harvard in which he argued that socialism would not create a new type of man because human beings will always be self-interested. Contrary to doctrine, he claimed that socialism could accommodate the shortcomings of human nature and even channel them toward socially constructive ends. Socialism, then, should not focus on turning people into what they ought to be. Instead, it should accept these selfish creatures for what they are and, as much as possible, give them what they need.[31]

In *A Preface to Politics*, written when he was still a socialist, Lippmann criticized the American Socialist Party for making "utopian proposals" that did not take into account human nature. Their policy recommendations, he said, "cover about as much of a human being as a beautiful hat does." In the same book Lippmann advised his readers to accept the fact that "human nature is a rather shocking affair." He assailed the claim that "business corruption is the work of a few inhumanly cunning individuals with monstrous morals" and even went so far as to say that capitalists "did not violate the public conscience" but rather "expressed it."[32] In other words, he saw the corruption and predatory behavior of capitalists as a reflection of human nature. So, even in his socialist phase, Lippmann did not believe in the innate goodness or perfectibility of human beings.

In the decades after he renounced socialism, Lippmann continued to see irredeemable defects in human nature, though global events may have dimmed his outlook even further. Writing in his newspaper column in the fall of 1941, he remarked that the "ice-cold evil" facing America reflected a darker side of human nature. "The modern skeptical world has been taught for some 200 years a conception of human nature in which the reality of evil, so well known to the ages of faith, has been discounted," he wrote. "Almost all of us grew up in an environment of such easy optimism that we can scarcely know what is meant, though our ancestors knew it well, by the satanic will. We shall have to recover this forgotten but essential truth."[33] Lippmann began to accept the view that at the core of human nature lies a "satanic will"—a propensity for "evil" that can be buried but never fully expunged.

After World War II, Lippmann became gloomier still. In the *Public Philosophy*, he chastised Rousseau for claiming "that there is no perversity in the human heart," and he also argued that people were disposed by nature to believe the "delusion" that "they have a commission to act as if they were gods," free of moral restraint and obligation. "Men have been barbarians much longer than they have been civilized," he said. "They are only precariously civilized, and within us there is the propensity, persistent as the force of gravity, to revert under stress and strain, under neglect or temptation, to our first natures."[34] Beneath the thin veneer of civilization lay a barbaric self, ancient and inexorable, awaiting an opportunity to rear its ghastly head and visit mayhem upon the world.

It is important to note that despite the deeply pessimistic overtones in his rhetoric, Lippmann did not see human nature as completely fixed or predictable. In fact, he thought deeply about how the influence of environmental factors made human nature variable. Lippmann believed that within each person reside "multiple selves," each of which is constituted in a particular social context—that is, by the people with whom one is involved in some way. So, for example, the self on display at work (the employee) is very different from the one at home interacting with children (the parent), and each of those selves has its own set of interests and concerns. Having multiple selves, of course, complicates what is in a person's interest. That which serves the interests of one side of a personality may be anathema for another, and there is no way of telling how a person will choose among these conflicting interests. This is all by way of saying that Lippmann perceived the complexity and unpredictability of human nature. "Men purse their interest," he said. "But how they shall pursue it is not fatally determined."[35]

Lippmann slammed the "socialist theory of human nature" for failing to appreciate this fact, reducing identity to the economic class to which a person belongs. Operating under the assumption that each person would behave solely in accordance with his class interest, the socialist was guilty of economic determinism. "That theory," said Lippmann, "assumes that men are capable of adopting only one version of their interest, and that having adopted it, they move fatally to realize it. It assumes the existence of a specific class interest." The socialist believed that exposing a person to certain environmental inputs would lead to predictable behavioral outputs. Socialists made this mistake, said Lippmann, because they did not appreciate "the inordinate variety of human nature."[36] They did not understand that just because human nature was malleable did not mean that, like a mold of clay, it could be easily shaped and fashioned in accordance with some ideal form. Malleability did not imply predictability.

His aversion to determinism notwithstanding, Lippmann did not discount the possibility of forming or educating character. Indeed, in *A Preface to Morals*, he pointed to the many religious and philosophical traditions throughout history that sought to "transform the will" through renunciation and self-denial. He praised such luminaries as Socrates, Buddha, Jesus, Plotinus, and Spinoza for embracing an ethos of disinterestedness, teaching that "the good life is impossible without asceticism, that without renunciation of many of the ordinary appetites, no man can really live well." Because competing desires generated conflict, renunciation lay at the root of any viable moral system. "There is not room enough, there are not objects enough in the world to fulfill all human desires," said Lippmann. "Desires are, for all practical purposes, unlimited and insatiable, and therefore any ethos which does not recognize the necessity of putting restraint upon naïve desire is inherently absurd."[37] Tortured by passionate desires, people can only find peace if they learn to regard the world around them with a certain degree of detachment, not caring so much whether life gives them what they want. Through the arduous work of habit formation, said Lippmann, people can reach a level of maturity in which they are not governed by their appetites and desires. While their underlying primal nature will never disappear, they can learn to control it with a well-formed second nature.

As his views about human nature grew more pessimistic, Lippmann became convinced that most of us could not possibly become masters of our passions without the benefits of tradition. People received from tradition a sense of purpose and meaning in life, and they also inherited a set of rules, norms and practices, that structured their behavior. Without this guidance, said Lippmann, leading a moral life was exceedingly difficult. "Morality, if it is not fixed by custom and authority, becomes a mere matter of taste determined by the idiosyncrasies of the moralist."[38] Tradition inculcated clear moral standards by which people should live, thereby making certain that they did not simply equate the good with their preferences. People who were severed from the moorings of tradition found themselves cast adrift in a sea of subjectivity and relativism, whereupon it was far more likely that the barbaric side of their nature—their "satanic will" and "perversity"—would come to the surface.

"The traditions of civility"

Lippmann did not always believe that tradition played a critical role in the redemption of humankind. In his youth, he clearly saw tradition as an impediment to progress, the tyranny of ancestors whose ideas and practices were now woefully obsolete. "Tradition," he wrote in *A Preface to Politics*, "is nothing but a record and a machine-made imitation of the habits that our ancestors created."[39] Progress demanded that people stop slavishly imitating their forefathers and start harnessing the power of science and reason to take charge of the future. In his second book, *Drift and Mastery*, Lippmann acknowledged that the eclipse of tradition led to aimlessness but maintained that the scientific method could restore that lost sense of purpose and direction and enable communities to control their fate. "Rightly understood," he wrote, "science is the culture under which people can live forward in the midst of complexity, and treat life not as something given but as something to be shaped."[40]

But by the late 1920s Lippmann began to reassess his earlier enthusiasm for science, realizing that, unlike many hallowed religious traditions of the past, it could not offer moral certainty. In his undeservingly overlooked *American Inquisitors*, which contains a number of dialogues clearly inspired by his reading of Plato, Lippmann revealed his ambivalence about the displacement of religious traditions in the modern world. An exchange between Socrates and Thomas Jefferson is especially revealing. In response to Socrates' question about the official beliefs of the United States, Jefferson says there are none because the Founders believed in "free inquiry and reason." "I don't understand you," Socrates replies.

> You say there were many people in your day who believed that God had revealed the truth about the universe. You then tell me that officially your citizens had to believe that human reason and not divine revelation was the source of truth, and yet you say your state had no official beliefs. It seems to me it had a very definite belief, a belief which contradicts utterly the belief of my friend St. Augustine for example. Let us be frank. Did you not overthrow a state religion based on revelation and establish in its place the religion of rationalism?[41]

Founded in the spirit of science, the Jeffersonian liberal order remained neutral and open-minded about normative questions and applied reason in its search for solutions to social problems. But Socrates shows that the liberal order rested on its own dogma. Jefferson and other liberals promoted the values of open-mindedness and rationality.

The problem was that this "religion of rationalism"—which extolled incredulity, free thinking, and the suspension of belief—did not offer the certainties that most people needed. "[M]en cannot endure not being confident of their conclusions," says Socrates. "An easy and tolerant skepticism is not for them. They want ideas which they can count upon, sure cures, absolute promises, and no shilly-shallying with a lot of ifs and perhapses. The faith of the people is always hard, practical, and definite. And that is why your religion of reason is not for them."[42] About a decade after he had disparaged religious traditions for perpetuating outdated habits and standing in the way of progress, Lippmann now recognized that the triumph of science came at a cost—the loss of meaning and moral certainty.

A year later, in *A Preface to Morals*, Lippmann pondered this loss at great length. "We are living in the midst of that vast dissolution of ancient habits which the emancipators believed would restore our birthright of happiness," he wrote. "We know now that they did not see very clearly beyond the evils against which they were rebelling." There was a time when our ancestors enjoyed "the gifts of a vital religion" that instilled in them a faith "that there was an order in the universe which justified their lives because they were a part of it." But, unfortunately, the "acids of modernity have dissolved that order for many of us."[43] When Lippmann referred to the "acids of modernity," he meant science, reason, and technology, the triumvirate of forces that challenged traditional sources of authority and uprooted people from traditional communal life. The rise of this triumvirate had devastating consequences. "By the dissolution of their ancestral ways," said Lippmann, "men have been deprived of their sense of certainty as to why they were born, why they must work, whom they must love, what they must honor, where they may turn in sorrow and defeat."[44]

While Lippmann regretted the effects of this dissolution, he did not yearn or call for a return to ancestral ways. He understood that many old traditions, hopelessly inflexible and antiquated, could not be restored because they reflected a simpler time. "Life in the ancestral order was not only simpler and contained within narrower limits than it is to-day," said Lippmann, "but there was a far greater unity in the activity of each individual."

The average person had few, if any, competing loyalties, and he lived in a community in which people could easily forge a unity of purpose. In the modern world, on the other hand, each person was pulled in a number of different directions, fraught with a bewildering array of interests, commitments, and responsibilities. "Each man finds himself the center of a complex of loyalties," said Lippmann. "The multiplicity of his interests makes it impossible for him to give his whole allegiance to any person or to any institution."[45] It was not hard to understand why most people in the modern world, hopelessly conflicted and complicated, were averse to the old traditions, which demanded strict conformity with moral codes and practices. Whereas a certain tradition might agree with some loyalties and interests to which a person felt drawn, it might conflict with others. The old traditions were simply too narrow and rigid for the vast majority of people in the modern world, bearing no relevance to the conditions of their lives.

Reactionaries longing for outmoded traditions and moralistic commands to which most people were averse, insisting that they were an antidote to the disorders of modernity, failed to understand how the world had changed. "The trouble with the moralists is in the moralists themselves: they have failed to understand their times," said Lippmann. "They think they are dealing with a generation that refuses to believe in ancient authority. They are, in fact, dealing with a generation that cannot believe it." Even if they wanted to believe in the ancient authority, most people could not do so. Modern man could not so easily convince himself of the righteousness of a tradition on which an ever-changing empirical reality and far-ranging opinions and practices cast serious doubt. "An authoritative code of morals has force and effect when it expresses the settled customs of a stable society: the pharisee can impose upon the minority only such conventions as the majority find appropriate and necessary," said Lippmann. "But when customs are unsettled, as they are in the modern world, by continual change in the circumstances of life, the pharisee is helpless. He cannot command with authority because his commands no longer imply the usages of the community."[46]

Because "simple customs are unsuitable and authoritative commandments incredible" in the modern world, Lippmann espoused the recovery of a kind of meta-tradition that tapped into the wisdom of the ancestral order but at the same time eschewed rigid moralism and adapted to changing circumstances. In *A Preface to Morals*, Lippmann celebrated what he called high religion, an ethical position that can be found in many philosophical and religious traditions throughout history. Lippmann held "that in all the great religions, and in all the great moral philosophies from Aristotle to Bernard Shaw, it is taught that one of the conditions of happiness is to renounce some of the satisfactions which men normally crave." Moreover, these traditions taught that renunciation is necessary to live not only contentedly but also ethically. For "wherever men have thought at all carefully about the problem of evil and of what constitutes the good life, they have concluded that an essential element of any human philosophy is renunciation."[47] Asceticism and renunciation lay at the heart of this high religion because, as we saw earlier, they provided an antidote to the wayward tendencies of human nature. The person who could control his desires and approach life disinterestedly would not incite conflict or bring harm to others, for his modest demands would never exceed what the world could readily supply. But what distinguished high religion from any particular religious tradition was that it extolled the virtues of asceticism and detachment without imposing specific restrictions or directives, and it gave people the freedom to walk their own crooked path toward salvation.

In *The Good Society*, Lippmann identified another meta-tradition, which he called the higher law. "The denial that men may be arbitrary in human transactions *is* the higher law," said Lippmann. The purpose of the higher law was to restrain the barbaric nature of man and to prevent tyranny and the abuse of power. "The dim apprehension that there must be a law higher than the arbitrary will of any man has driven civilized men forward seeking to tame the barbarian that is in us all."[48] Any society that wished to remain civilized, securing both liberty and order for its people, needed to comply with the higher law and make sure that no one was exempt.

Lippmann made it clear that this higher law was not to be found in the heavens but in the experiences of people seeking protection from arbitrary power. "For more than two thousand years, since western men first began to think about the social order, the main preoccupation of political thinking has been to find a law which would be superior to arbitrary power," said Lippmann. "This is the meaning of a thousand years of struggle to bring the sovereign under a constitution, to establish for the individual and for voluntary associations of men rights which they can enforce against kings, barons, magnates, majorities, and mobs."[49] Over time people came to realize that any hope for civilization rested on the widespread belief in a higher law that prohibited arbitrary power.

While the higher law may not appeal to ambitious politicians or pedantic theorists, it became indispensable for civilization nevertheless.

"The conviction that there is a higher law, higher than statutes, ordinances, and usages, is to be found among all civilized peoples," said Lippmann.

> Though the existence of any such higher law in human societies is constantly repudiated in practice and is even condemned in theory, it derives from an intuition which mankind is unable to abandon. For if there is no higher law, then there is no ground on which anyone can challenge the power of the strong to exploit the weak, there is no reason by which arbitrary force can be restrained.[50]

Lippmann understood that his celebration of a higher law would face criticism—and it certainly did from liberals and progressives who saw it as an apology for limited government, imposing unnecessary constraints on government attempts to promote the general welfare—but his observations of the rising totalitarian regimes in Europe and Asia convinced him that an appeal to universal principles was necessary.

"The predominant teachings of this age are that there are no limits to man's capacity to govern others and that, therefore, no limitations ought to be imposed upon government," said Lippmann. As global events made increasingly clear, this naïve faith in the capacities of men and governments courted disaster. In order to avert the calamity toward which modern societies careened, Lippmann called for the restoration of "the older faith," which taught that "the exercise of unlimited power by men with limited minds and self-regarding prejudices is soon oppressive, reactionary, and corrupt."[51] Contrary to conventional wisdom in the 1930s, Lippmann believed that progress did not require an expansion of government power but rather a healthy respect for limits. His reasoning was quite simple: governments comprised fallible men who could do great harm if vested with unfettered power.

This was why government, despite the nobility and wisdom of its aims, always had to operate within a constitutional framework. "Constitutional restraints and bills of rights, the whole apparatus of responsible government and of an independent judiciary, the conception of due process of law in courts, in legislatures, among executives," said Lippmann, "are but the rough approximations by which men have sought to exorcise the devil of arbitrariness in human relations."[52] In order to avoid violations of the higher law, said Lippmann, governments had to be structured so as to hold even the most powerful people in check. The various institutional mechanisms that keep governments and men of power at bay are the "approximations"—or concrete manifestations—of the higher law. They are the higher law made tangible.

Nearly two decades later Lippmann returned to the higher law in *Essays in the Public Philosophy*. He changed his nomenclature, now referring to the natural law or the public philosophy instead of the higher law, but his core argument did not change all that much. Now writing in the mid-1950s, a decade after World War II and in the darkest years of the Cold War, Lippmann once again posited a transcendent law to which all men and institutions should conform. Much to the chagrin of many critics, Lippmann was rather elliptical in his discussion of the natural law or the public philosophy. Toward the end of the book, however, he became more direct. The public philosophy, he said, required a constitutional system in which everyone had clearly defined rights and duties under the law. The reason for this was quite simple. "Without this, that is without constitutional government, there is no freedom," wrote Lippmann. "For the antithesis to being free is to be at the mercy of men who can act arbitrarily. It is not to know what may be done to you."[53] Once again Lippmann revealed his aversion to arbitrary power and his belief that the higher law, now called the natural law or the public philosophy, must ensure that people do not become, like flies to wanton boys, the playthings of capricious sovereigns.

The felt need for checks on arbitrary power led to what Lippmann called "the traditions of civility," which over the centuries were expounded by philosophers, practiced by lawyers, codified in groundbreaking laws and constitutions, and developed in judge-made common law.[54] According to Lippmann, the traditions of civility permeated Western political thought and institutions of the last two thousand years, creating norms and procedures that harnessed the exercise of power. These traditions, however, had become unfashionable in the twentieth century, leading to the rise of totalitarian regimes throughout the world. By the mid-1950s Lippmann wrote with a sense of urgency, declaring that the fate of civilized democracies was in peril if the public philosophy and its traditions of civility were not restored to their rightful place.

Lippmann clearly saw his theoretical writing as an act of recovery. Because "the art of governing has to be learned," it also "has to be transmitted from the old to the young, and the habits and the ideas must be maintained as a seamless web of memory among the bearers of the tradition, from generation to generation." Unfortunately, the link connecting past and present, passing along the traditions and knowledge required in the art of governing, was broken. Having forgotten "the traditions of how the good life is lived and the good society is governed," the liberal democracies suffered from a "kind of collective amnesia."[55] Lippmann sought to remind people of their lost inheritance, the traditions for which their ancestors had sacrificed and labored. The public philosophy, said Lippmann, "does not have to be discovered or invented. It is known. But it does have to be revived and renewed."[56]

"RATIONAL PROCEDURE IS THE ARK OF THE COVENANT OF THE PUBLIC PHILOSOPHY"

Lippmann believed that the restoration of this lost inheritance, the revival of the higher law and the public philosophy, was essential for civilized societies to move forward. In fact, in his view, a society guided by the wisdom of the higher law had a far better chance of achieving real progress, because it avoided the pernicious extremes of political inaction and sweeping change, *laissez faire* and totalitarianism. However enlightened they might consider themselves, he said, people cannot maintain and advance a civilization without looking to the past for guidance. A new generation cannot ignore its ancestors, re-inventing and re-discovering everything on its own, and hope to make any progress. "Men can know more than their ancestors did if they start with a knowledge of what their ancestors had already learned," observed Lippmann. "That is why a society can be progressive only if it conserves its traditions."[57]

Laws that truly served the public interest, he believed, should be able to run the gauntlet of constitutional checks and balances and procedural rules. In fact, these mechanisms should not hinder but facilitate progress. As he put it, "the very condition of progress was the limitation of power to the capacity and the virtue of the rulers."[58] He also remarked that "the progress of human emancipation" has largely involved "a series of restraints upon the exercise of power by men over men" and the establishment of "laws and usages which seek to limit coercive authority, traditional prerogatives, vested rights, and all manner of predatory, violent, fraudulent dealing among men."[59] Echoing the views of Edmund Burke, Lippmann contended that only when the higher law was enshrined in the law and custom could the march toward progress continue unabated.

Drawing a connection between tradition and progress, conservatism and liberalism, Lippmann seemed to embrace a paradoxical idea. As one might expect, progressives did not share this enthusiasm for tradition, calling it a shameless attempt by powerful interests to "prohibit the improvement of human affairs" and to "defend vested rights and obstruct reform." But Lippmann contended that one needed to distinguish between the higher law and traditional law. He agreed with progressives that the latter often "put the living under the dominion of the dead" and denied the living "the power to remedy injustice and improve their condition."[60] In other words, the traditional law often imposed specific standards of conduct or secured specific rights, privileges, and immunities that were no longer relevant or useful to people in the modern age.

The higher law, on the other hand, aimed for the "rediscovery and the reconstruction of general political standards," and it eschewed blind adherence to specific traditional practices. Lippmann acknowledged, for example, that the liberal tradition, which at one time identified good reasons for limiting the powers of government and enforcing equality under the law, eventually became a justification for *laissez faire* long after its usefulness came to an end. Classical liberalism prohibited government intervention in the economy, but the higher law or the public philosophy could easily justify a more active state because corporations had come to exercise arbitrary power over a significant portion of the general population. Invoking traditional law to defend corporate power defied the "substance" or "spiritual essence" of the higher law—that no person should be able to exercise arbitrary power over others. The classical liberal notion of the absolute right to property merely provided cover—or "ceremonial disguise"—for corporations acting with unaccountable "caprice and willfulness."[61]

The true liberal, then, never lost sight of the higher law and refused to follow traditional principles, such as the absolute right to property, when they no longer served the purposes for which they were created. The right to property was meant "not to satisfy the acquisitive and possessive instincts of the primitive man" but rather to serve "the grand ends of civil society"—that is, to promote "peace and security." When existing private property rights became destructive of those broader goals, government had to make the necessary adjustments. Because they erected impediments to corrective reform, the public philosophy could not abide absolute principles. "In the public philosophy an absolute right to property, or to anything else that affects other men, cannot be entertained," Lippmann concluded. "To claim it is to be outside the law and the bounds of civility."[62]

Instead of strict conformity to absolute principles, the public philosophy demanded adherence to procedures and protocols. "Rational procedure," he wrote, "is the ark of the covenant of the public philosophy."[63] The method or means by which governments achieved their goals mattered even more than the noble ends for which they strived. Political actors who followed procedures inherited from the traditions of civility operated under constraints that curbed their power, moderated their behavior, and slowed down the pace of change. As a young man, Lippmann was too impatient to care much for procedure, calling for bold policy initiatives and prescriptions at every turn, and echoing the Progressive view that the Constitution erected needless barriers to meaningful change. But, as his respect for tradition grew in the 1920s so did his belief in the importance of procedure and constitutional limits. For the whole point of tradition was to ritualize behavior—to create procedures that reduced the degree of arbitrariness and extremism in politics. Governments bound by tradition acted predictably and responsibly, adhering to written rules and established practices.

In this context, it is easier to understand what seemed to be Lippmann's inexplicable turn against the New Deal in 1937. Initially an outspoken if somewhat qualified supporter of the New Deal, Lippmann reversed course when FDR tried to push his infamous court-packing plan through Congress. Lippmann was apoplectic, accusing the president of being "drunk with power" and of trying to stage a "bloodless coup d'état which strikes a deadly blow at the vital center of constitutional democracy."[64] Lippmann was alarmed by FDR's willingness to undermine the integrity and independence of the judiciary. The president seemed to have utter contempt for the system of checks and balances and for the idea that judicial review played a vital role in safeguarding individual liberty. Bent on getting his way, he obviously had little regard for the importance of established procedure and tradition. But this did not mean that Lippmann no longer had sympathy for the goals of the New Deal. As Lippmann made clear in *The Good Society*, his supposedly anti-New Deal book, he continued to favor progressive economic policies. And in his columns, Lippmann also assailed what he saw as the Court's narrow reading of the commerce clause, insisting that most of the New Deal legislation struck down by the Court was constitutional. Still, the disappointing performance of the Court did not justify such a flagrant breach of the Constitution and the higher law.

In *The Good Society*, Lippmann tried to show how a modern welfare state could address economic insecurity and at the same time remain compliant with the higher law. So, despite what his critics claimed, Lippmann never abandoned his support for what he called free collectivism in his earlier work, *The Method of Freedom*. He merely focused on the procedures by which the welfare state could achieve its goals without exceeding established limits and infringing on individual liberties. Whenever possible, he suggested, the state should refrain from exercising social control directly and allow the common law to do its work. When one party has a grievance against another, it should first seek redress in the courts. In lieu of an imperious administrative state issuing commands from above, governing behavior through the enforcement of arbitrary rules and regulations, Lippmann envisioned "social control by a common law which defines the reciprocal rights and duties of persons and invites them to enforce the law by proving their case in a court of law." Compliance with the law would stem not from state interference but rather from court rulings that set precedents on "the reciprocal rights and duties of persons" in particular circumstances. Precedent enabled people to identify those actions for which they would be held liable in a court of law. Always in search of a middle way between the aggrandized state and *laissez faire*, Lippmann found much to commend in the common law.[65]

His enthusiasm for the courts and the legal tradition notwithstanding, Lippmann acknowledged that complex modern societies often required administrative solutions offered by bureaucrats and government officials. Judges and legislators did not always have the time or the expertise to address specific technical problems. As a result, there was no avoiding the fact that legislatures had to delegate authority to administrative agencies in government. This was not necessarily a problem so long as government officials with clearly defined regulatory powers were "subject to challenge and review before a tribunal." As legislatures saw an increasing need to delegate authority to these unelected officials, it became more essential that "the state, through the courts and through the legislature itself, should regard itself as a tribunal to review the conduct of these specialized lawmakers." In other words, the modern liberal state had to remain vigilant in its regulation of the regulators. This was consistent with the liberal idea that all men, officials and citizens alike, are equal under the law. The government official was "simply a man among men, with certain rights which he may not exceed and certain lawful duties which he may not neglect." Whenever they failed to observe proper procedures, government officials had to be held accountable either in the court of law or through congressional oversight.[66]

Although he saw a need to stem the tide of administrative tyranny, Lippmann never relinquished hope that the liberal state could address modern problems. "A liberal society must, of course, provide schools, hospitals, recreation centres, and all manner of socials services just as it must have a police force and an army," he wrote. "But it remains liberal only if the social servants, the school authorities or the managers of electric plants, perform specific chartered functions and are accountable under the law."[67] The health of the liberal state is assured when all government officials operate within established guidelines, never exceeding the specific powers with which they are vested, and never defying the protocols with which they are charged. Only by remaining faithful to procedure could the state avoid extremism and effect change in a deliberate manner.

"Truths are like the clothes of a growing boy, not like the shroud of a corpse"

Lippmann believed reform had to proceed cautiously for the simple reason that human beings did not have the capacity to discover absolute truths on which they could base bold policy innovation. He insisted on the epistemological fallibility of humankind. People arrived at truths by drawing on their concrete experiences and sharing information in prolonged discussions. But these truths were provisional, for their observations of this ever-changing world were necessarily imperfect and incomplete. In all likelihood, new facts would come to light, challenging the truth claims to which people had become attached. As a result, they needed to brace themselves for an overhaul of their beliefs, either scrapping them altogether or at the very least modifying them to a considerable degree. Given the human propensity for error, the person who claims to know the truth should remain humble and recognize that the search will never end. This condition of uncertainty precluded the utopian visions on which totalitarian regimes justified the radical reconstruction of society and sweeping change.

Despite his search for enduring truths and higher laws later in life, Lippmann never relinquished this pragmatic epistemology. His introduction to this theory of truth came during his undergraduate years when he met William James, the famous Harvard philosopher, and began having weekly discussions with him over tea. Instilling in Lippmann an interest in the scientific method and an aversion to the quest for certainty, James disabused him of the idea that deductive logic could lead to unassailable and everlasting truth. He also learned from James the virtues of open-mindedness and tolerance. Because our tentative truths are grounded in shared experience, a person should never insulate himself from the perspectives of others, even those who seem disagreeably eccentric or unfamiliar.

When James died in the summer of 1910, Lippmann praised the renowned philosopher in a short tribute published in *Everybody's Magazine*. "James knew that he didn't know," said Lippmann. "He never acted upon the notion that the truth was his store of wisdom. Perhaps that is why he kept on rummaging about in other people's stores, and commending their goods." This willingness to learn from others did not prevent James from having strong beliefs and arguing fervently on their behalf. But it did mean that he refused to express his views with "the expert's arrogance toward the man in the street." What distinguished James from most intellectuals—indeed, from most other human beings—was that "he listened for truth from anybody, and from anywhere, and in any form. He listened for it from Emma Goldman, the pope, or a sophomore; preached from a pulpit, a throne, or a soap-box; in the language of science, in slang, in fine rhetoric, or in the talk of a ward boss." One would be hard-pressed to escape the conclusion that James was "perhaps the most tolerant man of our generation."[68]

Although Lippmann would never be so open-minded, his teacher left a marked and lasting influence on his epistemology. Throughout his life Walter Lippmann celebrated empirical observation and experimentation and disparaged arid intellectualism. His indebtedness to James was especially pronounced in his early years. When doctrinaire socialist Louis Wetmore attacked him for writing a glowing review of William James' posthumously published *The Problems of Philosophy*, Lippmann responded with a spirited defense of epistemological humility. As we experience changes in our concrete reality, he said, we must adapt our truths accordingly. "Truths are like the clothes of a growing boy, not like the shroud of a corpse." We must also accept the provisionality of our truth claims in a changing world and recognize that we can never know anything for certain. "Mr. Wetmore must explain how he knows that any one of his beliefs is an absolute truth," he wrote. "Supposing that he has one, how does he know he has it? By what birthmark does he distinguish an absolute truth from any mean little pragmatic hypothesis?"[69]

In a second response to Wetmore, Lippmann argued that it was dishonest for people to convince themselves that they had absolute knowledge about anything. "Intellectual integrity demands that they should see their limitations," he said. "And if as a result they are less cocksure, man's spiritual progress in this world will have less bluster, and more real humility." Although a refusal to recognize absolute truths made the universe a lonely and hostile place in which we might feel lost, Lippmann felt confident that most people could "accept the uncertainty of life without regret." In the end, Lippmann saw greater danger in "bluster" than in "uncertainty." Whereas the latter might produce temporary fear and anguish, the former could inspire brazen—and even violent—attempts to impose a particular worldview on other people.[70]

In his early years, Lippmann saw science as the antidote to the tyranny in which absolutist thinking inevitably resulted. "As Absolutism falls, science arises; it is self-government," he wrote in *Drift and Mastery*. "For when the impulse which overthrows kings and priests and unquestioned creeds becomes self-conscious, we call it science."[71] In other words, science employed and refined the familiar method of critical thinking, challenging the assumptions on which hitherto unassailable belief systems rested. But science did not just facilitate the toppling of tyrannical kings and creeds; it also enabled a community of inquirers to reach tentative conclusions based on empirical observations. "The discipline of science is the only one which gives any assurance that from the same set of facts men will come approximately to the same conclusion," he wrote in the same book. "And as the modern world can be civilized only by the effort of innumerable people we have a right to call science the discipline of democracy."[72] One cannot help noticing in these passages the influence of John Dewey, the pragmatist who famously described democracy as the scientific method writ large. Lippmann would not accept for very long the Deweyan notion that all citizens could assume the habits of the well-trained scientist, but he would never relinquish the view that a community of intelligent inquirers observing and sharing empirical facts could reach a tentative agreement about the truth.

Throughout his career, Lippmann continued to see truth as an agreement reached by a community of inquirers. In *A Preface to Morals*, he favorably quoted pragmatist philosopher Charles Peirce for equating truth with agreement. "What modern science means by the truth has been stated most clearly perhaps by the late Charles S. Peirce when he said that 'the opinion which is fated to be ultimately agreed to by all those who investigate, is what we mean by the truth, and the object represented in this opinion is the real,'" said Lippmann. "When we say something has been 'explained' by science, we really mean only that our curiosity is satisfied."[73] In Jamesian fashion, Lippmann suggested here that the truth is that which a group of inquirers considers satisfactory. The truth is what "works" for them at the moment.

But even as Lippmann became less enthralled with science later in his career, he still insisted that truths were derived not from deductive logic but rather from empirical observation and experimentation. Writing in the 1930s, he found common cause with those "who, needing a political faith by which they can live, would prefer to found it not upon a grandiose reconstruction of the whole of human history but upon observation of existing conditions and such knowledge of the art of government as they are able to draw upon." These are the people, he continued, who "agree with Burke that 'the science of constructing a commonwealth, or renovating it or reforming it, is, like every other experimental science, not to be taught *a priori*.' "[74] In fact, what Lippmann liked about the New Deal was that it valued experimentation and did not receive inspiration from any kind of doctrine. While ideologues on both the left and the right criticized the New Deal for not conforming to some a priori truths from which an indisputable policy agenda could be derived, Lippmann accused these critics of failing to understand "that simple logical deductions will not yield workable policies amidst the contrariness of human nature." Lippmann enjoyed ridiculing the critics of the New Deal for their foolish consistency. In his column he remarked, "America is the despair of all those who like their politics to be neat and logical, of Marxists, for example, and rugged individualists and planners and upholders of laissez-faire, and all others who have an internally consistent philosophy."[75]

Even later in his career Lippmann saw the grave political implications of absolutism. Underlying the view that human beings could attain absolute truth, he argued, was a pernicious hubris for which the world had paid a terrible price throughout the twentieth century. In *US War Aims*, Lippmann advised against renewing a Wilsonian attitude, an error that had visited disaster upon humankind.

> It is the error of forgetting that we are men and of thinking that we are gods. We are not gods. We do not have the omniscience to discover a new moral law and the omnipotence to impose it upon mankind. When we draw up lists of general principles which we say are universal, to which we mean to hold every one, we are indulging in a fantasy, we are imagining ourselves as beings who are above and outside mankind, detached from the concrete realities of life itself, and able to govern the world by fiat. But in fact we are inside the human world. We are mere mortals with limited power and little universal wisdom.[76]

Positing that absolute truth was within the grasp of some human beings led to their apotheosis and, therefore, gave them carte blanche to do whatever was necessary to remake the world in the image of their abstract blueprints. But the world was far more unpredictable and muddled than the absolutist cared to admit. Any attempts to impose theories on concrete reality would likely have catastrophic consequences. After all, people were "mere mortals" without the requisite foresight and wisdom "to govern the world by fiat."

Lippmann was so conscious of the pitfalls of absolutism that there were moments in his career, especially early on, when he seemed to flirt with relativism. He appeared far more comfortable dwelling in the gray areas between absolutes, and he was averse to making moral claims when discussing political issues. "Before you can begin to think about politics at all," he said in *A Preface to Politics*, "you have to abandon the notion that there is a war between good and bad men."[77] He echoed this sentiment over a decade later as he described, in Nietzschean fashion, the genealogy of rights and duties in *The Phantom Public*. "The prevailing system of rights and duties at any time is, at bottom, a slightly antiquated formulation of the balance of power among the active interests of a community," he wrote; "a right is a claim somebody was able to assert, and a duty is an obligation somebody was able to impose." In the same book he laid his relativism bare, arguing that truth claims are merely a matter of historical and social context. "An opinion of the right and the wrong, the good and the bad, the pleasant and the unpleasant, is dated, is localized, is relative," he said.[78]

Over time Lippmann grew increasingly ill at ease with this kind of overt relativism. He came to believe that relativism paved the way for a world where everything is permissible and might makes right. In a relativistic world, the weak and vulnerable lived at the mercy of arbitrary powers who anointed themselves the final arbiters of truth. It was at this point that Lippmann began searching for a higher law, which was not relative to time and place, and to which everyone would have to answer. But this did not mean that he would swing to the opposite extreme and embrace absolutism, for Lippmann found a middle way by grounding his higher law in the common experiences of humankind. In other words, the higher law was derived inductively, not deductively.

In *The Good Society*, Lippmann claimed that the higher law grew out of past experience and did not spring from the mind of a brilliant philosopher working out a logical proof in the lonely confines of his scholarly hermitage. Only after enduring oppression at the hands of tyrants who exercised arbitrary power with impunity did people begin to conceive of a higher law. "The older faith, born of long ages of suffering under man's dominion over man," he said, "was that the exercise of unlimited power by men with limited minds and self-regarding prejudices is soon oppressive, reactionary, and corrupt." The higher law only dawned on people after centuries of torment and misery, and, through the slow process of accumulating wisdom from these experiences, they eventually began to see that the solution to their woes could be found in the establishment of formal checks on political power.

> But I think it is not misleading to say that some such dim but pregnant apprehension as this has been hammered out on the anvil of long experience, that it is no abstract and a priori speculation arrived at in the eighteenth century and declared to mankind by William Ewart Gladstone, but that it is much older, has its roots in centuries of confused struggle with all manner of censorship and inquisition, prerogative and privilege.

Rather than coming about as the result of "abstract and a priori speculation" during the Enlightenment, the higher law was wrought on "the anvil of long experience" and can be traced back to "centuries of confused struggle."[79]

The higher law did not just emerge out of historical struggle but also continued to evolve and take shape as a result of ongoing experience. "To those who ask where this higher law is to be found," said Lippmann, "the answer is that it is a progressive discovery of men striving to civilize themselves, and that its scope and implications are a gradual revelation that is by no means completed." The higher law was not an immutable truth awaiting discovery after people had drawn on centuries of experience. Instead, it was a living, breathing tradition that developed as people responded to new circumstances. While these materializations of the higher law embodied truths that had stood the test of time, they were also provisional, reflecting an ongoing evolution that would never come to an end. Meanwhile, the higher law found concrete expression in specific laws and usages—including constitutions, bills of rights, checks and balances, judicial review, and due process—"by which men have sought to exorcise the devil of arbitrariness in human relations."[80] These laws and usages were the reification of the higher law—provisional political truths given concrete form.

Even when Lippmann asserted the need for natural law in *Essays in the Public Philosophy*, he rooted this concept in concrete experience.

Alexander the Great, he said, offered a perfect example, for he "discovered empirically" the need for "a superior common law" that would transcend the plurality of interests in his empire. He did not use logic or benefit from divine inspiration in his discovery; he merely saw the need for this common law as a way of maintaining peace and stability in his vast dominion. "The common law is 'natural' in the sense that it can be discovered by any rational mind, that it is not the willful and arbitrary positive command of the sovereign power," said Lippmann. "This is the necessary assumption, without which it is impossible for different peoples with their competing interests to live together in peace and freedom within one community."[81]

Lippmann also grounded ethical traditions in past experience and concrete relations. One could not say that a particular desire or action was bad without looking to the likely effects on other people. Once again, abstract or a priori thinking did not offer any help. Lippmann began his analysis by making the point that moral judgments are only necessary in a world where sentient creatures face the scarcity of desired goods. "The categories of good and evil would not apply if there were no sentient being to experience good and evil," said Lippmann. "In a world where no man desired what he could not have, there would be no need to regulate human conduct and therefore no need for morality."[82] Human beings are sentient creatures that suffer when they experience privation. Moral systems have emerged out of this cruel reality, not out of an intellectual vacuum.

Slowly, people came to realize that disinterestedness and renunciation, the chief virtues of what he called high religion, were sensible ways of dealing with the pain and anguish associated with unsatisfied desire. Lippmann saw disinterestedness as the "inner principle" of many religious and philosophical traditions and the main inspiration for such well-regarded "virtues as courage, honor, faithfulness, veracity, justice, temperance, magnanimity, and love." It was crucial to understand, said Lippmann, that these "virtues are grounded in experience; they are not idle suggestions inadvertently adopted because somebody took it into his head one fine day to proclaim a new ideal." Over time, as human experience demonstrated the value of these virtues, they became accepted as traditional wisdom. Indeed, "the cardinal virtues correspond to an experience so long and so nearly universal among men of our civilization, that when they are understood they are seen to contain a deposited wisdom of the race."[83]

In the end, Lippmann regarded high religion and the higher law as enduring truths that were forged in the crucible of experience. Regardless of the time or place, these truths withstood close scrutiny and rigorous testing for many generations. At the same time, however, these enduring truths had been particularized in a variety of ways throughout history. Each community found its own way of reifying these truths, devising customs and usages that worked in that particular context. These specific customs and usages, then, were the embodiments of *provisional* truths that can be traced back to the ancestral order. As long as they continued to work, succeeding generations would continue to follow these traditions and, after a length of time, see them as venerable deposits of wisdom without which the good life could never be achieved. Although traditions and customs were hardly infallible, often requiring refinements and alterations in accordance with changing circumstances, they offered guidance for the average person, who had little chance of successfully navigating the world without them.

People might have learned from experience out of which they carved traditions, but there was a reason why this process was so slow and painstaking. Human beings were slow learners. It took many generations before they could derive lessons from their common experiences and fashion customs that would make discernible improvements in their lives. The modern world was an especially harsh school, for people were deluged with cascades of information and experiences of which their minds had difficulty making sense. The political world was especially remote and incomprehensible to most people. "The world that we have to deal with politically," said Lippmann, "is out of reach, out of sight, out of mind."[84] Woefully uninformed, most people received distorted information about political issues from unreliable news media and from special interests that used propaganda to manufacture consent.[85]

But even when people had access to objective facts and unbiased analyses, and the time to digest all of this material, they were still likely to form a picture of the world in their heads that bore little resemblance to reality. This was because people viewed the world through a particular lens that colored their perceptions and opinions. "For the most part we do not first see, and then define, we define first and then see," said Lippmann. "In the great blooming, buzzing confusion of the outer world we pick out what our culture has already defined for us, and we tend to perceive that which we have picked out in the form stereotyped for us by our culture."[86] In other words, people saw the world through preconceived notions, or stereotypes, instilled in them by their culture and social set. They never enjoyed an unmediated view of their environment. It was always refracted through the prism of their stereotypes.

So when we meet a person for the first time, "we notice a trait which marks a well known type, and fill in the rest of the picture by means of the stereotypes we carry in our heads."[87] A man's apparel, for example, might suggest to us that he is a criminal, prompting us to discriminate against him if he is applying for a job or a mortgage. The problem, of course, is that the pictures that we form in our heads, informed by our stock of stereotypes, are often way off base. Perhaps most troubling is the fact that people rely on stereotypes to form opinions about anything that they encounter in the world of which they do not already have intimate knowledge.

Lippmann certainly recognized the economy, even the necessity, of relying on stereotypes. People could not manage the complexities of modern life without them. As he put it, "the attempt to see all things freshly and in detail, rather than as types and generalities, is exhausting, and among busy affairs practically out of the question."[88] Stereotypes function as useful shortcuts that help us navigate our busy lives. But the tool that helped people deal with the buzzing confusion of the outer world also introduced political hazards. When people try to make sense of the political world, they often rely on ideology, which Lippmann saw as a certain kind of stereotype. Painting a clear and simple picture of the political world, ideologies helped people interpret and explain events and to form opinions about leaders and various policy proposals. The problem was that in most cases the picture did not correspond with reality whatsoever. And when people acted as if these pictures did reflect reality, they could do great harm.

It should not come as a surprise that Lippmann concluded *Public Opinion* on a pessimistic note, underscoring the epistemological limits under which people operate in the realm of politics. "Our rational ideas in politics are still large, thin generalities, much too abstract and unrefined for practical guidance," he wrote. "The number of human problems on which reason is prepared to dictate is small."[89] As will be discussed in the next section, the epistemological limitations of most human beings prompted Lippmann to reassess traditional democratic theory and to reconsider the role that elites should play in politics.

"In our age the power of majorities tends to become arbitrary and absolute"

According to what theorists have posited for centuries, democracy requires the full engagement of a knowledgeable and rational citizenry. Lippmann claimed that traditional democratic theory rested on the fallacy of the "omnicompetent citizen" who had a "consuming passion" for politics and an "instinct" for the "art of government."[90] In truth, he said, the average citizen was imbued with stereotypes and prejudices that prevented him from satisfying the demands of traditional democratic theory. Neither well-informed nor rational, the average person allowed his emotions and prejudices to influence his opinions. His "stereotypes are loaded with preference, suffused with affection or dislike attached to fears, lusts, strong wishes, pride, hope."[91] In addition, people were busy working, raising families, and enjoying what little leisure time they had left. Understandably, they did not have much time for, or interest in, thinking seriously about civic issues.[92] Most people, therefore, were not qualified to assume the weighty responsibilities of government. Because their views about political issues were ill-informed and capricious, it was almost certain that the aggregate of those opinions—or what is often called public opinion—would not agree with the public interest.

In his darker moments, Lippmann could speak of the masses in the most unflattering terms. "The mass of absolutely illiterate, of feeble-minded, grossly neurotic, undernourished and frustrated individuals, is very considerable, much more considerable there is reason to think than we generally suppose," he wrote. "Thus a wide popular appeal is circulated among persons who are mentally children or barbarians, people whose lives are a morass of entanglements, people whose vitality is exhausted, shut-in people, and people whose experience has comprehended no factor in the problem under discussion."[93] It is little wonder why he thought the people were not fit to govern. "We must assume that a public is inexpert in its curiosity, intermittent, that it discerns only gross distinctions, is slow to be aroused and quickly diverted," he said; "it personalizes whatever it considers, and is interested only when events have been melodramatized as a conflict."[94]

Accordingly, Lippmann believed that a popular majority, if left unchecked, would almost certainly rule unwisely—and perhaps even tyrannically. The Scopes trial showcased perfectly, in his view, the fatuous and repressive tendencies of unchecked majorities. In 1925, with overwhelming majorities in both chambers, the Tennessee legislature passed a bill making it unlawful to teach Darwinian evolution in public schools. The ensuing trial in Dayton captured national attention, becoming a vivid reminder of the never-ending conflict between individual freedom and popular sovereignty. Imposing its religious fundamentalism in the classroom, the democratic majority staged an all-out assault on reason and intellectual freedom, the pillars of scientific inquiry. While to some extent he sympathized with the fundamentalists, sharing their concern about the acids of modernity, he saw the Scopes trial as a cautionary tale. In *American Inquisitors*, partly a response to the Scopes trial, Lippmann concluded, "In our age the power of majorities tends to become arbitrary and absolute."[95]

When Lippmann seemed to abandon his support for New Deal liberalism in *The Good Society*, he was actually expressing his concern over the threat to individual rights posed by modern democracies. Causing much confusion among his readers, Lippmann argued that "gradual collectivism," the benign form of collectivism found in countries such as the United States and the United Kingdom, might very likely degenerate into the "absolute collectivism" found in Nazi Germany or the Soviet Union. Although this line of reasoning seemed to suggest that Lippmann endorsed the slippery slope argument made famous a few years later by Friedrich Hayek in *The Road to Serfdom*, he did not fault gradual collectivism for providing economic security to the masses. The flaw in gradual collectivism was not its reasonable goals but its attachment to the idea that popular sovereignty must always prevail. "The gradual collectivist believes in the absolutism of the majority" and "in the dictatorship of random aggregations of voters," said Lippmann. "In this theory the individual has no rights as against the majority, for constitutional checks and bills of rights exist only by a consent of the majority."[96] So, gradual collectivism tended to give way to absolute collectivism because it failed to recognize the value of "constitutional checks" that placed limits on the popular will.

This is why Lippmann soured on the New Deal after FDR hatched his notorious Court plan: it was inspired by the idea that the popular will should always prevail, constitutional checks and balances be damned. Had the plan been successful, Lippmann argued, a dangerous precedent would have been set, allowing FDR and future administrations to push through popular and increasingly collectivist policy proposals. Lippmann shuddered at the thought. "For when public opinion attempts to govern directly it is either a failure or a tyranny."[97]

One could not defend democracy, then, on the grounds that giving the reins of government to the majority would yield the best results for society. "The justification of majority rule in politics is not to be found in its ethical superiority," Lippmann said.

> It is to be found in the sheer necessity of finding a place in civilized society for the force which resides in the weight of numbers. I have called voting an

act of enlistment, an alignment for or against, a mobilization. These are military metaphors, and rightly so, I think, for an election based on the principle of majority rule is historically and practically a sublimated and denatured civil war, a paper mobilization without physical force.[98]

In other words, democracy is a peaceful alternative to civil war. In lieu of the battlefield, opposing sides in a democracy face off at the polls. Because majorities enjoy a numerical superiority that would likely translate into victory on the battlefield, it only makes sense that they should prevail on Election Day. Failure to accommodate majorities in this way might compel them to pursue their goals by violent means.

Lippmann was acutely aware of the bind in which democracies find themselves. Accommodating majorities is a necessary substitute for war, yet the masses cannot be trusted to exercise power responsibly. Because democracies choose accommodation, majorities have ample opportunity to show their fallibility. The best solution to this dilemma is to impose limits on popular sovereignty and to fragment power through a rather cumbersome system of checks and balances. "And therefore, it may well be that to limit the power of majorities, to dispute their moral authority, to deflect their impact, to dissolve their force, is now the most important task of those who care for liberty."[99] The purpose of a constitution is neither to inhibit nor to indulge popular will. Instead, "the function of a constitution is to refine that will."[100]

In Lippmann's view, refining the popular will required disinterested government officials to act as trustees of the public interest rather than delegates of public opinion. He had in mind a "statesman" who embodies the high religion and the Burkean concept of representation. Such a leader "stops trying merely to satisfy or to obfuscate the momentary wishes of his constituents, and sets out to make them realize and assent to those hidden interests of theirs which are permanent because they fit the facts and can be harmonized with the interests of their neighbors." The statesman tells the people what they need to hear and gives them not what they want but what they will learn to want. He explains that they cannot always get what they want and have to make compromises so as to accommodate the desires of their fellow citizens. "The politician says: 'I will give you what you want.' The statesman says: 'What you think you want is this. What it is possible for you to get is that. What you really want, therefore, is the following.' The politician stirs up a following; a statesman leads."[101]

Lippmann recognized that government officials had a better chance of acting as trustees if they were insulated from the temporary whims and passions of the people. This is why he advocated a limited role for democratic citizens. "To support the Ins when things are going well; to support the Outs when they seem to be going badly, this in spite of all that has been said about tweedledum and tweedledee, is the essence of popular government," said Lippmann.[102] In other words, the job of democratic citizens is to give their periodic stamp of approval or disapproval and then to go on their merry way, allowing elected officials to handle the nitty-gritty of governing free of undue interference. The people, then, serve as a vital check on the power of elected officials by throwing them out if their policies have not yielded desirable results over the course of an election cycle. The hope that they could weigh in on policy matters and contribute substantially to public affairs is sheer delusion. "A false ideal of democracy can lead only to disillusionment and to meddlesome tyranny," he said. "The public must be put in its place."[103]

When democratic citizens stick to their limited role, elected officials can draw on the knowledge that they have accumulated as political insiders and on the information and analysis of experts who, Lippmann hoped, would play an increasingly prominent role in government. He envisioned the creation of intelligence bureaus that would be housed in every federal government department and agency. Experts working for these bureaus would perform research and analysis for elected officials, remaining impassive about the outcomes of their efforts and detached from partisan conflict.[104] Even more than the elected officials who enjoy some insulation from public opinion in Lippmann's preferred democratic state, the expert personifies disinterestedness. Trained in some technical field, typically a natural or social science, the expert pursues the truth in accordance with defined protocols and practices and without personal investment in the end result. The scientific method requires his impartiality. Lippmann noted the connection between science and disinterestedness in *A Preface to Morals*: "It is no exaggeration to say that pure science is high religion incarnate."[105]

The benefits of a more prominent elite in politics were significant, in Lippmann's view. If when enacting policy elected officials could ignore the caprices of public opinion and, instead, heed the disinterested findings of experts, government would do a far better job of serving the public interest. In his discussion of the compensated economy in *The Method of Freedom*, Lippmann lamented the fact that the people would not support many of the measures advocated by most economists, such as the

Keynesian policy of countercyclical spending.[106] A political system wherein the public is "put in its place" and officials have the freedom to do what is best for the country could actually implement these compensatory economic policies. The upshot of this rather elitist arrangement, according to Lippmann, would be the preservation of free collectivism. Quite simply, striking a balance between the extremes of *laissez faire* and absolute collectivism requires less democracy.

Although Lippmann hoped that insiders and experts would go on to exercise greater influence in the political system, he did not place them on a pedestal. He had realistic expectations about what they could accomplish and never saw them as inherently superior to outsiders and laymen. They just happened to have a unique perspective and knowledge set that allowed them to make modest contributions to the commonweal. This meant that insiders and experts were no more likely to achieve omnicompetence than the average citizen. Lippmann himself was no exception. "I find it so myself for, although public business is my main interest and I give most of my time to watching it, I cannot find time to do what is expected of me in the theory of democracy; that is, to know what is going on and to have an opinion worth expressing on every question which confronts a self-governing community," said Lippmann. "And I have not happened to meet anybody, from President of the United States to a professor of political science, who came anywhere near to embodying the accepted ideal of the sovereign and omnicompetent citizen."[107] Insiders and experts may have special knowledge from which the public would certainly benefit, but it is restricted to specific areas and never certain. In those areas outside their expertise, they are just as ignorant as the rest of us. And even within their bailiwicks, they remain prone to error.

CONCLUSION

At least on the surface, Lippmann did not appear to bequeath a conservative legacy at the end of his life. A strong supporter of the Great Society and a vocal opponent of the Vietnam War, the elderly Lippmann fell in line with the liberal intelligentsia and even shared with many on the left a feeling of restlessness about conditions at home and abroad. In a curious turn of events, he increasingly found common cause with the likes of E.F. Stone and other left-wing journalists and became an object of derision inside the White House for railing against the war in Vietnam. Then again, Lippmann supported Nixon in 1968 and vehemently opposed

McGovern's candidacy in 1972, calling him a "Jacobin" for his allegedly utopian tendencies.[108] In truth, it was hard to pinpoint where Lippmann fell on the ideological spectrum throughout his career. Whether he was commenting on political events or engaging in philosophical reflection, his position depended on the issue at hand and on the time in which he was writing. This was why many of his critics have uncharitably concluded that he was a confused and inconsistent political commentator and thinker.

This indefinable quality to Lippmann can explain, at least in part, the waning interest in his career since his death. Because he defied ideological labels, Lippmann has not been fully embraced by intellectuals on either the left or the right. He languishes in an ideological gray zone, and, as a result, people on each side of the spectrum can find much in his commentary and thought with which they do not agree. It should not come as a surprise, then, that scholarship on his life and thought has been largely critical and has become increasingly scarce as the years have gone by. In fact, the only comprehensive biography of Lippmann, a sympathetic treatment by Ronald Steel, came out 35 years ago, and almost all of the scholarly works about him were released at least 20 years ago.

This neglect reflects the polarizing times in which we live. Lippmann's ongoing search for a middle way, his Burkean resistance to ideological branding, are woefully unfashionable today. This is unfortunate. Lippmann's political thought, both subtle and provocative, challenges readers to reexamine their cherished assumptions—to consider sending their sacred cows to the slaughterhouse. Nothing escaped his razor sharp analysis, whether it was socialism, progressivism, democracy, or liberalism. Instead of remaining committed to a particular cause or creed, Lippmann always sought pragmatic solutions to the problems his country faced. As he grew older, he saw the value of upholding ancient traditions that had stood the test of time. He also recognized that democracy gave proof to the adage that there can be too much of a good thing. Serving the public interest—and even saving democracy itself—might actually require qualifying popular sovereignty. These are hard lessons that deserve a wider audience.

NOTES

1. Reston, "Conclusion: The Mockingbird and the Taxicab," in Marquis Childs and James Reston, eds., *Walter Lippmann and His Times*, 227, 229.
2. Steel, "The World We're In," *New Republic* (April 14, 1973), 17.

3. Wright, *Five Public Philosophies of Walter Lippmann*, 11. See also Hari N. Dam, Heinz Eulau, Charles Forcey, Christopher Lasch, David Elliott Weingast, and Morton White.

4. Lippmann quoted in Steel, *Walter Lippmann and the American Century*, 27–28.

5. Lippmann, *A Preface to Politics*, 201.

6. Lippmann quoted in Steel, *Walter Lippmann and the American Century*, 39–40.

7. Lippmann, *The Method of Freedom*, 47, 106–107.

8. See Lippmann, *A Preface to Politics*, 201; *The Method Freedom*, 114.

9. See Lippmann, *The Good Society*, 210–240

10. Ibid., 25, 27.

11. Lippmann, *The Good Society*, 242–243.

12. Ibid., 182, 208.

13. Ibid., 186–187.

14. Lippmann, *The Method of Freedom*, 107.

15. Lippmann, *The Good Society*, 190.

16. Ibid.

17. Ibid., 258.

18. Ibid., 189.

19. Lippmann, *Essays in the Public Philosophy*, 119.

20. Lippmann, *The Good Society*, 201.

21. Lippmann, *Essays in the Public Philosophy*, 167.

22. Lippmann, *The Method of Freedom*, 41, 57.

23. Ibid., 50–51, 58–59.

24. Lippmann, *Essays in the Public Philosophy*, 146.

25. Lippmann, *The Method of Freedom*, 98–99, 112–113.

26. Riccio, *Walter Lippmann: Odyssey of a Liberal*, 45.

27. Lippmann quoted in Steel, *Walter Lippmann and the American Century*, 258.

28. Ibid.

29. Ibid., 18–19.

30. Ibid., 27.

31. Riccio, *Walter Lippmann: Odyssey of a Liberal*, 5.

32. Lippmann, *A Preface to Politics*, 42, 148, 35.

33. Lippmann quoted in Steel, *Walter Lippmann and the American Century*, 390–391.

34. Lippmann, *Essays in the Public Philosophy*, 86.

35. Lippmann, *Public Opinion*, 120–121.

36. Ibid., 119–121.

37. Lippmann, *A Preface to Morals*, 155, 164–165.

38. Ibid., 166.

39. Lippmann, *A Preface to Politics*, 13.
40. Lippmann, *Drift and Mastery*, 275.
41. Lippmann, *American Inquisitors*, 18–19.
42. Ibid., 45–46.
43. Lippmann, *A Preface to Morals*, 6, 8.
44. Ibid., 21.
45. Ibid., 267–268.
46. Ibid., 316–317.
47. Ibid., 320, 156.
48. Lippmann, *The Good Society*, 346, 333.
49. Ibid., 5–6.
50. Ibid., 334.
51. Ibid., 40.
52. Ibid., 346.
53. Lippmann, *Essays in the Public Philosophy*, 167.
54. Ibid., 98–99.
55. Ibid., 135–136.
56. Ibid., 101.
57. Ibid., 136.
58. Lippmann, *The Good Society*, 40.
59. Ibid., 352.
60. Lippmann, *The Good Society*, 344–345.
61. Ibid., 345–346.
62. Lippmann, *Essays in the Public Philosophy*, 119–120, 116.
63. Ibid., 133.
64. Lippmann quoted in Steel, *Walter Lippmann and the American Century*, 317.
65. Lippmann, *The Good Society*, 265–266, 269.
66. Ibid., 298–302.
67. Ibid., 303–304.
68. Lippmann, "An Open Mind: William James," 800–801.
69. Lippmann quoted in Riccio, 164.
70. Ibid.
71. Lippmann, *Drift and Mastery*, 275–276.
72. Ibid., 285.
73. Lippmann, *A Preface to Morals*, 129.
74. Lippmann, *The Method of Freedom*, 7.
75. Lippmann quoted in Riccio, 105–106.
76. Lippmann, *U.S. War Aims*, 181–182.
77. Lippmann, *A Preface to Politics*, 7.
78. Lippmann, *The Phantom Public*, 90, 87.
79. Lippmann, *The Good Society*, 40, 358–359.

80. Ibid., 346–347.
81. Lippmann, *Essays in the Public Philosophy*, 106–107.
82. Lippmann, *A Preface to Morals*, 168, 145.
83. Ibid., 221–222, 226.
84. Lippmann, *Public Opinion*, 18.
85. Incidentally, Lippmann coined the term "manufacture of consent" in *Public Opinion*. He used the term in his concluding remarks about propaganda, the use of symbols to rally the masses behind a particular cause. This idea has been popularized more recently by luminaries on the left such as Noam Chomsky.
86. Lippmann, *Public Opinion*, 54–55.
87. Ibid., 59.
88. Ibid.
89. Ibid., 260–261.
90. Ibid., 195.
91. Ibid., 78.
92. Lippmann cited a study reporting that 70–75% of American adults read the newspaper for about 15 minutes a day and typically pay less attention to serious political news and more to stories about sports and entertainment. See *Public Opinion*, 37–40.
93. Ibid., 48.
94. Lippmann, *The Phantom Public*, 55.
95. Lippmann, *American Inquisitors*, 111.
96. Lippmann, *The Good Society*, 107.
97. Lippmann, *The Phantom Public*, 60–61.
98. Ibid., 48.
99. Lippmann, *American Inquisitors*, 111.
100. Lippmann, *The Good Society*, 259.
101. Lippmann, *A Preface to Morals*, 280–283.
102. Lippmann, *The Phantom Public*, 117.
103. Ibid., 145.
104. Lippmann, *Public Opinion*, 241–243.
105. Lippmann, *A Preface to Morals*, 239.
106. Lippmann, *The Method of Freedom*, 74.
107. Lippmann, *The Phantom Public*, 10–11.
108. Riccio, 214.

CHAPTER 4

Reinhold Niebuhr: Prophetic Conservative

Introduction

Like Walter Lippmann, Christian ethicist and theologian Reinhold Niebuhr enjoyed considerable renown as a public intellectual. In 1915, he began his career as a pastor at the Bethel Evangelical Church in Detroit, where he presided over a predominantly German-American congregation. While he dazzled his parishioners with thoughtful and energetic sermons, Niebuhr delegated many of his pastoral duties to his widowed mother so that he could spend more time addressing larger ethical and political issues and extending his influence beyond his local community. His out-sized ambitions fueled his tireless work as a lecturer and writer, and it was a rare evening or weekend that he did not devote most of his energy to these activities. A gifted orator who could captivate secular and Christian audiences alike, Niebuhr delivered guest lectures and sermons around the country. Because he was equally comfortable with, and adept at, speaking from the lectern and the pulpit, he received invitations from both colleges and churches. Similarly, he wrote for both secular and religious publications, commenting on the political issues of the day, usually from a Christian perspective, with remarkable subtlety and sophistication for such a young man.

Niebuhr left his Detroit pastorate in 1928 for a professorship at the Union Theological Seminary, and by the early 1930s he emerged as a first-rate public intellectual who could expound on both current events and more abstruse philosophical issues. After World War II, he earned

© The Author(s) 2016
R.J. Lacey, *Pragmatic Conservatism*,
DOI 10.1057/978-1-137-59295-8_4

a reputation as a great mind whose insights into the frailties of human nature offered indispensable lessons for a totalitarian age. His celebrity culminated with his appearance on the cover of *Time* in 1948, an unprecedented achievement for a theologian. Upon his death in 1971, the same magazine lionized Niebuhr as "the greatest Protestant theologian in America since Jonathan Edwards."[1]

Since his death over 40 years ago, Niebuhr's star has not dimmed. Unlike Lippmann, he continues to receive an enormous amount of scholarly attention, especially from theologians, ethicists, intellectual historians, and political theorists. Niebuhr is perhaps remembered best as a thinker in the realist tradition. His admirers praise him for disabusing intellectuals on the left and the right of their utopian faith in the perfectibility of human beings and the inevitability of social progress, teaching them that our best hope in this irretrievably sinful world is not to achieve perfect justice but rather to prevent injustice. He warned that naïve optimism about the political and ethical capacities of human beings can blind us to the will-to-power, which resides within everyone, however virtuous their motives and actions may appear, and which, if left unchecked, will breed misery and injustice. In particular, Niebuhr was attuned to how easily optimism can turn into hubris, a mix of ideological certainty and self-righteousness that inevitably leads to political overreach.

One can see why his message resonated in his time—and continues to do so today. These are the times of ideological ardor, nightmarish political experimentation, and awe-inspiring technological innovation. To insist on marching toward the future with the resolve of a crusader, Niebuhr warned, is to court unmitigated disaster. In both the domestic and international spheres of politics, he said, it behooves us to proceed with caution, ever mindful of unintended consequences, and to operate under the assumption that people will almost always be motivated by self-interest and the will-to-power. The realist demands an honest assessment of the facts and, in doing so, recognizes the limits to what people can achieve ethically and politically. Never forgetting that the empirical (what *is*) rarely lives up to the normative (what *ought to be*), realists moderate their hopes accordingly. They adopt a prudent course of action by eschewing political enterprises that promise perfect justice and try to maintain a balance of power among competing interests out of which a tenuous peace can be fashioned. "The very essence of politics," said Niebuhr, "is the achievement of justice through equilibria of power."[2]

It is important to stress, however, that Niebuhr qualified his realism with Christian faith. As a proponent of what is often called Christian realism, he believed that it is essential to temper a sober acceptance of reality with transcendent principles which rouse people from their moral complacency and motivate them to make a better world. In his view, crude realism justifies a cynical dismissal of any ethical standards, only advising restraint for prudential reasons—that is, when one does not have sufficient power to achieve one's desired ends. That one should not pursue such ends in the first place does not enter the discussion. An ethically sound realism cannot sanction self-interest run amok. "No political realism," said Niebuhr, "which emphasizes the inevitability and necessity of a social struggle, can absolve individuals of the obligation to check their own egoism, to comprehend the interests of others and thus to enlarge the areas of co-operation."[3]

In the Christian faith, Niebuhr found an ethical system which demands what he called an "impossible possibility."[4] It offers the crucifixion as a symbol (and, for the believer, a rare historical instance) of sacrificial love (or agape). Agape is an ethical ideal that no one can be expected to follow unwaveringly—for, after all, it meant defying the instinct of self-preservation—yet, nevertheless, it stands in judgment of all who fall short of it in their actions. Agape serves as a transcendent principle by which all people should be inspired, even though they know that, at best, they can only achieve pale approximations of it. While the crude realist just accepts his own failings without remorse, the Christian realist directs his critical gaze inward. In the glaring light of divine judgment, he acknowledges, with great humility and contrition, his own shortcomings without ever giving up hope. This means that Christian realism demands ethical action, working toward a better and more just world, without ever daring to think that this end can be fully realized.

One does not have to look hard for evidence that Niebuhr's ideas continue to endure. While interviewing Barack Obama in April of 2007, *New York Times* columnist David Brooks asked the presidential candidate if he had ever read Reinhold Niebuhr. The clearly fatigued senator, who had been giving careful and uninspiring answers up to that point, perked up. "I love him," he said. "He's one of my favorite philosophers." Brooks then asked him what he took away from reading Niebuhr. "I take away," Obama replied,

the compelling idea that there's serious evil in the world, and hardship and pain. And we should be humble and modest in our belief we can eliminate those things. But we shouldn't use that as an excuse for cynicism and inaction. I take away...the sense we have to make these efforts knowing they are hard, and not swinging from naïve idealism to bitter realism.

As even the rather condescending Brooks had to concede, this was a fairly impressive impromptu summary of Niebuhr's views, especially for a sleep-deprived presidential candidate who was leaving the Senate chamber as he spoke.[5] What Obama clearly understood was that, according to Niebuhr, a responsible political ethics must find a middle way between "naïve idealism" and "bitter realism." The inevitability of sin should steer us away from the naïve quest for human perfection, but that does not mean we should simply resign ourselves to the evils of this world. Progress is always possible, Niebuhr averred, but only if we remain self-critical and modest about what we can accomplish.

Perhaps Niebuhr's message has found its most lasting legacy in his well-known "Serenity Prayer," a slightly altered version of which has become a motto for Alcoholics Anonymous (along with many other twelve-step programs). Originally composed in the early 1940s, the prayer captures the essence of Niebuhr's Christian realism: "God, give us grace to accept with serenity the things that cannot be changed, courage to change the things that should be changed, and the wisdom to distinguish the one from the other."[6] With remarkable concision and elegance, this prayer reflects the balance between pessimism and optimism, between despair and hope, between resignation and audacity, for which Niebuhr searched throughout his long career. It also expresses his pragmatic belief that wisdom starts with an honest account of the world as we find it. Empirical reality must always temper and clarify the higher ideals to which we have obligations. As Niebuhr saw it, any ideals worth following must agree with historical facts and experience. He was wary of abstract principles because they often insist that we try to change the things that cannot be changed or to ignore the things that can and should be changed. As history can certainly testify, stubborn adherence to abstract principle can wreak serious havoc.

As this chapter will make clear, this intermingling of pragmatism and principle—or what he sometimes called "Christian pragmatism"[7]—places Niebuhr quite comfortably in the Burkean tradition. At the core of his thought is the Christian doctrine of original sin. Primarily motivated by self-love, people are prepared to dominate or ignore others in accordance with their own interests, especially when they act collectively. Because of our innate capacity for cruelty and indifference, Niebuhr saw the need for traditions, both religious and secular, that promote faith in something larger than ourselves and instill a deep sense of communal and ethical obligation. His respect for tradition notwithstanding, Niebuhr did not espouse a slavish adherence to the status quo, for he understood that changing circumstances create the need for reform. What he feared was radical change and inertia, extremes inspired by principles that have no grounding in concrete reality. Particularly harmful are ideologies that embrace a utopian faith in human perfectibility. His is a pragmatic episte-mology, a theory of truth that insists on the primacy of induction, making specific observations of the human experience out of which broader, albeit provisional, generalizations can be built. Even religious traditions must prove their empirical relevance, and the most resilient of them, time-tested for many generations, become living or embodied truths that inspire ethi-cal action. Although opposed to hierarchies based on inherited privilege, Niebuhr believed that elites and experts have an important role to play in upholding traditions and promoting responsible change.

It is important to note that Niebuhr's affinities with Burkean conser-vatism became more explicit as his political thought matured. In his early years, especially while a pastor in Detroit and then a fledgling professor at Union, he exhibited an impetuous streak that grew out of his frustration with injustice. But even in the 1930s, ostensibly the most radical period of his life, when he was an active member of the Socialist Party who tended to view most social and economic problems through a Marxian lens, his somber outlook on human nature and his pragmatic theory of truth pre-vented him from becoming a political extremist or an ideologue. Over time his views about human nature and truth deepened his appreciation for tradition, incremental change, and some hierarchical structures. While his Burkean tendencies were latent early in his career, Niebuhr evolved into a bona fide pragmatic conservative in the years after World War II.

"Edmund Burke, the great exponent of the wisdom of historical experience"

While this is not exactly an orthodox take on Niebuhr, a number of scholars and commentators have characterized him as a Burkean or pragmatic conservative. In 1955, conservative political journalist and thinker Will Herberg was the first to shine a light on the Burkean con-nection in Niebuhr's work. "Reinhold Niebuhr," he wrote, "is to be counted among the 'neo-conservatives' of our time, who own kinship with Edmund Burke, rather than among the liberals, who draw their inspiration from Tom Paine and the French Enlightenment."[8] Peter Viereck and Eduard Heimann, also contemporaries of Niebuhr, echoed these sentiments quite fervently.[9] Revisionist interpretations of Niebuhr as a Burkean conservative have not abated since his death.[10] Theologian Vigen Guroian has devoted more effort than anyone else to carrying the torch first ignited by Herberg, shedding further light on the similarities between Burke and Niebuhr and on the persistent confusion about the meaning of the terms "liberalism" and "conservatism." "Niebuhr and Burke," he argues, "represent an Anglo-American tradition of political conservatism which is distinguishable from much of that which has passed for both liberalism and conservatism in this country."[11]

One obvious problem with this thesis is that Niebuhr was not particularly fond of being called a conservative. "I am sorry that Will Herberg persists in linking me with conservatism," he wrote to his friend and biographer June Bingham.[12] The reason is that Niebuhr associated conservatism with cynical apologies for a status quo that upheld rank injustice and undeserved privilege. When asked in an interview toward the end of his life what he thought of "the neoconservative political movement," Niebuhr made no effort to hide his contempt. "I disdain it for the reason that American conservatism is nothing but moribund realism," he said. "That's Goldwater's liberalism. This moribund liberalism is an effort to make the bourgeois ideals of individual liberty and freedom from all restraints, on which the bourgeois classes rose to power and created a free society, into an absolute."[13]

Interestingly, Niebuhr found fault with conservatism primarily because of its commitment to liberal values. In particular, he bemoaned its defense of classical liberalism, an outdated mode of thought that regards *laissez faire* as a universal standard of justice, even though it actually serves the interests of one class—the bourgeoisie. "In the political development of America our 'conservatives' are conservative only in the sense that they resist innovation and defend the *status quo*," said Niebuhr. "The *status quo*, until the Rooseveltian era, permitted a degree of non-interference by the state in economic process which must make America a paradise for all true devotees of *laissez faire*."[14] Of course, Niebuhr understood quite well that this "paradise" promised by conservative defenders of *laissez faire* was chimerical in the modern industrial age. An idea that brought freedom to owners of capital in an earlier age would introduce new forms of tyranny for workers of the industrial revolution. There is little wonder why he recoiled from any association with the label.

Although he did not accept the conservative moniker, Niebuhr made a point of identifying the affinities between his own ideas and Burke's.

Niebuhr was always glowing in his references to Burke, once describing him as the "the great exponent of the wisdom of historical experience as opposed to the abstract rationalism of the French Revolution."[15] He understood that Burke represented a traditional conservatism that bore little resemblance to the modern American version. While one can never justify the kind of conservatism that simply defends a status quo from which a privileged elite benefits unjustly, Niebuhr said that "it is necessary to regain that part of the conservative creed" that resonates quite clearly "in British history." He praised this creed for its emphasis on "historical rather than abstract modes of social engineering" and for recognizing "the perennial sources of recalcitrance to moral norms in human life." This brand of conservatism sees "politics as the art of the possible" and always remains "cautious not to fall into worse forms of injustice in the effort to eliminate old ones." He continued:

> Perhaps the creed of such a conservatism is most adequately expounded in Edmund Burke's *Reflections on the Revolution in France*. This type of conservatism is on the one hand the product of experience, particularly of the type of experience which includes all of the problems of man's collective life rather than merely the economic ones.[16]

Niebuhr admired Burke for his prudent approach to politics, relying on the lessons of historical experience and recognizing the limits to what can be achieved in this imperfect world.

Much to Niebuhr's chagrin, modern American conservatism showed no signs of such prudence. Either cynical apologists for the privileged or stubborn adherents of abstract principles, modern conservatives made enormous efforts to restore what was clearly a fading and largely discredited status quo. This is why Niebuhr said that he could see "no social locus in America for a valid 'conservative' philosophy." What he saw was a conservative ideology held captive by business interests. "The more parochial part of the business community," he said, "is bound to develop a conservatism in which a decadent laissez-faire liberalism in domestic politics is compounded with nationalism."[17] This was Barry Goldwater conservatism in a nutshell.

Yet Niebuhr did not break with conservatism and fall breathlessly into the waiting embrace of liberalism. He envisioned a convergence of the liberal and conservative traditions, which required taking the best elements of each. This involved bringing together a liberalism "stripped of its utopian errors" and a conservatism "rescue[d] from the error of aristocratic pretentions." He referred to this amalgamation as "realistic liberalism," but it is virtually indistinguishable from the "valid conservatism" that he associated with Edmund Burke. Niebuhr seemed to conflate the terms purposefully, for he saw little difference between the responsible left and the responsible right in the United Kingdom and other stable democracies in the West. "The debate between a responsible Right and a responsible Left is both inconclusive and insoluble," he argued, "because the degree of emphasis which must be put on planning or spontaneity, on control or freedom, cannot be solved in terms of fixed principles."[18] In other words, both the "valid conservative" (of the responsible right) and the "realistic liberal" (of the responsible left) will address social problems by examining specific conditions rather than simply applying "fixed principles" a priori. Niebuhr added to the conflation (or perhaps confusion) of terms by once calling Burke a "circumspect liberal."[19] This terminological inconsistency is quite telling. It reveals the profound ambivalence of a thinker searching for a creed shorn of ideological pretension and a middle way between extremes. Ultimately, Niebuhr found kinship with "the moderate conservatism of Edmund Burke [which] provided a more adequate analysis both of human nature and of political community."[20]

"Here Manual Labor is Drudgery and Toil is Slavery"

Even though many scholars, including Niebuhr himself, have recognized his affinities with Burke, he is not an obvious candidate for inclusion in the conservative canon, for he was known as either a radical or a liberal throughout his career. Niebuhr came of age under the influence of the Social Gospel and progressivism during his years at Eden Theological Seminary and Yale Divinity School. Niebuhr was never as utopian as Walter Rauschenbusch, the most famous Social Gospel theologian, who believed that carrying the banner of the Kingdom of God meant that "God's will shall be done on earth, even as it is now in heaven."[21] Nor did he agree with John Dewey, who believed that widespread ignorance was the cause of injustice and that organized social intelligence could provide answers to all important political and economic questions. Yet underlying his commitment to innumerable liberal causes during his tenure as a Detroit pastor was an ardent belief that the application of Christian tenets and rational intelligence to social problems could make the world a better place.

As a young pastor serving in the industrial heartland of America, Niebuhr became especially concerned about the plight of the working class and threw his support behind the labor movement. In his writings and speeches, he grew increasingly critical of the exploitative practices of corporate giants such as Ford, which made a practice of turning its workers into commodities. "We went through one of the big automobile factories today," he wrote in his diary in 1925. "The heat was terrific. The men seemed weary. Here manual labor is a drudgery and toil is slavery. The men cannot possibly find any satisfaction in their work. They simply work to make a living. Their sweat and their dull pain are part of the price paid for the fine cars we all run."[22] In a series of articles published the following year in *Christian Century*, Niebuhr condemned Ford for increasing profits at the expense of its workers. It managed to do so by reducing workers' hours—and hence earnings—and then speeding up the assembly line to maintain the same level of production.[23]

Concerned that grim working conditions would destroy the "personality" of workers by turning them into other-directed automatons, Niebuhr called for workplace democracy in the mid-1920s. "It may not be possible to make the machine process itself interesting," he said, "but if some of the efficiency of the industry is sacrificed for the sake of introducing democratic procedure in the factory, it may be possible to give the worker some sense of personal relationship to the entire manufacturing process, and some satisfaction in the total product manufactured."[24] Niebuhr maintained that workers would continue to suffer from alienation unless they were given some measure of control over factory conditions and the manufacturing process. Around the same time, Niebuhr also grew to believe that the problem of alienation demanded a more radical solution: the socialization of major industrial enterprises. For only if they owned the means of production could workers make their voices heard and receive a decent wage.

Niebuhr endorsed socialism not only because it would improve conditions for workers but also because it was the best way of dealing with "the tremendous centralization of wealth and power in the hands of the few."[25] He joined the Socialist Party in 1929, not long after he moved to New York City to begin his new teaching position at Union. His stature in the Socialist Party grew so quickly that it nominated him twice for public office, once for the state senate in 1930 and then for Congress in 1932. Although he suffered overwhelming defeats at the polls both times, Niebuhr's commitment to socialism only grew stronger throughout the 1930s. Responding to the desperate conditions created by the Great Depression, he declared that "capitalism is dying" and "ought to die."[26]

Niebuhr even came to see Marxism as "an essentially correct theory and analysis of the economic realities of modern society," which recognized the inevitability of class conflict, saw private ownership of the means of production as the main cause of cyclical economic crisis and international conflict, and insisted that "the communal ownership of the productive process is a basic condition of social health in a technical age."[27] But Niebuhr never became a doctrinaire Marxist or communist for the simple reason that he could never accept the claim that abolishing private property, and therefore economic inequality, would necessarily eliminate unjust concentrations of political power.[28]

Despite his aversion to ideological rigidity, Niebuhr did not much admire the pragmatism of Franklin D. Roosevelt during his first two terms. He considered FDR "a messiah rather than a political leader committed to a specific program" and the New Deal a disappointing series of half-measures that did not get to the root of the social and economic problems from which so many Americans suffered.[29] Even after he resigned from the Socialist Party in 1940 over a disagreement about international issues, he remained committed to its core principles and continued to find the Democratic Party uncongenial to his political beliefs.

By the mid-1940s, however, Niebuhr was beginning to come around and support the New Deal and Keynesian economics. He grew to appreciate the piecemeal experimentalism of the New Deal and, at the same time, became increasingly disenchanted with socialism for its more naïve assumptions about human nature. In the 1930s, when millions suffered from the mischief of their corporate and plutocratic overlords, Niebuhr believed that only the socialization of the means of production could bring about justice. After the war, with the revived economy and the obvious successes of the New Deal, Niebuhr saw the need to rethink his position. From this new historical vantage point, justice seemed to demand not socialism but a mixed economy. Niebuhr spent the rest of his life defending the modern liberal state, praising modest expansions of the New Deal under Truman and Eisenhower, and even giving his stamp of approval on the more ambitious Great Society. Niebuhr opposed the war in Vietnam not only because it was a quixotic and hubristic enterprise which did not serve American interests but also because it threatened to undermine what he considered to be the worthwhile efforts of the Great Society.[30]

While Niebuhr understandably earned a reputation as a member of the liberal establishment during these post-war years, his positions on the issues and his political philosophy were rooted in the principles of Burkean conservatism. Like Lippmann, he was a liberal for largely conservative reasons. He championed liberal reforms as a way of preserving those values and traditions that represented the best of Western civilization, and he always remained free of any illusions about what the people or the government could accomplish. His is a political philosophy that remains hopeful about the possibility of making social progress but never expects perfection. Central to his cautious optimism was his belief in the sinful nature of human beings.

"THE SIN OF MAN IS THAT HE SEEKS TO MAKE HIMSELF GOD"

Niebuhr is perhaps best known for elucidating the Christian doctrine of original sin, arguing that the frailties of human nature should make us question, and recognize the dangers of, the modern faith in the perfectibility of man and the inevitability of historical progress. That such a faith was commonplace in his time may seem quaint, if not preposterous, to those of us who live in a more ironic age. But many intellectuals remained boundlessly optimistic about what human beings could achieve, even during the years of disillusionment after World War I, and even when a pall of doom descended upon the world once again 20 years later. "There is a constant trend in human affairs toward the perfectibility of mankind," wrote political scientist Charles Merriam in 1939. "This was plainly stated at the time of the French Revolution and has been reasserted ever since that time, and with increasing plausibility."[31]

As Niebuhr made clear, this optimism about the unlimited capacities of human beings has a long and distinguished lineage. It first found expression in ancient Greece, enjoyed a comeback during the Renaissance, acquired further credibility in the French Enlightenment, gained favor among champions of democratic populism and socialism in the nineteenth century, and culminated in the radical ideologies of the twentieth century. According to Niebuhr, history has shown that overweening confidence in humanity and its future has often led to political excess and untold misery. Preventing such catastrophes from happening again requires an honest and realistic assessment of human nature.

His reputation as a clear-eyed realist notwithstanding, Niebuhr began his career with a fair amount of youthful optimism. Under the influence of the Social Gospel and progressivism during his early years as a pastor, he believed that an innate goodness resides within most people and that favorable conditions could change people for the better. His diary from that period includes a number of observations that reflect this sunny outlook. "There doesn't seem to be very much malice in the world," he wrote in 1923. "There is simply not enough intelligence to conduct the intricate affairs of a complex civilization." Two years later he remarked that people in a community are generally ready to devote their energies to helping others if encouraged to do so. "Most people lack imagination much more than they lack good," he concluded. "If someone points out what can be done and what ought to be done there is usually someone to do it." He was even so bold as to suggest that there is "no reason why we can not cure people of greed by making them conscious of both the nature and the consequences of their expansive tendencies."[32] If only people had the opportunity to expand their imagination and intelligence, Niebuhr argued, they could become increasingly selfless.

Yet, even during his callow youth, Niebuhr clearly recognized that human potential operates under definable limits. In 1923, he conceded that "[n]ot merely ignorance but callousness to human welfare is an ingredient in the compound of social and personal evil." Niebuhr did not just see people as coldly indifferent toward the suffering of others; he also believed that the lust for power motivated their behavior. "Man is imperialistic and even parasitic in his nature," he wrote in 1925. "He lives his life at the expense of others." Finding a middle ground between the optimists and the pessimists, Niebuhr concluded that the woes of civilization were "partly an expression of a universal tendency and partly a vice peculiar to a civilization with our kind of productive process." As a result, he remained somewhat hopeful about the "reformation of human nature" but also saw the need for "a constant reorganization of social processes and systems" that served to "mitigate the native imperialistic impulses of man."[33] Making social progress must rely on efforts that help people develop their capacities and reach their potential, but it also requires devising institutional mechanisms that channel and redirect their dark yet unalterable passions toward more constructive ends.

By the early 1930s, the doctrine of original sin took a more prominent place in Niebuhr's discussions of human nature. Although he still identified a "gregarious impulse" and "a specific impulse of pity" in human beings who often feel compelled to come to the "aid of stricken members of [their] community," Niebuhr argued that "the force of egoistic impulse is much more powerful" than most people are willing to accept.[34] This natural inclination toward egoism, "making the self the center of the world," is what Niebuhr meant by original sin.[35] "This doctrine," said Niebuhr, "asserts the obvious fact that all men are persistently inclined to regard themselves more highly and are more assiduously concerned with their own interests than any 'objective' view of their importance would warrant."[36] That we love ourselves more than anyone else is an inescapable fact of our existence.

"The very basis of self-love is the natural will to survive," Niebuhr said. "In man the animal impulse to maintain life becomes an immediate temptation to assert the self against the neighbor."[37] Self-preservation is an instinct common to all animals, but human beings have a unique tendency to transmute the will-to-live into the will-to-power. Even if it comes at the expense of others, they will do almost anything not only to save themselves but also to secure (and augment) the sources of their livelihood. "Man is insecure and involved in natural contingency; he seeks to overcome his insecurity by a will-to-power which overreaches the limits of human creatureliness," Niebuhr said.[38]

This happens because, unlike any other animal, human beings have the gift—or curse—of self-consciousness. "Self-consciousness means the recognition of the finiteness within infinity," said Niebuhr. "The mind recognizes the ego as an insignificant point amidst the immensities of the world. In all vital self-consciousness, there is a note of protest against this finiteness."[39] Niebuhr put it more bluntly when he said, "Man is the only mortal animal who knows that he is mortal...the only creature imbedded in the flux of finitude who knows that this is his fate."[40] Acutely aware of his own mortality and insignificance in the universe, he will do everything he can to stave off the inevitable and to aggrandize himself in the process. That other people often suffer the consequences of these efforts hardly matters to someone who fears his own death far more than he cares about the misfortunes of others. "The root of imperialism is therefore in all self-consciousness."[41]

In his theological writings Niebuhr developed further his ideas about how the human condition becomes fertile soil in which sin and evil can grow. Because they can anxiously envisage a world in which they would rather live, human beings are paradoxically both finite and infinite, both determined and free. Not merely the pawns of necessity, people have some measure of freedom to transcend the forces of biology and history. While transcendence can be a source of wondrously creative enterprises from which humanity can reap immense benefits, it can just as easily be expressed as a willful act of rebellion. "According to the myth of the Fall, evil came into the world through human responsibility," said Niebuhr. "The origin of evil is attributed to an act of rebellion on the part of man."[42]

In Christian theology evil stems specifically from rebellion against God, imagining that there are no limits to what we can do and that we can replace the divine as the center of the universe. "The sin of man," he said, "is that he seeks to make himself God."[43] Even if they have the best of intentions, people with inordinate ambitions and self-esteem, presuming that they can usurp God as the source of beauty and truth, will bring evil into the world. Niebuhr crystallized the problem quite succinctly when he said, "Man is mortal. That is his fate. Man pretends not to be mortal. That is his sin."[44] The idea that sin stems from rebellion against God situates Niebuhr in the Augustinian tradition. Like Augustine, he rejected the Manichean idea that the spirit is good and the body is bad, believing instead that sin "lies at the juncture of nature and spirit."[45] We sin because our spirit or consciousness endows us with the will to rebel against the limits that God and nature impose on us.

Niebuhr's theological musings on human nature also resonate with secular audiences because the Christian story that evil comes from the sin of rebelling against God can be seen as a metaphor for the dangers of pride. The person who rebels against God in the biblical narrative is the same person who, brimming with confidence and self-satisfaction, refuses to acknowledge the limits of his nature or "creatureliness" and believes that his bold ambitions and exertions of power are always for the good. Anyone this proud is bound to commit the gravest forms of injustice. "The ego which falsely makes itself the centre of existence in its pride and will-to-power," Niebuhr said, "inevitably subordinates other life to its will and thus does injustice to other life."[46] Entertaining delusions of grandeur and righteousness, the proud do not see the harm that they cause. Instead, they believe that the world, full of sorrows and injustices awaiting relief, beckons them to act. The fate of the world rests on their weary shoulders. "This ability to stand outside and beyond the world," Niebuhr said, "tempts man to megalomania and persuades him to regard himself as the god around and about whom the universe centres."[47]

Niebuhr's view of human nature, that the inclination toward self-love and pride resides within all of us, has clear political implications. It suggests that we should never overestimate our own virtues—or those of our fellow human beings—and construct a polity on the basis of that assumption, and it also urges us to be wary of ambitious enterprises spearheaded by demagogues who promise heaven on earth. In short, his sober outlook is the cornerstone of his realism—his Augustinian "disposition to take all factors in a social and political situation, which offer resistance to established norms, into account, particularly the factors of self-interest and power."[48]

Niebuhr added another dimension to his realism, however, in his discussion of human nature as manifested by groups. With his first major work, *Moral Man and Immoral Society*, Niebuhr produced a classic statement on political realism in which he lacerated both secular and religious liberals for failing to account for the moral inferiority of collective egos—or groups. He argued that, while individuals "may be moral in the sense that they are able to consider interests other than their own," it is far "more difficult, if not impossible, for human societies and social groups" to do likewise. "In every human group there is less reason to guide and to check impulse, less capacity for self-transcendence, less ability to comprehend the needs of others, and therefore more unrestrained egoism than the individuals, who compose the group, reveal in their personal relationships." Groups are less capable of reason, empathy, and moral action largely because they exist in the first place to serve shared interests and desires. Because it "achieves its cohesion" by being "united in a common impulse," a group compounds and magnifies the egoism of the individuals who constitute it.[49] With even more vehemence and consistency than the individual, groups will always assert themselves, never hesitating to exercise dominance over others or to ignore pleas for help when it suits them. Niebuhr observed that this is true of all collective egos in the world of politics, including nations, economic and social classes, races and ethnicities, religions, and other groups that coalesce around a shared interest or belief.

Since the world of politics involves competition among morally obtuse groups, it is unrealistic to expect that appeals to either reason or love will enlighten the masses and bring about social harmony. Even if every citizen were sufficiently educated to see the light of reason, the problem of group egoism would persist. "Since reason is always, to some degree, the servant of interest in a social situation," said Niebuhr, "social injustice cannot be resolved by moral and rational suasion alone." People will always find a way of using reason to justify a self-serving political agenda. "The will-to-power uses reason, as kings use courtiers and chaplains to add grace to their enterprise," Niebuhr said. "Even the most rational men are never quite rational when their own interests are at stake." Thus we must accept the hard truth that politics cannot deliver social harmony. At best it can achieve a balance or equilibrium of power in a world beset by a continual struggle between competing groups. "Conflict is inevitable, and in this conflict power must be challenged by power," said Niebuhr.[50]

This is why, even at the most radical stage of his career, Niebuhr found himself at odds with Marxists and liberals of all stripes. He faulted Marxists in particular for their cock-eyed optimism, believing that inter-group conflict could be averted through the revolutionary transformation of human nature. Niebuhr considered Marxism to be a useful analytical tool that improves our understanding of the relationship between economic and political power, and he agreed with its belief in the necessity of taming economic power, creating a "vigilant and potent state which substitutes political power for economic power." But he did not share its utopian teleology. Doctrinaire Marxists believed that abolishing the private ownership of the means of production would crush the class system and usher in an age of unprecedented social harmony. Niebuhr thought that Marxists blundered by assuming that human nature was so easily malleable. "The expectation of changing human nature by the destruction of economic privilege to such a degree that no one will desire to make selfish use of power, must probably be placed in the category of romantic illusions," he wrote. "If power remains in society, mankind will never escape the necessity of endowing those who possess it with the largest measure of ethical self-control."[51] Niebuhr understood that the will-to-power would not just disappear with the introduction of economic equality, for people could still find political and bureaucratic means of bringing about injustice, exercising undue mastery and control over their comrades.

Classical liberals are almost equally naïve about human nature according to Niebuhr. The only difference is that classical liberals believe that people already have moderate desires and will regulate themselves if given the chance to operate within unfettered markets. In their view, we do not need a revolution to mend our ways. As Niebuhr puts it, "Marxism expects men to be as tame and social on the other side of the revolution as Adam Smith and Jeremy Bentham thought them to be tame and prudential on this side of the revolution." Of course, the problem is that defenders of *laissez faire* such as Smith and Bentham laid the groundwork for injustice and social unrest by giving owners of capital the means of turning private property into "an instrument of aggression and usurpation."[52]

While Niebuhr gravitated toward modern welfare state liberalism by the mid-1940s, he took issue with the assurances, given by many in this camp, that the diligent application of intelligence to social and economic problems would propel humanity forward toward a better future.

This undying faith in progress, which Niebuhr associated with liberals like John Dewey, rests on the idea that people misbehave and commit injustices because they do not know better. Niebuhr described this "religion of modern culture" as follows: "Progress is guaranteed by increasing intelligence because human sin is attributed to ignorance which will be removed by a proper pedagogy." But as mounting historical evidence continues to make abundantly clear, there is little reason for such unbridled optimism. "History does not move forward without catastrophe, happiness is not guaranteed by the multiplication of physical comforts, social harmony is not easily created by more intelligence, and human nature is not as good or as harmless as had been supposed."[53] No matter how much intelligence and goodwill people devote to the cause of social justice, history does not offer any guarantees, for human nature remains forever flawed.

His doctrine of original sin notwithstanding, an important caveat should be noted. Niebuhr did not believe that all hope was lost, and he warned against the dangers of excessive pessimism. While we all desire more than we need and love ourselves more than others, it would be just as wrong to assume along with the pessimist that people are incapable of transcending self-interest and working toward the common good. Niebuhr saw that an excessive fear of the wickedness and unruliness of the people could justify tyranny. He cited the examples of Thomas Hobbes and Martin Luther, two political thinkers who saw only the worst in humanity and therefore concluded that "the business of government is to maintain order by repression." Consumed with the threat of anarchy, they forgot that rulers are just as prone to disorderly and immoderate behavior as their subjects. Concentrating power in the hands of rulers does not "provide checks against the inordinate impulses to power" to which they are all tempted.[54]

This is why governments have the function of not only checking antisocial behavior but also providing the means by which citizens, flawed but not irredeemable, can express their "sense of obligation to the community." Citizens can fulfill this obligation most readily by engaging in democratic processes that hold rulers accountable for their actions—that vest citizens "with political and constitutional power to resist the inordinate ambitions of rulers." Governments must have the means by which they can control the governed, and in turn the governed must have opportunities for civic participation so that they can control the government. Democracy creates possibilities for people to work toward a higher good and at the same time provides mechanisms that safeguard their inevitable expressions of self-love. Or as Niebuhr put it, "Man's capacity for justice makes democracy possible; but man's inclination for injustice makes democracy necessary."[55]

In the end, Niebuhr offered a powerful defense of democracy based on a realistic view of human nature. Like Abraham Lincoln, he saw democracy as the "last best hope of earth." But he understood that it was not a panacea or a utopian ideal. Nothing can prevent the insinuation of injustice into daily life. Some people will enjoy material comforts and privileges at the expense of their compatriots, and power will rest disproportionately in the hands of an elite class which does not always have the wisdom and discipline to wield it responsibly. For people will always be susceptible to sin, inclined toward excessive self-love and pride. We must find hope not in eliminating those tendencies but in curbing them.

"TRADITIONS AND CUSTOMS HALLOWED BY AGE THROUGH WHICH OUR PASSIONS ARE ORDERED"

The regrettable frailties of human beings did not completely dash Niebuhr's hopes about the future. He was convinced that under the chastening influence of tradition people will have a chance of acting contrary to their nature, accepting communal responsibilities and treating each other with respect and fairness. He often expressed his gratitude for tradition in his sermons, highlighting its benefits for the social order. "We are grateful," he said in a prayer, for "traditions and customs hallowed by age through which our passions are ordered and channeled."[56] He believed that tradition is the glue that creates social bonds, bringing people together and giving them a shared sense of purpose and identity. Without it, he said, people see themselves as free agents who focus on gratifying their desires and never give a thought to serving the commonweal.

Although his appreciation for tradition deepened over time, Niebuhr recognized its salutary effects even during his early years. While still serving as a pastor in Detroit, Niebuhr observed the trials of urban life on a daily basis and became alarmed by the rise in crime. He attributed this problem to the decay of traditions and customs that had placed restraints on previous generations. All of our cities have "a crime problem," he said, because the "great masses of men in an urban community are undisciplined and chaotic, emancipated from the traditions which guided their fathers and incapable of forming new and equally potent cultural and moral restraints." Niebuhr saw the industrial city as a teeming "mass of individuals" who do not enjoy any sense of community or share any moral standards from which they can receive guidance. Only the "productive process" of industrial society holds these "spiritually isolated" people together. In such a mass society, Niebuhr lamented, "it is difficult to create and preserve the moral and cultural traditions which each individual needs to save his life from anarchy." Fortunately, however, many people do not experience such moral chaos, and their ability to "escape it" stems from their "loyalty to religious, moral and cultural traditions which have come out of other ages."[57]

Niebuhr often pointed to the example of Great Britain, whose traditions held in check the rapacity of the wealthy classes and the resentment of the lower classes. Most relevant were "older conceptions of property, derived from an agrarian and feudal world," which mitigated tensions between the bourgeoisie and the proletariat. These feudal inheritances impressed upon the bourgeoisie that the social order requires limits on individual liberty and property rights and persuaded the workers to see the virtue in some hierarchical institutions and social inequality. Despite their differences, these classes found common ground in a set of inherited principles and institutions for which they showed a willingness to sacrifice some of their interests. More likely to resist abstract appeals to liberty and equality, the British did not experience the social upheaval and unrest that beset France and other countries in Europe.[58] "It may be significant," said Niebuhr, "that the nation which produced Edmund Burke's *Reflections on the Revolution in France* and expressed its preference for the 'rights of Englishmen' rather than the 'rights of men' should have a more stable government and no less liberty and justice than the home of the French Revolution."[59]

Like Burke, Niebuhr preferred traditional rights (e.g., "the rights of Englishmen") to abstract rights (e.g., "the rights of men") for a simple reason: Rooted in the soil of shared experience, traditional rights grow organically within a particular community and, over time, win the loyalty of the people. While tradition cultivates "mutually and historically acknowledged rights and responsibilities," said Niebuhr, the "'inalienable' rights" derived from abstract reasoning "are worthless if no community acknowledges them."[60] For people live not in "abstract universal societies" but in "historic communities" in which "peace, order, and justice" are "the product of ages of development." It is this organic aspect of community, he argued, that "justifies Edmund Burke in regarding historic rights and duties as more important than abstract rational rights and duties."[61] Traditional rights and duties emerge out of common experience and, slowly and unconsciously, become the values around which a political community coalesces.

Formulated in an intellectual vacuum, abstract rights do not resonate with most people and thus cannot possibly bring them together.

Because they enjoy such broad appeal, traditional rights and duties are far more likely to temper the natural impulses of people, changing for the better how they behave and treat others. Burke and other conservatives in British history understood this quite well. The wisdom of British conservatism, which "runs from Ireton through Edmund Burke to Winston Churchill," said Niebuhr, lies in its understanding that "the inordinacy of the ambitions of fellow men, which imperils our rights, are checked with more effect by historical habits than by appeals to reason."[62] The traditional values of honor, chivalry, and noblesse oblige, for example, restrained the overweening ambitions of the British aristocracy and, to a lesser extent, curbed the excesses of the bourgeoisie. More than just rational appeals to leading a good and moral life, feudal traditions had been effective because they were deeply engrained habits, acknowledged and revered for generations, and had come to define members of the elite. Abstract arguments about justice can never be as effective as the collective habits with which people are instilled at a young age and then comply for the rest of their lives.

Niebuhr conceded, however, that because these traditions grew out of the European experience, any attempts to transplant them to America, in which feudalism never set root, would inevitably fail. From the other side of the Atlantic, we could admire but never hope to emulate those British traditions that did not play a role in our history. We had to identify traditions relevant to our shared experience and history if we wanted to chasten the worst characteristics of human nature. In the American context, Niebuhr found hope ultimately in the Christian tradition. It is important to note that Niebuhr did not fit the Protestant stereotype of viewing faith in individualistic terms, and he rejected the fundamentalist pretension that Christianity offered certainty or absolute truth. Sounding almost Catholic at times, he actually believed that "faith is sustained by a vast company of the living and the dead," and he referred to Christianity as "the faith of our fathers by which we claim kinship with the past and gain strength for the present."[63] In other words, he regarded faith not as a solitary enterprise through which one found God but rather as a tradition that spanned generations of collective experience and thereby made faith a greater possibility. Only if we embrace this tradition, becoming a part of a community and participating in its rituals and practices, could we hope to find some kind of meaning by which we could order our lives.

Though his preferences clearly lay with Christianity, Niebuhr extolled any religious faith that conformed to what he called the "prophetic tradition." Prophetic (or profound) religions posit a God who is the creator, judge, and redeemer of humanity. God rebukes his beloved sinners for straying from the righteous path but ultimately blesses them with his radiant gaze of forgiveness. "The myth of the Creator God offers the possibilities for a prophetic religion in which the transcendent God becomes both the judge and the redeemer of the world," said Niebuhr. "In genuinely prophetic religion the God who transcends the created world also convicts a sinful world of its iniquities and promises an ultimate redemption from them."[64]

Prophetic religions demand impossibly high moral standards. The inevitable failure to meet these standards evokes divine condemnation, in the face of which the followers of prophetic religion experience a profound sense of humility and contrition. "Faith in a moral perfection which transcends human perfection is the basis of the note of contrition in all great religion," Niebuhr said. "Man does not feel himself an outraged innocent in the evil world. Indeed, he accepts some of the evil which befalls him in the world as a just punishment for his sin."[65] Having disappointed God, people become acutely aware of their own limitations and feel remorse for their sinful ways. When God forgives them, they can only feel immense gratitude for the gift of life. This is why the "dominant attitudes of prophetic faith are gratitude and contrition; gratitude for Creation and contrition before Judgment; or, in other words, confidence that life is good in spite of its evil and that it is evil in spite of its good."[66]

The impossible standard in the Christian tradition is what Niebuhr called the law of love (or agape). As exemplified in the story of Christ, the law of love requires self-sacrifice for the sake of others. But, except in the rarest of circumstances, the law of love is an historical impossibility. "Men living in nature and in the body," said Niebuhr, "will never be capable of the sublimation of egoism and the attainment of the sacrificial passion, the complete disinterestedness which the ethic of Jesus demands."[67] For this reason, the law of love is an ideal that stands as a constant reproach, a reminder of the fallen state in which all Christians woefully find themselves. The Cross represents for Christians not only "the love of God" to which they should aspire but also "the exceeding sinfulness of human sin" from which they can never escape in their corporeal existence.[68]

Thus, the Christian regards the law of love as the ultimate ideal after which he should pattern his life, but he must humbly and contritely accept that as a sinner he will fall short. The realization that there are limits to what people can achieve, that the Kingdom of God is an historical impossibility, will prevent them from engaging in ambitious enterprises born of sinful pride. "The real evil in the human situation, according to the prophetic interpretation," said Niebuhr,

> lies in man's unwillingness to recognize and acknowledge the weakness, finiteness and dependence of his position, in his inclination to grasp after a power and security which transcend the possibilities of human existence, and in his effort to pretend a virtue and knowledge which are beyond the limits of mere creatures. The whole burden of the prophetic message is that there is only one God…and that the sin of man consists in the vanity and pride by which he imagines himself, his nations, his cultures, his civilizations to be divine. Sin is thus the unwillingness of man to acknowledge his creatureliness and dependence upon God and his effort to make his own life independent and secure.[69]

In reminding people of their weakness and finiteness and of their dependence on the one God who created and judges them, the prophetic tradition excoriates the "vanity and pride" from which the belief in their own perfectibility emanates. When religious faith serves as "a constant fount of humility" for its followers, it will "moderate their natural pride."[70]

Even though people must humbly accept that the law of love is unattainable, they should not forget that it represents a moral ideal from which they should receive inspiration. "For the Christian only the law of love is normative," Niebuhr said. "He would do well to remember that he is a sinner who has never perfectly kept the law of God. But neither must he forget that he is a child of God who stands under that law."[71] Because he stands under the law of love, the Christian should always operate under its moral guidance. "The law of love is thus not something extra to be added to whatever morality we establish in our social relations," Niebuhr said. "It is their guiding principle."[72] No one should give up on trying to make the world a better place just because they are acutely aware of their own sinfulness. It is true that the prophetic tradition cannot abide political overreach born of pride, but it is just as intolerant of complacency and inaction, for they also grow out of self-love and a willful disregard for the injustices and tragedies that cause undue suffering. "A profound religion will not give itself to the illusion that perfect justice can be achieved in a sinful world," Niebuhr said. "But neither can it afford to dismiss the problem of justice."[73]

Unfortunately, Niebuhr said, "Christians are tempted by their recognition of the sinfulness of human existence to disavow their own responsibility for a tolerable justice in the world's affairs." Once they see that the law of love is an unrealizable ideal, these Christians wash their hands of any social and political obligation. Along with those Christians who retreat from worldly responsibility, Niebuhr recognized that justice is not the same thing as the law of love. After all, justice "presupposes the conflict of life with life and seeks to mitigate it" by creating a balance of power among competing self-interested groups. That certainly does not sound anything like love. But Niebuhr insisted that when justice promotes equality, it can also function as "an approximation" of the law of love.[74] "The principles of equal justice are thus approximations of the law of love in the kind of imperfect world which we know and not principles which belong to a world of transcendent perfection," Niebuhr said. "Since the law of love demands that all life be affirmed, the principle that all conflicting claims of life be equally affirmed is a logical approximation of the law of love in a world in which conflict is inevitable."[75]

Equal justice pales in comparison to the law of love because it does not involve heedless and Christ-like sacrifice, but it does evoke the idea of mutual (or brotherly) love, doing what we can to help others in need with the understanding that we are entitled to reciprocity should circumstances require it. Equal justice demands that people make reasonable sacrifices for their fellow human beings, giving up some of what they want so that the less fortunate can get their fair share. Because "sacrificing one's life for another cannot be formulated as an obligation," Niebuhr said, the law of love must give way to conceptions of distributive justice and mutual love, in which "the self, individual and collective, seeks both to preserve its life and to relate it harmoniously to other lives." But such mutually beneficial arrangements are not sufficient. For they must also draw "inspiration from a deeper dimension of history." Without an element of heedless or sacrificial love, they can easily "degenerate from mutuality to a prudent regard for the interests of the self; and from the impulse towards community to an acceptance of the survival impulse as ethically normative."[76] In other words, the law of love cannot triumph in our imperfect world, but it can leaven lesser forms of love and justice, preventing their descent into mere calculations of self-interest.

In prophetic religion Niebuhr found a home that was hospitable to his calls for reform. Insisting that people must not shirk their ethical obligation to promote justice but must also remain humble about what they can actually accomplish, prophetic religion strikes a balance between impetuous change and complacent inertia. This is especially true of the

Christian tradition, in which the law of love stands as a constant reminder to its followers of their limitations and, at the same time, as a reproach for their inability to meet its impossibly high standard. Christianity not only demands change in accordance with transcendent notions of social justice but also warns against the pretensions of saintliness. We are sinners trying to make modest improvements in an imperfect world, never forgetting that the "Christ in us is not a possession but a hope, that perfection is not a reality but an intention," but that, even so, this reality "does not destroy moral ardour or responsibility."[77] This combination of moral responsibility and humility is the perfect recipe for reform efforts which proceed with circumspection and caution.

Niebuhr recognized the necessity of trying to strike a balance between tradition and iconoclasm, between blindly obeying our ancestral inheritance and mindlessly destroying everything that originated in the past. This required differentiating traditions that embodied enduring virtues and wisdom from those that had outgrown their relevance in contemporary life. Niebuhr observed that the young people with whom he had the opportunity to work as a pastor gravitated to either extreme: "There is always the temptation to be too rebellious or too traditional, to be scornful of the old standard even when it preserves obvious virtues, or to flee to it for fear of being lost in the confusion of new standards." Not many of them saw the need for "the readjustment of traditions to new situations," he complained. "With traditions crumbling and accepted standards inundated by a sea of moral relativity," he said, young people must find ways to "construct new standards adequate for their happiness," but they must never lose sight of those traditions that still bear relevance to contemporary life and, perhaps after some necessary readjustments, can still provide meaning and guidance in an ever-changing world.[78]

Niebuhr insisted that we can only move forward as a society and effect responsible change if we have a healthy respect for history and tradition. He used the example of the artist who can only break the rules of art after he has mastered them first. For artists and social reformers alike, knowledge of the past provides a framework for future endeavor and innovation. As they deepen their understanding of what has worked for their ancestors, they become more aware of what can and should be changed and are less apt to repeat past mistakes. Niebuhr was undoubtedly paraphrasing the famous adage by George Santayana when he said, "Ignorance of the past does not guarantee freedom from its imperfections. More probably, it assures the repetition of past errors." Although young people should "not accept the ideas of the past too slavishly," Niebuhr said, they should not be too dismissive either. In both art and life, "appreciation must come before criticism."[79]

Even as he moved into the more radical phase of his career, Niebuhr did not jettison his appreciation for past practices. He may have called for a major overhaul of the capitalist system, but he still recognized the risks that came with bold attempts to create a more just world. In *Moral Man and Immoral Society*, Niebuhr struck a remarkably Burkean tone with his formulation of the problem:

> The question which confronts society is, how it can eliminate social injustice by methods which offer some fair opportunity of abolishing what is evil in our present society, without destroying what is worth preserving in it, and without running the risk of substituting new abuses and injustices in the place of those abolished.

Niebuhr recognized the perils of wholesale change, throwing out the baby with the bathwater, indiscriminately destroying good and bad traditions. He feared that the working class was particularly prone to such recklessness. Although his sympathies lay with the workers at that time of economic hardship, Niebuhr accused them of having little compunction about decimating those traditions worth preserving. In their desperate state, he said, they see "nothing good in modern society which deserves preservation."[80]

Yet, Niebuhr found reason to be sanguine about the prospects for gradual reform in the industrial age. The fact that workers had been able to organize labor unions, win concessions from their employers, and enjoy modest improvements in their living conditions, all without undermining the capitalist system, "seems to cast grave doubts upon the Marxian theory of revolution through the increasing misery of the workers." Indeed, Marx's mistaken prophecies "seemed to justify the revision of socialism into an evolutionary doctrine," and recent events may have even supported the claim that "socialism could be achieved progressively by parliamentary action." Niebuhr was not entirely convinced that parliamentary action could produce meaningful reform, because he had doubts about whether socialists could garner support from any constituencies other than industrial workers. According to his analysis, if they did not win over a sizable number of middle-class urbanites and rural farmers, in addition to the workers, the Socialists would not be able to attain the majorities necessary to effect evolutionary change. Still, Niebuhr insisted that a non-violent victory for the Socialists, through parliamentary elections, was always preferable. Even a partial victory for the socialist cause, in which it was "robbed of the hope of a final and complete triumph," was better than the alternative. After all, "no community can live in a permanent state of civil war, which would result from a revolutionary socialism unable to press through to its goal."[81]

Niebuhr admired the British for taking this lesson to heart. Eschewing the impetuous and revolutionary fervor of the French, they saw the wisdom in incremental change. "Both a nation and an empire," he said, "were remolded gradually and therefore more wisely than by revolutionary fanaticism."[82] Niebuhr believed that the United States could learn from British history and their penchant for gradual and evolutionary change. "While the intensity and extent of technical interdependence have invalidated bourgeois conceptions of property and have placed the logic of history behind proposals for socialization," Niebuhr said, "a wise community will walk warily and test the effect of each new adventure before further advances."[83]

"THE BANEFUL EFFECT OF GENERAL AND ABSTRACT PROGRAMS UPON THE SOCIAL LIFE OF MAN"

This wariness of impetuous change, lest the new venture prove far worse than the old and familiar, lies at the heart of Niebuhr's epistemology. An unapologetic pragmatist and admirer of William James throughout his career, Niebuhr claimed that our truth claims are only as good as the consequences which flow from them, and that we must continually test our truths against the empirical data available to us and against the other truths by which we lead our lives. Even religious faith must run the gauntlet of this process of verification. This pragmatic bent to his theory of knowledge meant not only that we must recognize the provisionality of our truths but also that we can only know something from our own limited perspective. "We see through a glass darkly when we seek to understand the world about us," said Niebuhr.[84] We can never know truth in and of itself; at best we can have "truth from a perspective."[85] What may be true in a particular time and place may not hold in a different historical and cultural context. This relativistic standpoint "makes it impossible to accept *our* truth as *the* truth."[86] Because we can never be certain about our truth claims, Niebuhr called for epistemological humility.[87]

What inspired Niebuhr's pragmatic epistemology was his lifelong distrust of abstract (or deductive) reasoning, particularly when applied to moral, social, and political questions. In his view, it is neither wise nor safe to act on ideas that, while they may sound ideal in theory, bear no relevance to concrete experience. "If it is dangerous to entertain great moral ideals without attempting to realize them in life," he remarked, "it is even more perilous to proclaim them in abstract terms without bringing them into juxtaposition with the specific social and moral issues of the day."[88] He bemoaned the "baneful effect of general and abstract programs upon the social life of man," arguing that their "generalizations fail to take the endless contingencies of history into account" and that their "panaceas are stubbornly held and not easily amended by empirical data."[89] Proponents of policies based on abstract reasoning are inclined to become ideologues who cling to their belief system even when the historical record and empirical reality present irrefutable evidence to the contrary. In the years immediately after World War II, that bygone era of liberal consensus, Niebuhr praised the United States for eschewing ideological extremes and adopting a "pragmatic approach to political and economic questions which would do credit to Edmund Burke, the great exponent of the wisdom of historical experience as opposed to the abstract rationalism of the French revolution."[90]

As the miseries wrought by the French Revolution clearly demonstrate, said Niebuhr, political and economic questions "are not answered primarily by nice rational calculations." If anything, reason sheds light on the fact that "life in its essence is not what it is in its actual existence." In most cases, the exigencies and contingencies of the human experience do not support the conclusions reached by abstract reasoning. Niebuhr pointed to the example of Kantian ethics, in which there is "no effective contact between the real and the ideal world." Based on the law of rational consistency, the categorical imperative demands that we act in accordance with maxims that we are prepared to universalize. Or, as Niebuhr put it, "Act so as to make thy action the basis of universal law." While this makes rational sense, Niebuhr said, a vital question lingers: "what is to persuade men to obey the law?"[91] The categorical imperative demands, for example, that one never lies. But why should anyone take this imperative seriously when a lie will produce far more preferable results? If we assume there is no risk to his own safety, who in his right mind would not lie to the Gestapo agent asking the whereabouts of Anne Frank and her family? Philosophical ideals do not always square with what common sense clearly tells us is right.

This is the reason why Niebuhr rejected Kantian ethics. It made the mistake of emphasizing intentions over results. "Since it is very difficult to judge human motives, it is natural that, from an external perspective, the social consequences of an action or policy should be regarded as more adequate tests of its morality than the hidden motives," he said. "Does it have the general welfare as its objective? When viewing a historic situation all moralists become pragmatists and utilitarians."[92] We can never know for sure what lies in the hearts of others, whether their motives are noble or nefarious (or both). People are complex. Even the most admirable leaders, for example, are motivated by a concern for both the general welfare and a selfish desire for approval. As the famous parable in the Book of Matthew makes clear, it is not so easy to separate the wheat from the tares.[93] No matter how much lip service someone may pay to the general welfare, declaring that this is what inspires his tireless work each day and keeps him awake at night, his true motives will always remain a mystery. But we can ascertain, without much trouble, whether his actions have actually promoted the general welfare. As a practical matter, then, we are all consequentialists who judge the moral worth of a particular action by looking at the results. Quite simply we deem something good when it produces desirable outcomes.

In *Moral Man and Immoral Society*, Niebuhr famously showed his utilitarian colors in his discussion of political violence. Although Niebuhr believed that "power had to be challenged by power" in a just political order, he recognized a flaw in this realist position. Because injustice demands the exercise of power which then breeds further injustice, there seems to be no end to the cycle of violence. "If social cohesion is impossible without coercion, and coercion is impossible without the creation of social injustice, and the destruction of injustice is impossible without the use of further coercion, are we not in an endless cycle of social conflict?" Or, as Niebuhr also put it, "if power is needed to destroy power, how is this new power to be made ethical?" We must accept that society "will probably never escape social conflict" and focus our energies on finding ways of "reducing it to a minimum."[94] In accordance with the utilitarian moral calculus, Niebuhr sought to minimize the amount of pain that will beset a conflict-ridden world.

Ultimately, Niebuhr found hope in nonviolent resistance or coercion, which "is usually the better method of expressing goodwill" and of militating "against the resentments which violent conflict always creates in both parties." Those who practice nonviolent resistance prove their "freedom of resentment and ill-will" because they suffer more than the opposition does, and the "effects of these very vivid proofs of moral good-will are tremendous." Niebuhr continued:

> In every social conflict each party is so obsessed with the wrongs which the other party commits against it, that it is unable to see its own wrongdoing. A non-violent temper reduces these animosities to a minimum and therefore preserves a certain objectivity in analyzing the issues of the dispute.

Clear-headed and objective, the practitioners of nonviolent resistance understand that people "are never as immoral as the social situations in which they are involved" and thus resent not their oppressors but the unjust system from which they benefit. Meanwhile, nonviolent coercion compels the oppressor to reconsider his "moral conceit" that the established order maintains peace. Whereas violent "conflict arouses dormant passions which completely obscure the real issues of a conflict," nonviolent resistance "reduces these dangers to a minimum" and allows for ongoing discussion and negotiation as the resistance remains underway. A peaceful resolution of the conflict—and an end to the cycle of violence—becomes possible.[95] Thus, Niebuhr's defense of nonviolence was results-oriented and never relied on deontological ethics.

His enthusiasm for nonviolence notwithstanding, Niebuhr maintained that violent means of achieving just ends may be ethically permissible in some instances. "If a season of violence can establish a just social system and can create the possibilities of its preservation, there is no purely ethical ground upon which violence and revolution can be ruled out."[96] After all, the moral distinction between violent and nonviolent forms of coercion is not so clear. Both are designed to change the behavior of other people by bringing harm to their persons and property. Niebuhr gave as an example the boycott of British cotton in India, an act of nonviolent resistance that sought to bring about independence by using economic leverage. Thousands of workers and children in Manchester experienced economic pain as a result of the boycott. And that was the intention: to inflict enough hardship on the British people that their government would relent and give India independence. The ends may have been just, but the means were not morally pure. For Niebuhr, there is no moral purity in the world of action. Moral perfection can only precede the act; it exists in the realm of thought. "The action is therefore always sinful," as Niebuhr put it later in his career.[97] Because ethics and sin, good and evil, are not mutually exclusive categories in the political world—because they co-exist and intermingle in countless ways—one can never rule out the use of violence a priori. Ethics may demand violence in some instances.

When discussing political violence, Niebuhr even went so far as to defend the notorious maxim often attributed to Machiavelli—the ends justify the means. "This wholly pragmatic and relativistic analysis of the problem of violence obviously fails to arrive at an absolute disavowal of violence under all circumstances," he said.

> It is therefore tainted with the implied principle that the end justifies the means. This is supposedly a terrible Jesuitical maxim which all good people must abhor. Yet all good people are involved in it. Short of an ascetic withdrawal from the world, every moral action takes place in a whole field of moral values and possibilities in which no absolute distinction between means and ends is possible. There are only immediate and more ultimate values.[98]

Niebuhr suggested here that the Machiavellian motto has been treated unfairly. Compelled to act in an imperfect world, we must all make this moral calculus. Depending on the perspective from which we view it, every action can be considered a means or an end. We must muddle our way through a world without intrinsic moral truths and make choices that serve our most cherished values. We assess the comparative worth of those values on the basis of their likely "social consequences"—that is, we "evaluate them in the light of experience."[99] If experience teaches us that it is pernicious to sacrifice all of our freedoms at the altar of equality, for example, and violence is the only means by which to secure our freedom, shedding blood may very well be defensible.

In the end, Niebuhr embraced the Machiavellian idea that violence is only justifiable when it is used economically, devastating its victims with surgical precision and for a short duration. "If violence can be justified at all," he said, "its terror must have the tempo of a surgeon's skill and healing must follow quickly upon its wounds." It must achieve a "triumph quick enough to obviate the dangers of incessant wars."[100] Violence that strikes with blunt force for an extended period of time—and hence restarts the cycle of conflict—will not pass ethical muster, for the overall costs will almost certainly outweigh the benefits.

Niebuhr's views about violence are consistent with his social ethics in general. In a world without intrinsic goods and evils, we must all "become pragmatists and utilitarians" who make moral determinations in accordance with the net social consequences of a proposed action.[101] So neither violence nor nonviolence is inherently superior to the other. We must choose the option that yields the most desirable results overall in a given set of circumstances. So, for example, nonviolence is the only viable strategy for oppressed minorities, including African-Americans, because violence would elicit an overwhelming and terrifying backlash from which they could not adequately defend themselves. Indeed, "any appeal to arms must inevitably result in a terrible social catastrophe."[102] The fact that nonviolence disarms the oppressor more effectively in such cases attests to its moral superiority. If it could be proven otherwise, violent resistance would have moral worth.

Niebuhr applied pragmatic logic in the same way to the problem of property. He did not favor or oppose private property on principled grounds. As discussed earlier in this chapter, he was critical of modern conservatives who considered property an inalienable right, accusing them of embracing a naïve view of human nature. A thoughtful examination of history, he said, reveals that people are sinful creatures who will cause great harm if given unqualified property rights. Property is a form of power that, if left unchecked, people will use as "a tool of aggression and injustice."[103] Thus, anyone who draws lessons from historical experience can see "the advantage of viewing the 'right' of property with circumspection and of justifying it only relatively and not absolutely."[104] Of course, Marxists are equally wrongheaded for insisting that private property must be abolished because it is an unadulterated evil. History shows that "some forms of property are obviously instruments of social justice and peace," particularly those that promote "the security of the home" or "the proper performance of our social function."[105]

In the American context, Niebuhr understood that the dogma of *laissez faire* represents a more formidable threat. He lamented that "the absence of a Marxist challenge to our culture has left the institution of property completely unchallenged." This was unfortunate, for "it is not tenable to place the institution of property into the realm of the sacrosanct," he said. "Every human institution must stand under constant review. The question must be asked, what forms of it are viable under what specific conditions?"[106] No doubt private property has proven to be a viable institution under many different circumstances. But *laissez faire* rests on the dubious notion that private property is an unqualified good. In the end, Niebuhr saw *laissez faire* as an intellectually bankrupt theory whose survival depends on "the ignorant belief that the general welfare is best served by placing the least possible political restraints upon economic activity," said Niebuhr. "The history of the past hundred years is a refutation of the theory."[107]

The focus on observable results in his discussions of violence and property speaks to Niebuhr's overall preference for inductive reasoning. The "significant decisions between competing systems and political philosophies... must be constantly reviewed empirically and amended in the light of new evidence," Niebuhr said. "They are the resources of an inductive rather than a deductive social science. Such a science will not speak vaguely about general concepts such as property or planning."[108] It is not wise to make policy in accordance with principles derived from deductive reasoning, as they often do not cohere with reality. Instead, policymakers should reach tentative conclusions, always subject to further review, as a result of induction and make "significant decisions" in the light of empirical evidence. So, for example, one cannot rely on a one-size-fits-all formula to determine the extent to which social justice should be sacrificed for the sake of individual freedom. The appropriate balance between justice and liberty will depend on the specific circumstances, and it will require the expertise of social scientists who understand the dynamics of the situation and can determine what policies will produce the best overall outcomes. "The question how much liberty should be risked to establish justice, or justice sacrificed to preserve liberty," Niebuhr concluded, "will be illumined by able social scientists."[109]

Given his views about the elusiveness of absolute truth, Niebuhr comes across as a relativist, especially regarding political questions. "The principles of political morality," he said, "cannot be stated without the introduction of relative and contingent factors." But it is important to stress that Niebuhr's acceptance of relative truths did not make him a relativist. He strived for a middle way between skepticism and certainty, between relativism and absolutism. He feared that "secularism represents a form of skepticism which is conscious of the relativity of all human experience," and as a result "stands on the abyss of moral nihilism and threatens the whole of life with a sense of meaninglessness."[110] At the other extreme, "absolutists" generally refuse to entertain alternative points of view and "are inclined to hold to their position without regard to the political consequences which may flow from it." Whereas relativists may lead us down the path to nihilistic despair, absolutists are so certain about their truths that they may start imposing them on others. Niebuhr hoped to carve out an epistemological middle ground in which the virtues of relativism and absolutism could be brought together. He admired relativists for their flexibility, tolerating those people with whom they disagree and recognizing that "human society is governed by more than one principle."[111] Yet he also respected absolutists for remaining true to, and acting upon, their convictions. Niebuhr called for an epistemology that allowed people to hold on to their convictions without sacrificing flexibility.

This middle ground in Niebuhr's epistemology can be found in his belief in universal truths. Like absolutes, universal truths apply to all people, no matter the time or place. Unlike absolutes, however, universal truths are derived inductively from the experiences common to all of humanity and given a particular form in accordance with the circumstances of each concrete case. "It is very important to arrive at concepts of justice which draw upon the common experience of mankind," said Niebuhr. "But it must be recognized that insofar as such principles of justice are given specific historical meaning, they also become touched by historical contingency."[112]

Niebuhr gave as an example the universal claim about the sinful nature of human beings. "The Christian insistence on its universality," he said, "would seem to be attested by practical experience about as irrefutably as any truth can be established." Those who insist on the goodness of human nature are guilty of being "unscientific" and ignoring empirical facts. The sinful nature of human beings qualifies as a universal truth because "ambition and the lust for power" is a "general human phenomenon" or a "common element" that can be observed in every corner of the world throughout history. Depending on the time and place in which they live, along with many other factors, people may manifest these traits in different ways. But underlying the various displays of power, vanity, and envy throughout the world lie the "common characteristics" of humankind.[113]

Niebuhr also believed that universal principles of justice, such as the law of love in the prophetic tradition, stem from the common experiences of humankind. Although Niebuhr rejected Catholic natural law theory, he still saw a need for "principles of justice which transcend the positive enactments of historic states." At first, these principles seem "more specific than the law of love," for they "are generated in the customs and mores of communities." But "they may rise to universal norms which seem to have their source not in particular communities but in the common experience of mankind."[114] This suggests that the law of love itself—the most transcendent law in the Christian tradition—must receive validation from experiences shared by all of humanity. That is, it is universally true insofar as the concrete experiences of humanity as a whole demonstrate its usefulness.

It is not surprising, then, that Niebuhr also tested the universality of Christian faith. Though he did not believe that Christian faith could be proven definitively, Niebuhr argued that it can be at least tenuously validated. This is the task of what theologians call Christian apologetics. The negative "proof" of Christian faith involves showing how alternative understandings of human conduct and nature, especially those offered by modern culture, are not supported by the facts of history. It means pointing to the shortcomings of other interpretations of the human experience, and then inferring the superiority of the Christian view.[115] The "positive" proof "consists in correlating the truth, apprehended by faith and repentance, to truths about life and history, gained generally in experience."[116] Christian faith proves "true" to the extent that its tenets agree with historical experience.

Although "the acceptance of the truth of the Gospel is a gift of grace which stands beyond both forms of worldly wisdom," one can hardly abide by a faith that does not have discernible benefits in the here and now.[117] Faith does not rest alone on those empirical observations, but it cannot endure without them. Niebuhr said, "Religions grow out of real experience in which tragedy mingles with beauty."[118] It is in the crucible of worldly experience, full of triumphs and misfortunes, that people forge religious faith. "Faith in its essence is not an arbitrary faith," he said. "Once held, actual historic existence verifies it."[119] Although revelation may initially inspire faith, and thereby make life more meaningful, it can only be sustained and given life in the light of experience. "[Faith] illumines experience and is in turn validated by experience."[120] According to Niebuhr, prophetic (or profound) religions, including Judaism and Christianity, are especially grounded in historical experience.

Niebuhr traced the prophetic religious tradition back to the ancient Hebrews, who, unlike the Greeks, demonstrated an aversion to abstract reasoning and instead grounded enduring truths in concrete experience. Though "allegedly more crude and less rational" and "relegated to the sphere of 'pre-scientific' or 'pre-philosophical' thought," the Hebraic tradition is "more 'empirical' than the Greek tradition," Niebuhr said. "Its superior empirical accuracy consists in its understanding of the wholeness of the human self in body, mind and soul, in the appreciation of the dramatic variety of the self's encounters with others selves in history." In Niebuhr's view, the ancient Hebrews established truths whose "superior empirical accuracy" lies in its acute understanding of the human drama. Their experiences suggested that there was a "discontinuity between the self and God" and, therefore, it would be wrong for people to identify with the divine and to believe that they share a "rational faculty" with him. A more sensible faith will insist that the "self is related to God in repentance, faith and commitment."[121]

So, based on their observations of the human experience, the ancient Hebrews posited a transcendent God who stood in judgment of human actions and yet remained inscrutable. The chief benefit of this tradition was that it promoted contrition and humility before God. In the Greek tradition, the divine was immanent—ever present throughout the world—and thus more understandable and accessible to human reason. By assuming that the divine stood within their reach, the Greek tradition instilled a sense of pride in people and thus spurred their imperialistic impulses. This is how the Greek tradition revealed its empirical—and epistemological—inferiority.

Niebuhr applauded the prophetic tradition in Christianity—or what he sometimes called "Christian pragmatism"—for building on the virtues of the ancient Hebrews and continuing to look to experience for guidance. "This Christian 'pragmatism,' " he said, "drew upon Christian insights which were long obscured in the minds of even the most pious, but which have been clarified by historical experience even as they have clarified that experience."[122] Many of these insights are embodied in traditions inherited from the past. When people approximate the law of love in their actions, for example, it is "partly the consequence of historic and traditional disciplines which have become a part of the socio-spiritual inheritance of the individual."[123]

Niebuhr offered the example of the courageous soldier whose ability to transcend the instinct of self-preservation is "the fruit of a great tradition and the spirit of the military community." Knowing the law of love in the abstract is not enough. Only after they inherit deeply rooted traditions revealing its truth will people act on it. The soldier who sacrifices his own life for something greater, perhaps out of love for his country or comrades in arms, can only imagine performing such an act of heroism if he assimilates a set of traditional values about honor and duty. "The law of love is not obeyed simply by being known," Niebuhr said. "Whenever it is obeyed at all, it is because life in its beauty and terror has been more fully revealed to man. The love that cannot be willed may nevertheless grow as a natural fruit upon a tree which has roots deep enough to be nurtured by springs of life beneath the surface and branches reaching up to heaven."[124] Because of the frailties of human nature, we cannot simply obey the law of love through the exercise of sheer will. We do so, at least approximately, with the help of tradition. The law of love can only ripen on the tree of tradition, whose roots reach down and draw from the wellspring of life experience.

What that experience clearly reveals to the pragmatic or prophetic Christian is that the whole truth remains elusive. We can only hope to have a fragmentary understanding of the world around us. The problem lies not in our partial ignorance but in our refusal to acknowledge it. "The truth, as it is contained in the Christian revelation, includes the recognition that it is neither possible for man to know the truth fully nor to avoid the error pretending that he does."[125] The only truth of which we can be certain according to the prophetic tradition is that we can never have a firm grasp on the truth. Any assertions to the contrary will lead inexorably to pride, ambition, overreach, and injustice.

At its best, the prophetic tradition in Christianity embodies the spirit of empiricism. "The relevance of a genuine and vital Christian faith," Niebuhr said, "is that it unmasks the errors of a false and abstract idealism."[126] It accomplishes this task by preaching contrition, humility and forgiveness. People must be contrite for their sinful tendency to serve their inordinate interests at the expense of others. Once they see themselves as hopeless sinners in the eyes of God, they will become humble about what they can know and achieve in this world. They will also show a loving forgiveness for their fellow sinners who do wrong or have different beliefs. Recognizing their own moral and intellectual limits, they will see the error in condemning others too harshly. Only then will people stop insisting that they alone know the truth and walk the path of righteousness while brandishing their general ideals and schemes as weapons of self-interest. Instead, they will remain modest about their own truth claims and open-minded about those held by others. Ironically, Niebuhr believed that there could "be no genuine empiricism without religious correction of this tendency." In other words, we need prophetic religion to maintain a scientific attitude. We need it to avoid the pitfalls of deductive rationality and to see the advantages of drawing on empirical evidence and solving problems inductively.[127]

"DEMOCRACY HAS BROUGHT ARBITRARY POWER UNDER CHECK AND MADE IT RESPONSIBLE"

Prophetic religions encourage the scientific attitude by establishing traditions and institutions that inculcate the virtues of contrition, humility, and forgiveness. Although the church must play a key role in establishing traditions that inspire these ideals, Niebuhr also found hope in secular and political institutions. As the example of the self-sacrificing soldier shows, the military can cultivate customs and values that reify the law of love. But he came to find hope in democracy as the political manifestation of prophetic religion. The spirit of contrition, he said, "lies at the foundation of what we define as democracy. For democracy cannot exist if there is no recognition of the fragmentary character of all systems of thought and value which are allowed to exist together within the democratic frame." People in a democracy remain somewhat incredulous about all the laws and institutions under which they live, holding to the view that "no laws, ideals, structures, and systems should exist without the criticism which may disclose their ambiguous character and thereby prevent the evil in them from destroying the good."[128] Democracy embodies the Christian idea that, even at their best, political institutions are flawed and incomplete and therefore only improvable under a regimen of constant criticism and examination.

According to Niebuhr, democracy remains vigilantly self-critical with a system of "checks and counterchecks" in which opposing sides compete in a marketplace of ideas and fraudulent truth claims are exposed in the glaring light of intense scrutiny. He considered democracy "the best method of neutralizing special interests and of arriving at the truth by allowing various corruptions of the truth to destroy each other." Creating the conditions in which the sophistries of special interests cancel each out, democracy can actually "eliminate ideology from culture" and prevent "tyranny, whether rooted in priestly, military, economic, or political power."[129] Democracy evades the hazards of ideology and tyranny by striking a delicate balance between optimism and pessimism, between placing too much faith in human beings and giving up on them altogether. The former is an expression of pride; the latter leads to a withdrawal into a world of sensuality. Neither of these sins is conducive to a healthy polity, for pride fosters imperialistic tendencies, and sensuality becomes an escape from responsibility. Democracy creates opportunities for people to avoid both the sins of pride and sensuality, directing their energies toward a higher good while attenuating their inevitable expressions of self-interest. It not only gives people the hope that they can make a better future but also reminds them that no one has the key to the kingdom of heaven.

Niebuhr praised democracy in particular for finding proximate solutions to economic problems. After observing recent history in the United States and Europe, Niebuhr concluded in the years after World War II that the socialization of the means of production is not always wise. There is always "some peril of compounding economic and political power," he said. Deciding on the right course of action requires "continuous debate" and "continuous adjustment to new developments," and this can be accomplished most readily "within the framework of democratic procedure."[130] Only a democracy can avoid ideological schemes, which ultimately serve a particular set of interests, and make the adjustments necessary to maintain a balance of power among competing economic and political interests. In the end, Niebuhr saw democracy as the best way of achieving economic justice, creating a modern liberal state that adapts to changing conditions and charts a middle course between *laissez faire* and Marxism. Though often inefficient and chaotic, democracy proves to be far more effective than any other system by promoting epistemological modesty, problem-solving on the basis of empirical evidence, and continual discussion.

Though Niebuhr applauded democracy for promoting sensible reform based on observed facts and promoting economic justice and equality of opportunity, he could not abide the populist attack on hierarchical structures and elite institutions. He did not see democracy and hierarchy as mutually exclusive. "Democracy has brought arbitrary power under check and made it responsible," he said, "but it has not seriously altered the hierarchical structure of the community. Even democratic communities are integrated by military and civil bureaucracies and by local legislative assemblies and governors." Niebuhr saw hierarchy as yet another problem that required balance. We must acknowledge that while "hierarchy is necessary," it also produces "inordinate" expressions of "prestige, power, and privilege." We must protect "traditional and inevitable social hierarchies," particularly when they promote unity and stability, from "too simple applications of the criteria of liberty and equality." Yet, at the same time, we must make sure that these hierarchies are continually "subjected to the judgment of these criteria of justice and placed under the check of universal suffrage."[131] According to Niebuhr, there is a significant difference between "monstrous inequalities of power and privilege" and "justified inequalities of authority."[132] Finding the right balance meant allowing for hierarchies based solely on the latter.

Niebuhr praised the British for successfully striking this balance, creating a community that "could absorb, and profit from, both the middle class and the workers' rebellion without rending the wholeness of a traditional culture and community."[133] He credited hierarchical structures and elites in British history for upholding traditions that had defended society from the destabilizing effects of both bourgeois and proletarian radicalism. As the British example testifies, elites can serve as guardians of traditions that maintain social stability, particularly in times of great upheaval and uncertainty, without abusing their authority for personal gain. Largely because of the influence of the aristocracy, Niebuhr said, "civil conflict on the property issue was mitigated because older conceptions of property, derived from an agrarian and feudal world, mitigated both the extravagant individualism of the bourgeois classes and the doctrinaire collectivism of the industrial workers."[134] What he admired about Britain was that aristocratic notions of honor, chivalry, and *noblesse oblige* pervaded the entire social structure, persuading each class to sacrifice self-interest for higher ideals. Thanks to "traditional and inevitable social hierarchies" inherited from the aristocratic order, "a nation and an empire were remolded gradually and therefore more wisely than by revolutionary fanaticism."[135]

As noted earlier, Niebuhr understood that aristocratic traditions could not be transplanted into American soil. But, in his view, the absence of an aristocratic heritage did not negate the necessity of political and social hierarchy in the United States. In an essay that he contributed to a festschrift on Walter Lippmann, Niebuhr expressed his admiration for the distinguished columnist's democratic realism. Along with Burke and Lippmann, he subscribed to the trustee theory of democratic representation, in which elected officials think and act independently of what their constituents demand in the short term. Insulated to some degree from the temporary whims and passions of the people, trustees can use their judgment and exercise power on behalf of the public good. Niebuhr disparaged the idea that representatives need to act as delegates or errand boys for the people, making decisions that merely reflect their will. "Ideally," he said, "a free society creates various aristocracies and elite groups in various fields of culture and political affairs." Elites should not just occupy positions of power but also work for institutions—including newspapers, magazines, think tanks, and universities—that evaluate the policies enacted by government officials. He saw a great need for a natural "aristocracy of informed and knowledgeable men...who are able to judge the performance of their elected officials."[136]

Although he was a proponent of democracy, Niebuhr rejected the Enlightenment idea that the legitimacy of government rests on political equality and explicit popular consent. He praised Burke for understanding that "the authority of government to speak for the community is derived both from tradition and from its ability to harmonize and express the multifarious interests and passions of the various groups."[137] Along with Burke, Niebuhr believed that government must be judged by not how well it reflects popular opinion but whether it "makes power responsible" and "disperses power into as many centers as possible, thereby creating a system of checks and balances."[138] He praised traditional or Burkean conservatives for recognizing "the inevitability of social hierarchies" in an imperfect world, seeing that a just society does not guarantee equality but rather finds appropriate ways of "dealing with the factors of power and interest."[139]

Equating justice with equality laid the groundwork for the kind of radicalism for which Burke criticized the French Revolution. On two occasions, Niebuhr quoted with approval Burke's famous line about the revolutionaries' mad impulse to "level everything which had raised up its head."[140] They were so bent on imposing their abstract notions of equality that they were willing to sacrifice liberty. Niebuhr insisted that justice required placing equality and liberty in dialectical opposition to each other and finding an appropriate balance between them.[141]

CONCLUSION

In the summer of 1951, Niebuhr published a short piece entitled "We Need an Edmund Burke" in *Christianity and Society*. Despite the lack of maturity in American political thought, he said, "our pragmatic-historical approach to the issues of social justice has points of similarity with the position of Edmund Burke, when he challenged the rationalism of the French revolution with the history-informed wisdom which has always been the boast of English political thought."[142] In highlighting the Burkean virtues of America at that time, Niebuhr was referring to what he saw as the pragmatism of the New Deal, which averted revolution and social upheaval by curbing the excesses of capitalism.

Much to his chagrin, however, he saw something else going on in the United Kingdom at the same time. In his view, the leadership of the Labour Party espoused orthodox Marxism and as a result had become increasingly inflexible on matters of public policy. He faulted its leaders in particular for embracing wildly optimistic assumptions about human nature from which they deduced hardline policy positions. As a representative example of this kind of Marxist rationalism, Niebuhr pointed to Aneurin Bevan, a Member of Parliament who resigned from the government because he could not abide its willingness to make reasonable compromises. Committed to the belief that all medical services should remain absolutely free, Bevan found especially intolerable a provision in the new budget requiring a modest payment for such services as dentures. Although he was a proponent of universal health care, Niebuhr believed that many members of the Labour Party had become unreasonable, blinded by "too abstract Marxist concepts." According to Niebuhr, "moderate charges" for dentures made sense. For, unlike the Marxists who occupied the higher ranks of the Labour Party, Niebuhr thought that people make "inordinate demands" which, if left unchecked, could become quite costly to the government. "To assume that demands upon a scheme of socialized medicine can be met without any checks against inordinate demands is to assume, with Marxism, that human needs are determinate and human desires ordinate," he said. "Actually human desires are inordinate from some standpoint or other because needs are indeterminate."[143]

Because people have unpredictable and infinite desires in a world where supply is limited, societies must accept the bitter reality of trade-offs. People cannot always get what they want, so they must determine what they are willing to sacrifice in order to secure what is most important to them. But in a free society, Niebuhr believed, it is crucial that individuals be able to make choices based on their own priorities. If policymakers impose exorbitantly high taxes in order to pay for "the most ideal denture" and other desired services, people who would prefer to buy cheaper dentures so that they can spend the rest of their disposable income on something else are robbed of that option. In order to prevent that eventuality, those people who "want the best possible equipment of false teeth... ought to be asked to make some contribution to that end." Here we see Niebuhr trying to strike a balance between equality (or security) and liberty, endorsing a form of socialized medicine that controls costs and preserves individual choice by requiring people to pay "moderate charges" for the "most expensive solution."[144]

It is not important whether Niebuhr was right about this particular issue. What matters is that his pragmatic approach, even when he supported ostensibly left-wing policies, is consistent with Burkean conservatism. Niebuhr always analyzed issues from a realist and pragmatic perspective, working under fairly pessimistic assumptions about human nature which are supported by the historical evidence, and reaching conclusions on the basis of facts observed in the past and present. He had special reverence for principles that grew out of past experience and became reified in such traditions as prophetic Christianity.

Niebuhr supported initiatives and policies that at best could approximate the Christian law of love, never forgetting that the normative did not always agree with harsh reality or with competing principles. So, for example, the law of love mandates the finest health care for all, regardless of the cost, but our imperfect world requires policymakers to make compromises. They must do what they can to comply with the law of love without making undue sacrifices to other important principles and priorities (such as liberty and cost-saving). The prophetic tradition calls for a scientific approach in which decision-makers refrain from applying abstract formulas to social problems and instead make continual adjustments in accordance with the empirical evidence. In light of the injustices to which the quest for perfection will inevitably give rise, the prophetic tradition demands that we remain humble about our moral and intellectual capacities. Lest our putative remedy proves far worse than the problem to which we initially turned our attention, we must not get carried away with our hubristic ambitions. In the end, Niebuhr's political thought highlights the continued relevance of Burkean conservatism, proving it to be both modern and adaptable to a changing world.

NOTES

1. "Death of a Christian Realist," *Time*, June 14, 1971.
2. Niebuhr, *An Interpretation of Christian Ethics*, 189.
3. Niebuhr, *Moral Man and Immoral Society*, in Sifton, ed., *Reinhold Niebuhr: Major Works on Religion and Politics* (henceforth *Major Works*), 348.
4. See, for example, Niebuhr, *An Interpretation of Christian Ethics*, 58.
5. Brooks, "Obama, Gospel, and Verse," *New York Times*, April 26, 2007.
6. Niebuhr, "The Serenity Prayer," in *Major Works*, 705. For more on the origins of the prayer, see Sifton, *The Serenity Prayer: Faith and Politics in Times of Peace and War*. An editor and book publisher, Elisabeth Sifton is Niebuhr's daughter. She argues that this is the original version written by her father.
7. See Niebuhr, "Theology and Political Thought in the Western World," in *Major Works*, 868–869.
8. Herberg, "The Three Dialogues of Man," *The New Republic*, May 16, 1955. See also Herberg, "Christian Apologist to the Secular World," *Union Seminary Quarterly Review* 11:1 (1956); Herberg, "Reinhold Niebuhr: A Burkean Conservative," *National Review* (December 2, 1961).
9. Viereck, "Niebuhr in the Conformists' Den," *The Christian Scholar* 39:3 (1956); Heimann, "Niebuhr's Pragmatic Conservatism," *Union Seminary Quarterly Review* 11 (May 1956).

10. See Guroian, "The Conservatism of Reinhold Niebuhr: The Burkean Connection," *Modern Age* 29 (Summer 1985); Guroian, "The Possibilities and Limits of Politics: A Comparative Study of the Thought of Reinhold Niebuhr and Edmund Burke," *Union Seminary Quarterly Review* 36:4 (1981); Guroian, "On Revolution and Ideology: Convergence in the Political Legacies of Niebuhr and Burke," *Union Seminary Quarterly Review* 39:1–2 (1984), 25–40; Charles C. Brown, *Niebuhr and His Age: Reinhold Niebuhr's Prophetic Role in the Twentieth Century* (Philadelphia: Trinity Press, 1992); Lester, "British Conservatism and American Liberalism in Mid-Twentieth Century: Burkean Themes in Niebuhr and Schlesinger," *Polity* 46:2 (April 2014).

11. Guroian, "The Possibilities and Limits of Politics: A Comparative Study of the Thought of Reinhold Niebuhr and Edmund Burke," *Union Seminary Quarterly Review* 36:4 (1981), 190.

12. Niebuhr to June Bingham in a letter dated April 19, 1955. Quoted in Rice, "The Fiction of Reinhold Niebuhr as a Political Conservative," *Soundings* 98:1 (2015), 59–83. See Rice for a lucid criticism of the claim that Niebuhr was a conservative. It is worth noting that Rice does not challenge—and, in fact, implicitly agrees with—the view that Niebuhr shared commonalities with Burke. Rice is more concerned with the revisionist claims that Niebuhr provided an intellectual foundation for the ideas of William F. Buckley, Irving Kristol, and other luminaries on the right in post-war America. "Whatever degree of congeniality Niebuhr felt for Burke," Rice says, "it is clear that he disdained the brand of conservatism espoused by Buckley and his fellow travelers" (60).

13. Cogley, "An Interview with Reinhold Niebuhr," in *McCall's Magazine* 93:5, 167.

14. Niebuhr, "The Foreign Policy of American Conservatism and Liberalism," *Christian Realism and Political Problems*, 56.

15. Niebuhr, *The Irony of American History*, in *Major Works*, 528.

16. Niebuhr, "The Foreign Policy of American Conservatism and Liberalism," *Christian Realism and Political Problems*, 72.

17. Niebuhr, "Liberalism: Illusions and Realities," *The New Republic*, July 4, 1955.

18. Ibid.

19. Niebuhr, *The Structure of Nations and Empires*, 193.

20. Niebuhr, *Man's Nature and His Communities*, 61.

21. Walter Rauschenbusch, "The Kingdom of God," *Cleveland's Young Men* 27, quoted in Bodein, *The Social Gospel of Walter Rauschenbusch* (New Haven: Yale University Press, 1944), 7–8.

22. Niebuhr, *Leaves from the Notebook of a Tamed Cynic*, in *Major Works*, 57.

23. Fox, *Reinhold Niebuhr*, 95.

24. Niebuhr, "The Effects of Modern Industrialism on Personality," *Student World* 21 (October 1927), quoted in Fox, *Reinhold Niebuhr*, 98.

25. Niebuhr, quoted in Fox, *Reinhold Niebuhr*, 98.

26. Niebuhr, "After Capitalism—What?" *World Tomorrow* 16 (March 1, 1933).

27. Niebuhr, "Russia and Karl Marx," in *Major Works*, 614.

28. See, for example, Niebuhr, *Moral Man and Immoral Society*, in *Major Works*, 268–269, 288.

29. Niebuhr, "The National Election," *Radical Religion* 2 (Winter 1936), 3–4, quoted in Fox, *Reinhold Niebuhr*, 178.

30. Niebuhr, "Vietnam: Study in Ironies," in *Major Works*, 692.

31. Charles Merriam quoted in Schlesinger, *A Life in the Twentieth Century: Innocent Beginnings, 1917–1950*, 250.

32. Niebuhr, *Leaves from the Notebook of a Tamed Cynic*, in *Major Works*, 34, 58, 64.

33. Ibid., 34, 63, 64.

34. Niebuhr, *Moral Man*, in *Major Works*, 169, 179.

35. Niebuhr quoted in Fox, *Reinhold Niebuhr*, 179.

36. Niebuhr, *The Irony of American History*, in *Major Works*, 477.

37. Niebuhr, *An Interpretation of Christian Ethics*, 41.

38. Niebuhr, *The Nature and Destiny of Man*, I, 178.

39. Niebuhr, *Moral Man*, in *Major Works*, 180.

40. Niebuhr, *An Interpretation of Christian Ethics*, 67.

41. Niebuhr, *Moral Man*, in *Major Works*, 180.

42. Niebuhr, *An Interpretation of Christian Ethics*, 72–73.

43. Niebuhr, *The Nature and Destiny of Man*, I, 140.

44. Niebuhr, *Beyond Tragedy*, 28.

45. Niebuhr, *An Interpretation of Christian Ethics*, 76.

46. Niebuhr, *The Nature and Destiny of Man*, I, 179.

47. Ibid., 124.

48. Niebuhr, "Augustine's Political Realism," in *Christian Realism and Political Problems*, 119.

49. Niebuhr, *Moral Man*, in *Major Works*, 139–140.

50. Ibid., 141–142, 182.

51. Ibid., 268–269.

52. Niebuhr, *The Children of Light and the Children of Darkness*, in *Major Works*, 388, 410.

53. Niebuhr, "Optimism, Pessimism and Religious Faith—I," in *Major Works*, 713, 715.

54. Niebuhr, *Children of Light*, in *Major Works*, 380.

55. Ibid., 380–381, 354.

56. Niebuhr, "For Our Inheritance: A Thanksgiving Prayer," in *Major Works*, 697.

57. Niebuhr, *Leaves from the Notebook*, in *Major Works*, 81.
58. Niebuhr, *Children of Light*, in *Major Works*, 404–405.
59. Niebuhr, "Coronation Afterthoughts," *Christian Century* 70 (July 1, 1953), 771.
60. Niebuhr, "Liberalism: Illusions and Realities," *The New Republic*, July 4, 1955.
61. Niebuhr, "Do the State and Nation Belong to God or the Devil?" in *Faith and Politics*, 85.
62. Niebuhr, *The Self and the Dramas of History*, 179.
63. Niebuhr, "Prayers," in *Major Works*, 704, 697.
64. Niebuhr, *An Interpretation of Christian Ethics*, 29.
65. Niebuhr, "Optimism, Pessimism and Religious Faith—I," in *Major Works*, 721.
66. Niebuhr, *An Interpretation of Christian Ethics*, 105–106.
67. Ibid., 31.
68. Niebuhr, "The Christian Church in a Secular Age," in *Major Works*, 734.
69. Niebuhr, *The Nature and Destiny of Man*, I, 137–138.
70. Niebuhr, *The Children of Light*, in *Major Works*, 429.
71. Niebuhr, "The Christian Church in a Secular Age," in *Major Works*, 737.
72. Niebuhr, "Christian Faith and Social Action," *Faith and Politics*, 132.
73. Niebuhr, *An Interpretation of Christian Ethics*, 182.
74. Niebuhr, "The Christian Church in a Secular Age," in *Major Works*, 737.
75. Niebuhr, *An Interpretation of Christian Ethics*, 149.
76. Niebuhr, "Love and Law in Protestantism and Catholicism," *Christian Realism and Political Problems*, 159; *The Nature and Destiny of Man*, II, 96.
77. Niebuhr, *The Nature and Destiny of Man*, II, 125.
78. Niebuhr, *Leaves from the Notebook*, in *Major Works*, 73.
79. Ibid., 110. In 1905, George Santayana wrote his oft-quoted (or oft-misquoted) line: "Those who cannot remember the past are condemned to repeat it." See *The Life of Reason*, Vol. 1 (*Reason in Common Sense*), 284.
80. Niebuhr, *Moral Man*, in *Major Works*, 271.
81. Ibid., 280, 281, 298, 308.
82. Niebuhr, "Liberty and Equality," *Faith and Politics*, 196.
83. Niebuhr, *The Children of Light*, in *Major Works*, 419.
84. Niebuhr, *Discerning the Signs of the Times*, in *Major Works*, 761.
85. Niebuhr in a letter to Lewis Mumford (1941), quoted in Fox, *Reinhold Niebuhr*, 205.
86. Niebuhr, *Nature and Destiny of Man*, II, 214.
87. For other scholarly treatments of Niebuhr's pragmatic epistemology, see Diggins, *The Promise of Pragmatism* and *Why Niebuhr Now?*; West, *The American Evasion of Philosophy*; Lasch, *The True and Only Heaven*.
88. Niebuhr, *Leaves from the Notebook*, in *Major Works*, 5.
89. Niebuhr, "Christian Faith and Social Action," *Faith and Politics*, 125.

90. Niebuhr, *The Irony of American History*, 528.
91. Niebuhr, *An Interpretation of Christian Ethics*, 197, 205, 208.
92. Niebuhr, *Moral Man*, in *Major Works*, 273.
93. Niebuhr, "The Wheat and the Tares," in *Major Works*, 883.
94. Niebuhr, *Moral Man*, in *Major Works*, 317 & 319.
95. Ibid., 328–330.
96. Niebuhr, *Moral Man*, in *Major Works*, 279.
97. Niebuhr, *The Nature and Destiny of Man*, I, 278.
98. Niebuhr, *An Interpretation of Christian Ethics*, 194.
99. Niebuhr, *Moral Man*, in *Major Works*, 273; *Leaves from the Notebook*, in *Major Works*, 55.
100. Niebuhr, *Moral Man*, in *Major Works*, 308, 332. See Wolin, *Politics and Vision*, 197–200, for a discussion of "the economy of violence" in Machiavelli's thought. Also see Machiavelli, *The Prince*, 42, 65–66.
101. Niebuhr, *Moral Man*, in *Major Works*, 273.
102. Ibid., 333.
103. Niebuhr, *Irony of American History*, in *Major Works*, 538.
104. Niebuhr, *Children of Light*, in *Major Works*, 405.
105. Niebuhr, *Irony of American History*, in *Major Works*, 538–539.
106. Ibid., 539.
107. Niebuhr, *Moral Man*, in *Major Works*, 174.
108. Niebuhr, "Christian Faith and Social Action," *Faith and Politics*, 127.
109. Niebuhr, "The Christian Faith and the Economic Life of Liberal Society," *Faith and Politics*, 143.
110. Niebuhr, *The Children of Light*, in *Major Works*, 395, 428.
111. Niebuhr, "The Limits of Liberty," in *Major Works*, 634, 638.
112. Niebuhr, "God's Design and the Present Disorder of Civilization," *Faith and Politics*, 105.
113. Niebuhr, "Faith and the Empirical Method in Modern Realism," *Christian Realism and Political Problems*, 7–8.
114. Niebuhr, "Love and Law in Protestantism and Catholicism," *Christian Realism and Political Problems*, 148.
115. Niebuhr, "Coherence, Incoherence, and Christian Faith," *Christian Realism and Political Problems*, 202; "The Validation of the Christian View of Life and History," *Faith and History*, 186.
116. Niebuhr, "The Validation of the Christian View of Life and History," *Faith and History*, 187.
117. Ibid.
118. Niebuhr, *Does Civilization Need Religion?*, 200.
119. Niebuhr, *An Interpretation of Christian Ethics*, 219.
120. Niebuhr, *The Nature and Destiny of Man*, II, 63.
121. Niebuhr, *The Self and the Dramas of History*, in *Major Works*, 863.
122. Niebuhr, "Theology and Political Thought in the Western World," in *Major Works*, 869.

123. Niebuhr, *An Interpretation of Christian Ethics*, 215.

124. Ibid., 215, 220.

125. Niebuhr, *The Nature and Destiny of Man*, II, 217.

126. Niebuhr, "Christian Faith and Social Action," *Faith and Politics*, 129.

127. Niebuhr, "Christian Faith and Social Action," *Faith and Politics*, 129–131.

128. Ibid., 134–135, 129–130.

129. Niebuhr, "Ideologies," *New Leader* (16 August 1941), 4, quoted in Fox, *Reinhold Niebuhr*, 219.

130. Niebuhr, *Children of Light*, in *Major Works*, 419–420.

131. Niebuhr, "Liberty and Equality," *Faith and Politics*, 187–188, 196.

132. Niebuhr, "Liberalism: Illusions and Realities," *The New Republic* (4 July 1955).

133. Niebuhr, "Liberty and Equality," *Faith and Politics*, 196.

134. Niebuhr, *Children of Light*, in *Major Works*, 404.

135. Niebuhr, "Liberty and Equality," *Faith and Politics*, 196.

136. Niebuhr, "The Democratic Elite and American Foreign Policy," in *Walter Lippmann and His Times*, 173–175.

137. Niebuhr, *The Structure of Nations and Empires*, 57.

138. Niebuhr, "Unintended Virtues of an Open Society," *Christianity and Crisis* 21 (24 July 1961), 132.

139. Niebuhr, "Liberalism and Conservatism," *Christianity and Society* 20 (Winter 1954–1955), 3.

140. Niebuhr quotes this passage in *Pious and Secular America*, 71 and in *The Self and the Dramas of History*, 189.

141. For a useful discussion of how Niebuhr sought a balance between equality and liberty, see Robin Lovin, *Reinhold Niebuhr and Christian Realism*, 225–227.

142. Niebuhr, "We Need an Edmund Burke," *Christianity and Society* 16:3, 6.

143. Ibid., 6–7.

144. Ibid.

CHAPTER 5

Peter Viereck: Reverent Conservative

Introduction

A distinguished historian and poet who taught at Mt. Holyoke College for over 40 years, Peter Viereck played an important role in the formation of conservative thought in the years immediately after World War II—and is even credited with popularizing the term "conservative" and giving the "nascent movement a label."[1] But by the late 1950s, Viereck became *persona non grata* among most self-styled conservatives, relegated by leaders of the movement, especially William F. Buckley, to the "ranks of eccentricity."[2] With most of his works of political thought behind him, Viereck focused his energies on teaching history and writing poetry. Viereck continued to reflect on political questions and certainly made quiet efforts to promote his conservative ideas, mainly by getting new editions of his books into print before he died, but he never jumped back into the fray. He remained a marginal and largely forgotten figure in the conservative world, enjoying only a modest following among some intellectuals on both the left and the right. The leaders of the conservative movement never welcomed him back into the fold, for Viereck refused to accept what he saw as their extremism.

The issue that encapsulated the disagreement between Viereck and most of his fellow conservatives, perhaps more than any other, was McCarthyism. Viereck assailed the senator as a radical who did not aim to expose communist subversives in our midst so much as to satisfy his desire, motivated by a combustible mix of ambition and status resentment,

© The Author(s) 2016
R.J. Lacey, *Pragmatic Conservatism*,
DOI 10.1057/978-1-137-59295-8_5

to destroy members of the establishment and their cherished institutions. Much to Viereck's consternation, most conservatives either remained conspicuously silent about the senator's reckless antics or, in the case of Buckley, defended him outright. This was a crucial moment when conservatives could have taken the high road, condemning the senator from Wisconsin whose hateful demagoguery undermined the values of a free society and did more to discredit the fight against communism than to aid it. Instead, they decided to hitch their wagon to McCarthy's populist star. Reflecting on this moment half a century later, Viereck said, "I think McCarthy was a menace not because of the risk that he would take over—that was never real—but because he corrupted the ethics of American conservatives, and that corruption leads to the situation we have now. It gave the conservatives the habit of appeasing the forces of the hysterical right...I think that was the original sin of the conservative movement, and we are all suffering from it."[3]

So, according to Viereck's lament, post-war American conservatism lost its way, both ethically and intellectually, soon after it began to take off. In embracing McCarthyism, either tacitly or explicitly, Buckley and his crowd at *National Review* betrayed the core principles of conservatism. What were those principles? Influenced by the thought of Edmund Burke, Viereck believed that true conservatives are "by definition moderate in all things" and thus gravitate to the center.[4] Eschewing extreme positions, they seek balance and harmony. Because of their pessimistic view of human nature, they have a temperamental aversion to ideology and untested innovations and a reflexive trust in tradition and time-tested practices. They acknowledge the need to address existing social problems but insist on incremental reform, taking pains to work within a traditional framework. The primary concern of conservatives is to safeguard individual freedom, and they believe that a flagrant disregard for law and tradition breeds tyranny, the greatest threat to freedom. Only by conserving our treasured inheritance—laws, traditions, customs, and values—can we maintain the fragile civilization in which our freedoms thrive. Viereck was fond of summarizing the conservative position with a short poem called "Greek Architecture" by Herman Melville:

Not magnitude, not lavishness,
But Form—the site;
Not innovating willfulness,
But reverence for the Archetype.

Informed by a tragic sense of the human condition, conservatives demand a reverence for the law and established forms and remain forever suspicious of creative and outlandish invention. Whenever uncertainty reigns, conservatives err on the side of caution, preferring the old to the new, the known to the unknown, the tried to the untried, facts to theories, the concrete to the imagined. The law of unintended consequences never escapes the conservative mind.

According to Viereck, at the very heart of conservatism is a profound humility, an acknowledgment that human reason, even when functioning at its best, is fallible. There is no end to the blueprints and doctrines that we can devise if we put our minds to it, but we impose these abstract creations at our peril. Ideological dogma and systems may sound compelling in theory, even seem incontrovertible according to deductive reasoning, but they may lead to disastrous consequences when put into practice. McCarthyism was a case in point. The leaders of the conservative movement who excommunicated Viereck seemed blithely unconcerned about the dangers of hubris. They were at the forefront of a nascent movement that offered a blistering indictment of a liberal order that, in their view, failed to acknowledge the severity of the communist threat; the unsavory methods used by McCarthy were a necessary price to pay in the fight against this unmitigated evil. Their version of conservatism was not committed to concrete traditions and gradual change; rather, it stood resolutely for certain principles, adhering to them regardless of the potentially disruptive effects.

Even with the warnings of Viereck and other traditionalists, the leaders of the movement turned conservatism into an ideology composed of three strains: economic libertarianism, religious fundamentalism, and anticommunism. While there were obvious tensions between these strains, conservatives of different stripes were able to find agreement on several principles: unfettered economic freedom, religious piety, rugged individualism, and fierce opposition to any efforts by the state to promote the common good. Their unwavering adherence to these principles convinced them to embrace extreme measures, such as dismantling the welfare state and dispensing with due process and civil liberties in the fight against communist subversion. This shift from concrete tradition to abstract principle, from relying on history and experience to insisting on loyalty to categorical truths, is what alienated Viereck from most of his fellow conservatives. In his view, they had ceased to be conservatives in the Burkean sense of the term and had become "Jacobins" who were certain that they were right—so certain, in fact, that they could justify extreme, even destructive, measures that served ends consistent with their principles.

Despite Viereck's valiant struggle, the soul of post-war American conservatism soon belonged to these Jacobins, and his thought receded to the margins of both political and academic life in the United States. To the casual observer in the early twenty-first century, he appears to be nothing more than an idiosyncratic curiosity. But Viereck remains relevant and instructive, perhaps now more than ever in a time of bitter partisanship and ideological division. In the spirit of Edmund Burke he sought a much-needed middle way between seemingly irreconcilable opposites, including relativism (even nihilism) and absolutism, romanticism and enlightenment rationalism, individualism and collectivism, atomism and organic unity, freedom and order, revolution and stasis (or counterrevolution), and rule of the many and rule of the few. He saw conservatism not as an ideology or a creed but as a temperament informed by a keen sense of balance and proportion and a taste for moderation, deliberation, and gradual change. Viereck once called conservatism "the art of listening to the way history grows"[5]—a wonderful illustration of his insistence that politics requires attending to the continuities of lived experience for guidance, never adhering slavishly to formulas, theories, or systems.

In searching for a synthesis between opposites, Viereck developed a pragmatic conservatism that put him at odds with the prevailing movement. The fundamentals of his thought, which this chapter will address in detail, can be summarized in brief: Responding to the age of ideological extremism in which he lived, Viereck believed that only an abiding reverence for law and tradition could hold in check the darker impulses of human nature. If change is necessary, it must come gradually and grow organically out of traditional roots. Neither an absolutist nor a relativist, Viereck subscribed to what he called "universals"—truths commonly accepted throughout the civilized world but flexible enough to allow for diverse practices, truths that become particularized and concrete in a given time and place through the building of traditions, customs, and institutions. According to Viereck, our fallibility prevents us from ever knowing absolute truth with certainty. We must accept the provisionality of those reified truths, wrought in the crucible of past experience, which we inherit from our ancestors in the form of laws, institutions, and traditions. The same can be said of values or ethical truths, which are derived not from a priori reasoning but rather from an ever-expanding moral imagination informed by the lessons of the past. Viereck's final hope was that a renewed interest in the humanities among the best and the brightest would help create a new generation of elites dedicated to preserving these values while prudently adapting them to new circumstances.

"CHILDREN, DON'T OVERSIMPLIFY"

All but forgotten in the world of conservative political thought, Viereck became the object of revived interest, if only briefly, when *The New Yorker* published a lengthy and sympathetic profile of him less than a year before his death in 2006. Written by Tom Reiss, the piece was called "The First Conservative" and portrayed Viereck as the intrepid founder of a movement that quickly turned its back on him. This betrayal paved the way for a conservatism that would be captured by various extremists, including religious fundamentalists, war hawks, and supply-siders. Viereck obviously agreed with this interpretation of events, but the guardians of orthodox conservatism were quick to dismiss the *New Yorker* article as revisionism, a blatant attempt to discredit the Bush administration as radical. John J. Miller of *National Review*, for example, scoffed at the claim that "an anti-capitalist poet who wanted Adlai Stevenson to become president" was America's "first conservative." Although his *Conservatism Revisited*, published in 1949, was the first post-war book to use "conservatism" in the title, said Miller, Viereck had negligible influence on defining the movement that would emerge in the 1950s. In the end, his "achievement was largely semantic." He may have coined the term, giving him "naming rights" to the movement, but it took others to give it settled meaning.[6]

Viereck received a similar reception from most of his fellow conservatives in the early 1950s. They rejected his definition of conservatism and were reluctant to accept him as one of their own. Frank Meyer, a libertarian and senior editor of *National Review*, called Viereck's conservatism "counterfeit" and accused him of "passing off his unexceptionably Liberal sentiments as conservatism."[7] Willmoore Kendall, yet another senior editor at *National Review* who had taught Buckley at Yale University, called Viereck a "verbalist" who would tell people "how to be conservative and yet agree with the Liberals about Everything."[8] On the surface, Viereck *did* appear to be a liberal who merely called himself a conservative—that is, a conservative in name only. After all, not only did he oppose Joseph McCarthy, he also accepted much of the New Deal, supported Adlai Stevenson's candidacy for president, and warned against the dangers of unregulated capitalism. It is little wonder that, many years later, Buckley would reflect on the "expulsion" of Viereck from the conservative movement and say it was achieved quite easily.[9]

Although his arguments largely fell on deaf ears among conservatives, Viereck insisted that his positions on the issues were consistent with conservative values. He conceded that the New Deal could be excessive, resulting at times in unnecessary government intrusions in the private sphere. But the New Deal should be praised by conservatives because it was humane. In Viereck's view, conservatism does not subscribe to a particular economic program, and liberals should not be able to claim a "monopoly" on compassion. "If such humane reforms, over the centuries, were a monopoly of liberalism," said Viereck, "then who wouldn't be a liberal?"[10] Perhaps more important was the indisputable fact that the New Deal saved capitalism and prevented revolution. "The year 1933 killed radicalism and communism in America," said Viereck, and the New Deal proved "to the plutocrat-resenting masses that their aspiration for economic liberty could be met—via the Squire of Hyde Park—*within* the traditional Constitutional, semi-squirearchical framework." As a result, the masses found no reason to seek "socialist alternatives to the plutocrats."[11] To tear down that which prevented revolution would be radical. Consistent with conservative values would be "a government both accepting the New Deal and pruning, purifying it. This dual need would be fulfilled by Stevenson-style Democrats certainly."[12]

Viereck's admiration for Stevenson seemed boundless. When Viereck called the 1952 presidential campaign of Adlai Stevenson "the finest conservative episode in American history, since the miracle of the Federalist papers,"[13] he was being completely serious. While committed to preserving the New Deal, Stevenson favored curbing its "centralizing" tendencies and "nurturing local patterns." Instead of dismantling the New Deal, Stevenson wanted to improve on its legacy and ensure that it did not trample on the "rich variety of free local traditions."[14] As Viereck was fond of pointing out, even Stevenson saw himself as a conservative. "The strange alchemy of time has somehow converted the Democrats into the truly conservative party of this country—the party dedicated to conserving all that is best, and building solidly and safely on these foundations," said Stevenson on the campaign trail in 1952. "The Republicans, by contrast, are behaving like the radical party—the party of the reckless and the embittered, bent on dismantling institutions which have been built solidly into our social fabric...Certainly there can be nothing more conservative than to change when change is due, to reduce tensions and wants by wise changes, rather than to stand pat stubbornly."[15]

Along with Stevenson and the Democratic Party, Viereck understood that capitalism was not an unqualified good and should not be mistaken for a "sacred religion."[16] While most conservatives of the Buckley school championed limited government, unfettered markets, and big business, Viereck considered them apologists for plutocracy, celebrants of what he called the "cash-nexus," the acquisition of wealth and material goods above all else. They were not real conservatives. "A conservative sympathizes with aristocracy, never plutocracy," said Viereck. "Aristocracy serves; plutocracy grasps…The aristocratic spirit sustaining our democracy is whatever conserves not real-estate values but real values."[17] The modern conservative must acknowledge that *laissez faire* capitalism produces disastrous results for the economy, treats workers inhumanely, atomizes society, and threatens our values. Mindful of this reality, the conservative seeks a balance between "the atomistic disunity of unregulated capitalism" and the "bureaucratic, merely mechanical unity of modern socialism." Neither "the dehumanizing impersonality of capitalist competition" nor "the standardizing unity of statism" is an acceptable option. The conservative must find a middle way in which judicious state regulation of economic life serves to uphold the dignity of the individual without uprooting him from the community that makes life worth living. As long as government regulation of the economy does not undermine the spirit of "voluntary cooperation," which Tocqueville so famously observed in America—and perhaps does what it can to encourage this spirit—a reasonable balance can be struck between "the anti-individual unity of socialism and the anti-social individualism of capitalism."[18]

Viereck pointed to unions as an example of how spirited voluntary communities could temper the dehumanizing effects of capitalism. Although most conservatives were ardent enemies of unions, considering them bastions of radical socialism, Viereck called unions "our most conservative, revolution-preventing force," praising them in particular for "working *within* the capitalist system for increased living standards and increased civil liberties."[19] Even better, unions can achieve their objectives without having to rely on the intrusions of an ever-expanding bureaucratic state. So, for example, instead of benefiting from state-imposed wage controls, unionized workers can negotiate directly with their employer for higher compensation. But Viereck believed that unions do more than just improve the material conditions of workers. They give each worker "a human, cultural, social, and recreational unity with his neighbors, not merely an economic one… an organic sense of community, more medieval (guild-style) than modern." Unlike the modern liberal state, which dispenses benefits efficiently but in the process undermines community and voluntarism, unions cultivate a "sense of belonging" among workers who feel empowered to take control of their own destinies.[20] Few other institutions can legitimately claim to moderate the atomizing forces of both capitalism and the state.

Viereck's support for unions, endorsement of Stevenson, and moderate positions on economic issues put him on the fringes of conservatism. Some of his kindred spirits also considered themselves conservatives, including Clinton Rossiter, Thomas Cook, and Golo Mann (the son of the famous German novelist, Thomas Mann). But most of the people with whom Viereck found common cause and shared similar views came from the left. He even became fond of Norman Thomas, six-time presidential candidate for the Socialist Party. In a telegram sent to Thomas right before his 80th birthday, Viereck praised him as "mankinds [sic] most gallant warrior for justice and dignity against fascism, communism, and inhumanity."[21] Moderate liberal Arthur Schlesinger is a more typical example of an intellectual with whom Viereck forged an alliance. A friend of Viereck's from his undergraduate days at Harvard, Schlesinger urged liberals and conservatives to converge at the "vital center" and to recognize their commonality in the fight against extremism at home and abroad. Of course, associating with the likes of Thomas and Schlesinger provided additional fodder for his conservative critics, but Viereck agreed with Schlesinger that liberals and conservatives had more in common than they were willing to acknowledge.

Before American conservatism became an uncompromising ideology, Viereck also saw the possibility of a "liberal-conservative unity."[22] In fact, he insisted that these various categories or labels—"liberal," "conservative,""socialist"—were not mutually exclusive. For example, one could be a conservative liberal—that is, a liberal influenced by conservative ideas—or even a conservative socialist. This was because conservatism was not an ideology. "It is misleading that 'conservatism' contains the suffix 'ism'," said Viereck. "It is not an ism."[23] In fact, conservatism was "more an implicit temperament, less an articulate philosophy than the other famous isms." And because conservatism was not an ism, it intersected with a full range of ideological perspectives, running the "gamut... from extreme intolerant reaction to an evolutionary moderate spirit," from "authoritarianism" to "liberalism."[24] For this reason, Viereck rejected the rigid ideological demarcations that many of his fellow conservatives wanted to impose. To those conservatives who dismissed him as a closet liberal for his position on the New Deal and other issues, he replied,

"[C]hildren, don't oversimplify, don't pigeonhole; allow for pluralistic overlappings that defy abstract blueprints and labels."[25]

A perfect example of a conservative who refused to be pigeonholed is Prince Clemens Metternich, foreign minister for the Hapsburg Empire from 1809 to 1848, who figures prominently in Viereck's work, especially *Conservatism Revisited.* According to Viereck, the prince was a true conservative who was devoted to stability and internationalism and vehemently opposed to nationalism, radicalism, and relativism. He was also opposed to *laissez faire* capitalism because of its corrosive effects on society.[26] Calling himself in private letters a *"socialiste conservateur"* (conservative socialist), Metternich expressed concern about the proletarian miseries wrought by the industrial revolution and believed that the government "must restrain the new middle-class seizers of power and must subordinate their capitalism to the common welfare." At the same time, he "did not [favor] crushing the middle-class." He merely wanted to put "brakes on [its] rush to power."[27] In the spirit of true conservatism, Metternich resisted doctrinaire prescriptions and rigid ideologies, realizing that reasonable accommodations made to the working class were necessary to prevent social discord, even revolution. Viereck pointed out that there are other conservatives who have followed in Metternich's footsteps, including his protégé, Benjamin Disraeli. The British prime minister, who christened the Tories the Conservative Party upon the recommendation of Metternich, forged an alliance between the aristocracy and the proletariat in the struggle against the increasingly powerful—and rapacious—bourgeoisie.

In Viereck's view, the emphasis on balance and moderation was an appropriate—nay, a necessary—response to a totalitarian age. If any lesson could be learned from the savagery of Nazism and Stalinism, it was that we should remain forever wary of ideologies, ambitious political agendas, and promises of an idyllic future—whether they hail from the left or the right. Extreme libertarianism is just as utopian and romantic as communism for its blatant disregard for historical precedent and empirical reality. The conservative recognizes that humanity can ill afford such fanciful politics, for it always stands at the edge of a precipice, especially in the nuclear age. Understanding politics as the art of the possible, the conservative finds hope in erecting barriers between humanity and the abyss; he has no illusions about the possibility of flying or hovering over it.

Given the rise of totalitarianism and the resulting carnage of World War II, a conservative revival in the mid-twentieth century was not surprising. "A conservative outlook," said Viereck, "is often the result of having witnessed personally an unbearable degree of revolutionary disorder."[28] This was certainly true of Viereck himself. His father, George Sylvester Viereck, a committed German nationalist who had tarnished his reputation by publishing pro-Germany propaganda during World War I, found complete disgrace after he was arrested for conspiring with the Nazis in September 1941. Disgusted with his father, Viereck cleared out all his belongings from the family apartment in New York City and would remain estranged from his father for the next 16 years.[29] During his father's trial, Viereck published his first book, *Metapolitics*, a stinging indictment of Nazism and its intellectual ancestry. He argued that Nazism had deep roots in the German nationalist movements of the nineteenth century, which were inspired largely by the Romantics, including Richard Wagner and Houston Stewart Chamberlain. According to Viereck, the Nazis inherited from the Romantics a virulent hostility toward much of what is most laudable in the Western tradition and a mystical faith in the German Volk. Controversial upon its release, the book's thesis became more credible after the United States entered the war. While his father languished in prison, Viereck served in the Army's Psychological Warfare Branch, for which he analyzed enemy propaganda. His brother, who volunteered to serve in the Army right after Pearl Harbor, was killed in action at Anzio. Viereck saw his father's story as an object lesson in the dangers of delusional attachment to extreme ideologies. Viereck eventually reconciled with his aging father, who lived with his son's family for the last three years of his life. His father finally got around to reading *Metapolitics* at this time. When he finished, he said, "Peter, you were right."[30]

Although his personal story may have informed his thought, perhaps intensifying his revolt against ideology, Viereck had already shown himself to be an ardent conservative before the events just described. As a recent graduate of Harvard who had been awarded its top essay and poetry prizes, Viereck received an invitation from *The Atlantic Monthly* to write about "the meaning of young liberalism for the present age." In response, he submitted a long essay entitled "But—I'm a Conservative!"[31] Published in April 1940, the article called for a conservatism based on "common sense" and dedicated to the "conservation" of the "values basic to every civilized society and creed...in order that all may be free." Viereck identified both Nazi Germany and Stalinist Russia as equal threats to freedom and civilized values. Their surface differences notwithstanding, they shared a chilling enthusiasm for the omnipotent state. At home, he believed that both communist "fellow travelers" and libertarians ("self-styled Liberty Leaguers") were also equally harmful. Whereas fellow travelers failed "to repudiate Lenin's formulae of class war and proletarian dictatorship," Liberty Leaguers offered "only negative liberty to starve and be unemployed." At the end of the article, Viereck said it was his "great dream, perhaps young and naïve," that America could "synthesize cultural, spiritual, and political conservatism with economic reform." This synthesis would "be broad enough to include some economic ends of the radicals" but would "exclude the means of the communazis."[32] While sympathetic with reform efforts meant to achieve humane goals, conservatism rejects the chilling totalitarian (or "communazi") logic that the ends justify the means. For conservatism rests on "a humanist reverence for the dignity of the individual soul," precluding any measures that make people expendable or superfluous.[33] Every means to an end must be recognized as an end in itself. Likewise, all people must be recognized as ends in themselves.

But the tragedy of the human condition, said Viereck, is that the impulse to treat others as means to an end, to exercise mastery and control over them, will never disappear. It is our nature, sown into the fiber of our being. Anyone who has read George Orwell's *1984* will remember the bleak vision of the future described by O'Brien. "If you want a picture of the future," he said, "imagine a boot stamping on a human face—forever."[34] This is a perfect illustration of how Viereck viewed human nature.

"Every modern baby is still born a caveman baby"

Although conservatives may share humanitarian goals with many liberals, the primary bone of contention between them is their divergent views on human nature. The conservative, said Viereck, subscribes to the doctrine of original sin, either literally or metaphorically. Whatever the cause may be, human beings are fallen creatures, born with an immense capacity for wickedness and cruelty. "In his natural instincts," said Viereck, "every modern baby is still born a caveman baby."[35] The conservative must begin with the premise that "every human being is by nature barbarous, capable of every insanity and atrocity" and is "naturally prone to anarchy, evil, mutual destruction."[36] Liberals and radicals, on the other hand, believe just the opposite. They tend to maintain a "faith in the natural goodness of man, the infinite perfectibility of the masses."[37] No matter how often history and literature provide evidence to the contrary, "progressives still cling to their Rousseauistic faith in the infinite perfectibility of human nature."[38] In a nutshell, while the conservative calls attention to the moral frailties of human beings, the liberal sees an untapped potential for goodness.

Viereck was fully aware of the political implications of this difference of opinion about human nature. Because of their optimistic account of human nature, liberals have much greater confidence in the masses—and in their capacity for self-governance. They have no fear that pure democracy may result in majority tyranny; in fact, they believe social progress is all but certain so long as power rests in the hands of the people. Maintaining this optimism requires liberals to be "color-blind to tragedy" and "blind to the lessons of history."[39] This may be an unfair assessment on Viereck's part, for liberals certainly acknowledge the reality of evil and injustice in the world. Unlike conservatives, however, liberals believe that evil and injustice originate not in human nature but in social, economic, or political structures. Bringing an end to a particular injustice, then, simply becomes a matter of changing external reality. Viereck saw how this logic—taken to its extreme—could lead to a dangerously utopian political agenda. "If you deem evil external, if consequently you deem utopia just around the corner," said Viereck,

> then you cannot blame human nature or the masses for the failure of utopia to arrive. Instead, you are then tempted to blame some small aristocratic or plutocratic "conspiracy." The next step, while still believing in democracy and "the people," is to step up an undemocratic terrorist dictatorship in order to purge these "unnatural" aristocrats or plutocrats,...[the] sole obstacles to the mass utopia inherent in "nature."[40]

In other words, a belief in the malleability of human nature opens the door to totalitarianism. If someone believes in "the perfectibility of man," he can justify using "those freedom-destroying 'bad means' (totalitarianism) that promise the quickest shortcut to this 'good end.'" To paraphrase the Nobel Prize-winning poet Czeslaw Milosz, faith in the earthly paradise justifies all crimes. Destroying this faith can bring an end to the totalitarian temptation.

Viereck understood that most liberals did not take their optimistic view of human nature to its logical extreme. The end result would probably not be a totalitarian nightmare. But Viereck considered it important to show how liberal optimism about human nature creates opportunities for a more ambitious, even a more radical, political agenda, in which attempts to promote the general welfare compromise individual liberty. While liberals do not worry so much about the tension between equality and liberty, between the collective and the individual, conservatives are forever concerned about it. In their view, reformers almost always give precedence to social equality over individual liberty. As a way of resolving this dilemma, Viereck favored humanitarian reform that did not cross what he called the statist line. "This is the line beyond which the social gains are outweighed by the loss in private rights."[41] This solution is a perfect example of how Viereck searched for middle ground where both conservatives and liberals could find agreement.

But ensuring that reform did not cross the statist line was only possible if conservative pessimism was made to check the humanitarian impulse of liberalism, if a heavy dose of conservative realism was used to counteract liberal idealism. How could this be achieved?

> The conservative sees the inner, unremovable nature of man as the ultimate source of evil; sees man's social task as coming to terms with a world in which evil is perpetual and in which justice and compassion will both be perpetually necessary. His tools for this task are the maintenance of ethical restraints inside the individual and the maintenance of unbroken, continuous social patterns inside the given culture as a whole.[42]

Because evil is inherent to man, it cannot be eradicated. We must accept the barbarous nature of humanity and promote those values and traditions that serve to restrain its most dangerous impulses. While values do their work internally through the development of conscience, traditions operate externally by maintaining socially acceptable patterns and modes of behavior. In Freudian terms, values fortify the Super-Ego, the inner parent; traditions provide clear behavioral guidelines for the Ego, which adheres to the reality principle. Together, they domesticate the Id.

The problem with liberals and radicals, according to Viereck, is that they do not recognize the need for such restraints. Rousseau famously lamented that "Man was born free but is everywhere in chains." After quoting this passage, Viereck replied: "In chains, and so he ought to be." Unlike liberals heavily influenced by Rousseau, the conservative understood "the good and wise and necessary chains of rooted tradition and historic continuity… Without the chaos-chaining, the Id-chaining heritage of rooted values, what is to keep man from becoming Eichmann?"[43]

Interestingly, the doctrine of original sin that played such an important role in Viereck's thought was in tension with his view that "the need for value codes and the existence of ethics is innate in man." Human beings were sinful, barbarous creatures, but they contained within them the source of their own redemption. "Ethics inhere in man," he said; "values *are*." By nature man was an "evaluating animal" who discriminated between right and wrong. Viereck conceded that he had no way of proving that this was the case; he reached this conclusion from observations of human experience. "I do deeply believe that values and the Christian ethics not only are innate and universal but are the most important and most distinguishing characteristic of man."[44] Taken out of context, the preceding passage might suggest that Viereck agreed with the Rousseauean conception of human nature. Nothing could be further from the truth. He merely believed that human beings were ambivalent creatures. The better and worse angels of their nature waged a constant battle. In the end, however, there was reason for hope. Despite their fallen state, human beings were able to recognize the need for maintaining ethical values as a way of restraining the monstrous Id within.

"Aspirations of the Past"

The most effective means of restraining the darker impulses of human nature was clearly tradition. One of the "earmarks" of conservatism, according to Viereck, was "a trust in unbroken historical continuity and in some traditional framework to tame human nature."[45] Recall that, to his mind, every person is born a caveman. "What prevents today's baby from remaining a caveman is the conservative force of law and tradition, that slow accumulation of civilized habits separating us from the cave."[46] Law can be understood as the codification of tradition. Together, law and tradition represent a bulwark against anarchy and disorder. People must observe even bad laws and traditions until they can be changed through legitimate means. The consequences of rebellion and disobedience are grave. "He who irresponsibly incites revolutionary mob emotions against some minor abuse within a good tradition, may bring the whole house crashing down on his head and find himself back in the jungle—or its ethical equivalent, the police-state," said Viereck, echoing sentiments expressed by Abraham Lincoln in his famous Lyceum Speech. "You weaken the aura of all good laws every time you break a bad one—or every time you take a short cut around the 'due process' of a good one." This is why vigilante justice is never justifiable. "The lynching of the guilty is a subtler but no less deadly blow to civilization than the lynching of the innocent."[47]

The conservative demands unwavering reverence for law and tradition because they are an inheritance from our ancestors who fashioned them on the anvil of experience. To ignore the wisdom wrought from past experience is reckless. "Conservatism is a treasure house, sometimes an infuriatingly dusty one, of generations of accumulated experience, which any ephemeral rebellious generation has a right to disregard—at its peril." It is difficult for people to know how to behave if they rely only on abstractions or theories as a guide. But knowing that a particular way of doing things has stood the test of time gives us confidence that it is right. This is why Viereck insisted that "the best sanction is the community's experience of having lived it for centuries, the feeling of it 'always' being so and being there." In the end, this conservative reverence for law and tradition functions as "a social and cultural cement, holding together what western man has built."[48]

According to Viereck, the Western heritage has roots in the "moral commandments and social justice of Judaism"; the devotion to "beauty" and "intellectual speculation" of Hellas; the "exaltation of objective rule of law" and "universalism" of Rome; and the "love, mercy, and charity" (i.e., the Golden Rule) of Christianity.[49] Because the Western heritage has several traditions that create "inner contradictions" not always easily reconciled, it necessarily calls for "diversity within unity" and a "tolerant pluralism."[50] Despite the inevitable tensions and disagreements that will arise within this diverse tradition, a respect for the preciousness of the individual soul must remain paramount. It is not only the best way to maintain "diversity within unity"; it is also the one value common to all four traditions. Even the Greeks, who placed great emphasis on unity and the common good, extolled "the ideal of individual liberty, the ideal of free self-expression whether in philosophy, art, or politics." Thanks in part to this inheritance, Viereck argued, "we can talk today about civil liberties, the Bill of Rights, the 'Rights of Man.'"[51]

The link between individual liberty and tradition was inextricable for Viereck. Only within the parameters of a traditional framework can people actually enjoy freedom. "Painfully, over aeons, civilization stamps its traditional and conservative values upon men. Only within these values, or traffic lights, are freedom and objective justice possible." Viereck had great fondness for the metaphor of the "traffic light" that regulates behavior but ultimately serves the interests of freedom. A busy road system without traffic lights would create anarchy and confusion, leading to more accidents and injuries. This is why revolutionaries, who want to smash the traffic lights of law and tradition, are not freedom fighters but the forerunners of tyranny. "What actually keeps a free society free? Society is kept free by the traffic lights of law, not by the revolutionary lawlessness of well-meaning radicals and hasty innovators," said Viereck. "[Revolution] means the total economic and psychological disruption of the social mechanism, with disaster, starvation, and new tyranny."[52] Freedom can only exist in a well-ordered and stable society that finds a middle way between "anything goes" (anarchy) and "nothing goes" (tyranny). Neither extreme is a safe place for the individual.

Individual freedom continues to thrive so long as Western society continues to embrace "diversity within unity." In this context, people agree to disagree and feel free to speak their minds about existing problems while remaining respectful of precedent. Conservatism, then, does not call for a blind acceptance of the past. Moreover, it "never admires the past passively in sterile escapism. It must daily and actively re-experience, as if for the first time, the aspirations of the past—and then fulfill them in the future." This "fresh and creative traditionalism" requires us to act on the "aspirations of the past"—to put them into daily practice—in order that present and future concerns can be addressed.[53] Unwavering loyalty and conformity to past practices is what characterizes the reactionary. "But not all the past is worth keeping," said Viereck. "The conservative conserves discriminately, the reactionary indiscriminately." The conservative recognizes that history often gives lessons in what *not* to do. "By 'tradition' the conservative means all the lessons of the past but only the ethically acceptable events. The reactionary means all the events. Thereby he misses the lessons."[54]

All this suggests that traditions evolve. On top of ancient traditions sprout new ways of doing things. Most of the old roots remain, but above the soil a vibrant tree grows and stretches its limbs. The true conservative must be able to distinguish "living roots" from "lifeless ones." Living roots are traditions that build on the past but continue to have practical relevance today. Lifeless roots, "contrived by romantic nostalgia," are those that were "either never existent or no longer existent."[55] He accused faux conservatives—including most Old Guard Republicans, Buckley's *National Review* crowd, and even Russell Kirk—of yearning for lifeless roots or having a "rootless nostalgia for roots." In a similar vein, Viereck charged them with making an "unhistorical appeal to history" in their hope to recapture an imaginary or obsolete past. Instead of accepting the viable tradition in front of them, they sought to fashion one out of thin air or import another from a time and place alien to the American experience. "In contrast, a genuinely rooted, history-minded conservative conserves roots that are really there."[56]

The best example of this "rootless nostalgia for roots"—or what Viereck also referred to as the "traditionless worship of tradition"—was the dream among many post-war conservatives of restoring a pastoral agrarian society in which the government would be strictly limited to protecting negative liberties. "Such romanticizing conservatives refuse to face up to the old and solid historical roots of most or much American liberalism," said Viereck. "What is really rootless and abstract is not the increasingly conservatized New Deal liberalism but the romantic conservatives' own utopian dream of an aristocratic agrarian restoration" conjured by "writers like Russell Kirk."[57] As wonderful as this portrait of eighteenth-century America may appear, it hardly reflected the twentieth-century experience of most people in this country. Ignoring the challenges posed by the reality of an urban and industrial America, faux conservatives opposed the social reforms created under the New Deal, even after many of them had proven to save and improve capitalism and, after a generation, had established solid historical roots.

In Viereck's view, then, the New Deal represents a recent offshoot of ancient traditions. Faux conservatives did not see it that way. Their goal was to dismantle the New Deal legacy because it reflected liberal values. But conservatives needed to accept the fact that a significant part of the American tradition *is* liberal, much of it worth preserving because it grew out of even older traditions. While the New Deal certainly involved innovation and experimentation, both hallmarks of liberalism, it also built on many values inherited from the Western tradition, including Christian charity, Judaic social justice, Roman rule of law, and the classical liberal call for economic freedom. Nevertheless, the "rootless doctrinaires" who called themselves conservatives insisted on adhering to their abstract principles, refusing to build on "the concrete existing historical base" of which the New Deal was an integral part.[58]

According to Viereck, post-war conservatives became enamored with what he often called "Manchester liberalism"—a distorted version of classical liberalism—and jettisoned every other inheritance from the Western tradition. He used the term Manchester liberalism synonymously with *laissez faire* liberalism, and he deemed it a shameless apology for "the recent and rootless outlook of the Gilded Age robber-barons of the late nineteenth century." Despite what Old Guard Republicans contended, Manchester liberalism was "neither old nor traditional nor conservative."[59] It was a relatively new idea used to defend "a program of almost unlimited free enterprise, hostile to all social reform," and to provide intellectual cover for what amounts to unfettered greed. In the end, Manchester liberalism was not rooted in the Western tradition so much as it was a set of principles based on a priori reasoning.

As Viereck astutely pointed out, the same could be said of the French Revolution, which was inspired by the Enlightenment. Anathema to all conservatives because of its radical rejection of tradition, the French Revolution "had brought to power the anti-aristocratic, commercial middle class" who wanted to bring about "an atomistic society of laissez-faire liberalism and economic free enterprise" and once and for all bring an end to "the state-controls of an organic, monarchic society." In other words, *laissez faire* became the rallying cry for a group of radicals who wanted to destroy the traditional aristocratic order and replace it with a new bourgeois ruling class. In embracing *laissez faire* wholeheartedly, post-war conservatives revealed their contempt for tradition and proved themselves to be the heirs of the French Revolution. They were radical defenders of plutocracy disguised as Burkean conservatives.[60]

Viereck believed that the true conservative did not promise to crush the aristocratic order in the name of economic freedom for the middle class. In fact, the conservative had a reflexive distaste for the crass materialism of the bourgeois "shopkeeper" and was keenly aware of his community obligations, embracing such ideals as honor, chivalry, and *noblesse oblige*. It was the latter ideal especially that inspired Prime Minister Benjamin Disraeli, whose concern about inequality and poverty was so great that he enfranchised the working class with the passage of the Reform Bill of 1867. Other important reforms followed under his leadership, making Disraeli the symbol of what came to be known as "Tory socialism." The idea was to forge not just a politically convenient alliance between the aristocracy and the working class but a stronger bond between the rich and the poor more generally. Disraeli saw this bond as a necessary precursor to improving the lives of the poor. He also feared that, if given the opportunity, the bourgeoisie would turn Great Britain into "Two Nations" (rich and poor) at war with each other.

Disraeli's "Tory socialism" speaks to another crucial aspect of conservatism that often gets overlooked. Faux conservatives wanted to reorganize society in accordance with certain fixed principles and, once achieved, make sure that it remained forever the same. They supported radical change to bring about their ideal society, after which they would resist all change. But, according to Viereck, neither upheaval nor immobility is compatible with conservatism. The real conservative advocates incremental change within the parameters of a traditional framework. Viereck was fond of summarizing the conservative position on social change with the following statement by Disraeli: "In a progressive country change is constant; and the great question is, not whether you should resist change which is inevitable, but whether that change should be carried out in deference to the manners, the customs, the laws, the traditions of the people, or in deference to abstract principles and arbitrary and general doctrines."[61]

"OUR ROAD TO HELL WILL BE PAVED WITH GOOD INVENTIONS"

Like Disraeli before him, Viereck held that the real conservative acknowledges the inevitability of change but cautions against hasty innovation, trying to accomplish too much too quickly. In a time when everything seemed to be moving at breakneck speed, Viereck believed in slowing down the pace of change. This did not mean that the conservative envisions bringing everything to a standstill. Indeed, Viereck found many occasions to quote the following epigram from Burke: "A state without the means of some change is without the means of its conservation."[62] Viereck understood that a stubborn adherence to the status quo could actually stoke the fires of revolution or, at the very least, make people woefully unprepared for the change that is coming. Either way, clinging to the past indiscriminately could lead to disorder. If the aim of conservatism is to promote stability and harmony in the social order, then neither revolution nor reaction is constructive. The true conservative, then, is a reformer. He sees cautious reform as a middle way between the extremes of dynamism and stasis, revolution and reaction, initiating judicious change when necessary and also working to mitigate forces of change that emerge in society.

Before Viereck became a marginal figure in the movement, there was still considerable debate about what constituted the appropriate conservative response to capitalism. One could not dispute the fact that capitalism was a source of sweeping change in industrial societies, uprooting people from traditional ways of life and situating them in entirely new modes of economic production and social relation. According to Viereck, the truly Burkean conservative does not regret the rise of capitalism or long quixotically for a mythic agrarian past. He accepts the inevitability of capitalism and recognizes many of its obvious benefits, including significant increases in productivity and material wealth. Nevertheless, the conservative does not embrace capitalism uncritically. He sees the disruptive social and economic effects of unrestrained capitalism and thus considers it his mission to address the problem through social and economic reform.

The success of such reforms serves as a vital reminder that it is wrong to exaggerate the evils of capitalism or to predict its ultimate downfall. Marx's bold prophesies notwithstanding, capitalism did not collapse under the pressure of revolution because of its inherent contradictions. On the contrary, capitalism proved to be far more resilient and adaptable than many critics on the left were willing to admit. As recent history made evident, its energies could be channeled in more humane and socially productive ways.[63] At the same time, Buckley and others on the far right were equally wrong in their prediction that all liberal or socialist reforms push us down a slippery slope toward tyranny. In fact, said Viereck, conservatives have always understood that the absence of reform is more apt to produce tyranny. For "150 years" they have feared that "*laissez faire* liberalism was allowing industrial mechanization to become not the servant but the tyrant of man."[64] For this reason, they believe that "humane reform takes precedence over *laissez faire*."[65] While either capitalism or socialism taken to an extreme is clearly undesirable, a balance between the two results in prudent reform.

Those who represented the gravest threat in the twentieth century were not the reformers but the ideological extremists who called for constant innovation and revolution in an attempt to remake the world in the image of their utopian ideal. Both Stalinists and Nazis were ideologues committed to realizing their dreams without any regard for history or tradition and without concern for the inhumane consequences. Armed with the most powerful technologies available in the twentieth century, they faced few obstacles that could put a stop to their horrific ambitions. Reflecting on the lessons learned from the experiences of totalitarianism, Viereck often made the gloomy prediction that "our road to hell will be paved with good inventions."[66] By "invention" Viereck meant any kind of innovation, technological or otherwise.

The most important inventions that paved the way for communism, fascism, and Nazism were in fact ideas, according to Viereck. Originating in the nineteenth century, these ideas—including Romanticism, nationalism, utilitarianism, positivism, and Social Darwinism, to name a few—gave rise to a "revolution in values" that "liquidated the ethical restraints governing the means society used to reach their ends."[67] In other words, with the death of traditional sources of moral authority came the relativistic view that everything is permissible. The end result was a series of political revolutions that found it surprisingly easy to defy the values of Western civilization. Revolutionaries were able to effect significant changes, but the costs were immeasurable: the complete deprivation of individual freedom and dignity, untold bloodshed and terror, and the nightmarish experiment in total domination.

Compared to the ideological zealots who turned their backs on the Western tradition, conservatives, liberals, and even democratic socialists share humane goals and agree on the prudent means of achieving them. That said, there are key differences worth mentioning. By temperament the conservative is wary of change and therefore "puts the burden of proof on the innovator." He "sees change as disruptive to the traditional framework unless...it grows organically out of the concrete historical context." In his view, change to existing institutions should be natural, growing like a tree out of traditional roots. His liberal counterpart, frustrated with those who put obstacles in the way of progress, usually "puts the burden of proof...on the anti-innovator." He "plans change from abstract a priori generalizations"—from blueprints derived from logic—without regard for history or tradition.[68] Unmoored from the past, the liberal sees reform as the "mechanical moving-around of institutions as if they were separate pieces of furniture."[69] For liberals, reform is simply an exercise in making reality conform to an abstract plan. Tradition does not hold them back or create limits.

This posed a problem for Viereck. Nothing in the liberal's traditionless approach ensures gradualism. His appeals to reason and wariness of tradition open the door to reckless innovation. Even worse, if reason fails the liberal, as it did for so many in the nineteenth century with the emergence of relativism, he is left without any principles or truths to guide him. When his absolutes disappear, anything goes. Viereck said:

> liberalism unintentionally paved the way for Hitlerism and Stalinism. Liberalism always begins attractively by liberating men from absurd old prejudices and aristocratic excesses. It ends tragically by putting all men in the position of those few illuminati who, when initiated into the seventh circle of Syria's medieval Order of Assassins, were told the Order's secret of secrets: "*There is no truth; everything is permitted.*"[70]

But the conservative, having never relied on reason alone, can still stand on foundational truths forged by tradition. In so doing, he finds a middle way between absolutism and relativism (or nihilism), between "nothing goes" and "anything goes." It is to Viereck's conservative epistemology that we now turn.

"PARTICULARIZED UNIVERSALITY"

The problem with both relativism and absolutism is that they really just represent opposite sides of the same coin. Relativism taken to an extreme creates a situation where there is no way of settling disputes between competing conceptions of the good or truth; the final arbiter becomes power or might. As Bertrand Russell said, in a relativistic world, truth would be determined by the person with the largest Maxim gun. But absolutism introduces a similar problem because inevitably there will be disagreement on matters of the good and truth between groups that claim to be right on the basis of their unassailable logic or god. Compromise between these groups who are equally certain of their righteousness is impossible. Again, only conflict will settle the matter. Power will be the final judge on matters of right and wrong.

It should be made clear that, for Viereck, relativism was the main source of war and conflict in the age of totalitarianism.[71] For this reason, he reserved most of his criticism for liberals such as John Dewey. Because Deweyan liberals smuggled certain Western values into their philosophical systems, their relativism did not degenerate into a celebration of "might makes right."[72] That said, their refusal to accept any universal standards for distinguishing truth from falsehood, right from wrong, led ultimately to Hitler's chilling formulation that "the sole earthly criterion of whether an enterprise is right or wrong is its success."[73] Viereck was deeply concerned about the apathy that plagued many students coming of age in the mid-twentieth century. Too "sophisticated" to have "passionate commitments" of any kind, students had no way of responding to Hitler. In fact, they seemed decidedly blasé about the gravest threats to Western civilization. Viereck recalled reading with consternation about a student who, in the spring of 1942, approached her professor after class and said quite earnestly: "I can't see that we have any right to condemn Hitler. After all, he has a different standard of morality and has just as much right to his views as we have to ours." He blamed "moral relativism" not only for the Hitlers of the world, who believed "everything is permissible" and then acted on it, but also for the millions of others who lacked the conviction to condemn them.[74] This was especially troublesome, according to Viereck, as the United States tried to gather the strength and courage needed in the struggle against communism.

While Viereck considered relativism the more blameworthy culprit, he argued almost as vehemently that the solution was not absolutism.

Absolutism can actually create the conditions for relativism and disorder. "If you make no allowance for pluralism and aim at too much unity," said Viereck, "you will get no unity at all; you will only provoke the same internal strife and chaos that you condemn in those who seek too little unity." For this reason, the "alternative" to the "value-vacuum" created by Dewey and other liberals "is not the arbitrary imposition of values by a new Inquisition. 'Anything goes' is neither crushed nor cured by saying 'Nothing goes.'"[75] The problem with "Nothing goes" is that it always identifies a single authority as the source of truth and morality. Intolerant of diversity and unwilling to accept any compromise, the absolutist in effect throws down his gauntlet, making it clear that he is prepared to fight anyone who refuses to conform to his truth. Bloodshed ensues when two absolutists with different values occupy the same space.

In his search for a middle way between absolutism and relativism, Viereck borrowed heavily from the ideas of Burke. Viereck shared with the father of conservatism a deep suspicion of deductive logic and a priori reasoning, especially when people using these methods claim to have discovered immutable truths about politics. The descendants of Burke share an epistemological humility that prevents them from making assertions with complete certainty and then acting on them. The true conservative is forever mindful of the dangers associated with turning abstract blueprints into concrete plans for action. "Even the most logical formula," said Viereck, "even or especially the most brilliant, distorts some essential of the original concrete situation." Abstract ideas derived from other abstract ideas may be logically sound but they do not necessarily accord with reality. As a result, using them as plans for action could be perilous. Quite rightly, said Viereck, Burkean conservatives have often blamed "a priori 'eighteenth century rationalism'" for "the chaos and terror of the French Revolution."[76] They have also been quick to point out that other eminently rational ideas, above all Marxist–Leninism, resulted in political cataclysms.

Wary of applying abstract ideas to political reality, conservatives tend to be "anti-theoretical" and resist the impulse to make generalizations. According to Viereck, it is the liberal who revels in abstract formulas and theories, giving him a significant advantage when engaged in intellectual combat. "In ideological debates, the immediate winner will be the progressive, the man with a priori formulas for bettering society. The loser will be the conservative, the man who flounders confusedly, like some village idiot." It should come as no surprise that the conservative cannot defeat the liberal in a debate, for his "philosophy is inarticulate, inexpressible."

Viereck would often remind his readers that liberalism is a creed while conservatism is a temperament, a way of being. As he put it: "Liberalism argues, conservatism simply is."[77]

This does not mean that conservatism is fatuous or anti-intellectual. The crucial point to understand is that, for Burkean conservatives, there is no arguing one's way to the truth. However persuasive and logically sound an argument may be, its correspondence with truth is hardly certain. At the heart of conservative philosophy is a belief that human beings are epistemologically fallible, prone to making mistakes in the quest for knowledge and truth. Because he sees theorizing about politics as a foolhardy enterprise, the conservative has no interest in becoming practiced at debate. Instead, he receives guidance from "concrete history-evolved conditions which he is unable to verbalize."[78]

Unlike most liberals and progressives, Burkean conservatives believe that truths are ultimately "rooted in historical experience." As a result, they cannot support their arguments with just a few pithy syllogisms. Faced with a far more painstaking task, they must sift through the historical evidence and slowly build a case from the scraps of knowledge they gather along the way. Viereck praised Burke because he "was concrete and inductive; he preferred prudence and experience to deductive logic." Eschewing both the hyper-rationality of the Enlightenment and the anti-rationality of Romanticism, Burke "had his own kind of reasonableness; its base was neither deductive rationalism nor an instinct-exalting romanticism but a playing by ear, based on experience."[79] The conservative does not place his trust in either reason or intuition. He prudently draws on the facts of concrete experience from which he infers general truths.

Burke argued, for example, that rights cannot be derived through abstract reasoning but rather only in response to concrete problems requiring prescription. Hence, his preference for "prescriptive rights" over "abstract rights." Ever the Burkean, Viereck agreed that a claim on liberty becomes legitimate by virtue of "the prescriptive right of unbroken institutional continuity, the unspoken community sense of what is lawful…not expressible in precise economic abstractions of either capitalism or socialism." He said: "Historic liberties are legitimate because [they] evolved from concrete, lived experience, in contrast with liberalism's abstract, unlived Rights of Man."[80]

It is important to stress that conservatives such as Burke and Viereck do not refer to experience in the individual subjective sense. To determine what is right, not only must we turn to the experiences of our contemporaries;

we must also heed the lessons of our ancestors. Much of the debate between the left and the right—indeed, between Paine and Burke in the late eighteenth century—boils down to this very question: How much deference should be paid to past experiences? "Liberals favor universal suffrage horizontally in time," said Viereck. "Conservatives favor it also vertically…you must give the vote also to your ancestors."[81] The Burkean conservative says that we should never ignore the experience-based wisdom of our ancestors. After all, as the philosopher George Santayana famously said, those who do not learn from history are doomed to repeat it. It is for this reason that the conservative seeks guidance from traditions, customs, and institutions inherited from previous generations. They are the product of experience accumulated over time.

Burkean conservatives such as Viereck see tradition as the embodiment or reification of truth. As he put it, "Conservatism tends to embody truth, liberalism to know it."[82] This epigram encapsulates Viereck's view that truth inheres in the concrete world of past experience and practices, not in the abstract world of theories and formulas. While the use of reason has its place and can be useful, the truth is never made manifest until it is *lived*. This is especially the case with respect to values or ethical truths. "To make people live the ethical check instead of only theorizing it, the best sanction is the community's experience of having lived it for centuries, the feeling of it 'always' being so and being there," said Viereck. "Whether your source for our ethical code is natural or supernatural or that blurred borderline to which both science and religion tend, only this conservative experience of communal tradition will turn it from abstraction into a way of life." Knowing that past generations have already tested an idea and found it prudent "to formalize and institutionalize it" inspires people to accept it as truth and live by it.[83] Whether a truth originated in reason or religious faith is not nearly as important as the fact that it has stood the test of time. If it was good enough for our revered ancestors, then it is very likely to be good enough for us.

Seeing tradition as the reification of truth does not mean that we should accept everything we inherit from our ancestors. That would be the way of the reactionary. "The romanticizing reactionary swallows the past indiscriminately," whereas the "conservative assimilates it discriminately."[84] The conservative chooses selectively in his borrowing from the past largely because he knows he cannot ignore the present. In his utter contempt for contemporary life, the reactionary revolts against it. "The [reactionary] sometimes seems just as revolutionary against the existing present as the radical Jacobin or the Marxist, only in the opposite direction," said Viereck. "The Burkean, in contrast, does come to terms with the reality of inevitable change."[85] The conservative, then, does not see truth as an immutable treasure discovered ages ago by our ancestors, which the present generation need only pass on to the next generation unsullied and intact. Instead, said Viereck, he acknowledges that each generation must add its unique vantage point and work to keep inherited truths "fresh" and relevant to contemporary life. Each generation "daily and actively re-experience[s], as if for the first time, the aspirations of the past."[86] In the process it reveals the malleability of inherited truth.

At times, Viereck's epistemology revels in the particulars so much that it borders on relativism. He believed that ideas put into practice in one place may not work in another because of differences in tradition and history. In his discussions of freedom, for example, he often cited the Burkean view that "transplanting" a constitution and free institutions from one country to another will probably not work. This is because there is no such thing as an abstract conception of freedom with universal applicability. "Since freedom grows organically in its native soil and cannot be transplanted in 'liberal' fashion," said Viereck, it is foolish to think we can "schoolmasterishly" persuade another country to "adopt our foreign democratic constitution wholesale."[87] Each country must find its own path to freedom. This example points to an apparent tension between tradition and universal values in Viereck's thought. The belief that truth is tied to tradition, bound to a particular time and place, runs contrary to universalism.

Aware of this problem, Viereck tried to work out a synthesis of tradition and eternal values, of the particular and universal truth, which he called "particularized universality." In order to achieve this synthesis, he made an important distinction between absolute and universal values. Conceding that "nothing mortal is absolutely absolute," Viereck argued that it is preferable to speak of "universals" rather than "absolutes." "Universals," he said, "are those rediscovered values, transcending national, class, and individual differences, which are *relatively absolute*." (Emphasis added.) Despite the rich variety of traditions throughout the world, there are certain "relative absolutes" that grow out of those experiences common to all civilized peoples. "To the general laws of ethics, civilization subordinates the ego of any individual and the ego of Lenin's 'class' or of the fascist's 'nation.' This view is permanently innate in the experience of man," Viereck said. "But it must be newly learnt by every generation." What all people learn from "bitter experience" is that our precarious existence in this world cannot be sustained without guidance from transcendent values, even if they are not real.

> Suppose it were some day proved—as today alleged but unproved—that these universals ('relative absolutes') of right and wrong are indeed mere bourgeois prejudices. Suppose it were proved that right and wrong do not exist. Our instinctive comment would be: so much the worse for right and wrong. But our more reflective comment would be: so much the worst for existence. For we would learn soon enough, through bitter experience, that man can only maintain his individual and material existence through guiding it by the nonexistent: by the moral universals of the spirit. If to logic this sounds like paradox and untruth, then it is of such paradoxes that human truth is made.[88]

Even if the relativist proves he is right, that there is no universal morality, "so much the worst for existence." For humanity depends for its very survival on the common belief in an admittedly "nonexistent" (or certainly unsubstantiated) universal moral spirit. The implication here is that universal moral standards may not exist, but they are pragmatically true—that is, they have proven useful, and even necessary, in the human experience.

Viereck's preference for pragmatic thinking can be seen in his views on human nature. While he argued that universal moral standards are largely hewn from human experience, he also contended that they grow in part out of man's nature. As he put it, "the need for value codes and the existence of ethics is innate in man, innate only in man, innate in all men without exception." But Viereck added an important caveat. "This becomes obvious through experience, but can never be 'proved.'"[89] Viereck did not rely on deductive logic or reason to prove conclusively that ethics are innate in all human beings. That is not possible. The most he could do was make use of induction, trusting his observations of concrete experience and arriving at a tentative conclusion.

By stressing the importance of experience, however, Viereck indicated that it did not really matter where moral universals originate. Until they are applied—that is, given concrete life—in a particular time and place, they do not have any definite purpose. Values may stem from "the universal religion of Christianity," or even from human nature, but they "are ineffective abstractions unless meanwhile rooted internally in some concrete historic past."[90] In other words, universal truths about right and wrong only become real when they are reified in a particular tradition. There will most certainly be variation in the application of universal truths, which is why Viereck called them "relative absolutes," but these differences do not belie the fact that there are general laws to which we all look for guidance and inspiration. People worship different gods whose stories are recounted in a variety of sacred texts, but the universal grammar underlying these various traditions is evident. Viereck believed that this Burkean synthesis of the particular and the universal—what he called "particularized universality"—avoids both the runaway amorality of relativism and the fruitless abstractions of absolutism.

This synthesis gave Viereck a pragmatic flexibility in his policy positions. He accepted the generous welfare state, for example, so long as its efforts did not cross the "statist margin"—which "may be defined as the line beyond which liberty is sacrificed to security." Once public policy crosses this line, said Viereck, "the gain in local working conditions…is less than the loss of liberty, so that the balance sheet holds a net loss for society as a whole."[91] This formulation seems to conflict with Viereck's unequivocal rejection of utilitarianism, the view that overall success is the final criterion for justice. But Viereck's discussion of the statist margin is not utilitarian so much as it is pragmatic. He was trying to strike a balance between two legitimate goals—liberty and security—without sacrificing too much of either. Viereck always insisted that the Burkean conservative cannot adhere slavishly to abstract definitions of freedom when trying to determine the right course of action in a political matter. Instead, he must draw on past practices and present facts in his search for a feasible solution. Unlike the "fanatic ideologue," the conservative "knows the humble wisdom of the second best when the best is historically impossible."[92] Serving truth requires making an honest attempt to apply universal values to a particular time and place. It also demands a humble recognition of our fallibility, our limited knowledge, and capabilities.

"The aristocratic spirit"

For Viereck, "particularized universality" is realized most readily in art, especially literature. He believed that universal values stem not only from experience but also *imagined* experience. Each individual has a fairly narrow range of experiences, so he must picture what other human beings experience in order to arrive at universal moral standards. Great literature stirred the moral imagination, facilitating the discovery and reaffirmation of universal values. "The distinctive value of literature is that it enables one to share intensely and imaginatively the rich, varied experience of men of all ages who have been confronted with human problems."[93] Heightening our empathy for others, literature helps us imagine what it is like to walk in their shoes. It should come as no surprise that Viereck saw the humanities—especially the study of the Great Books in literature, art, and history—as a bulwark against the many threats to civilization. Those subjects give color to "the rich, varied experience of men of all ages" and make it easier for us to empathize. The value of the Great Books is that they are morally instructive without being didactic or preachy. They do not tell us how we must act; they give us, rather, a panoramic view of the human experience from which we can draw tentative moral lessons. In the end, "only a curriculum in the broad humanities can educate us to be good human beings."[94] If only more people had read Charles Dickens and cried for Amy Dorrit, perhaps Social Darwinism and *laissez faire* liberalism would have enjoyed less influence. Surely, George Bernard Shaw was not the only person who converted to socialism after reading *Little Dorrit*. Shaw's conversion illustrates what Viereck believed wholeheartedly: Aesthetic experiences necessarily inform ethical positions.

In his view, ethics is an art, not a science, and therefore it is "important to conserve our values humanistically...via poetry and the other arts and humanities; via the study of history and of the great Greek and Elizabethan tragedies."[95] He believed that the primary purpose of conservatism is not to push a certain political agenda but to promote a broad-based education in the humanities. "The proper start for a new American conservatism," Viereck claimed, "is in the world of literature, the arts and sciences, intellectual history, the universities, the humanities."[96] If the goal of conservatism is to conserve what is best from our past, the best place to start is in our schools and universities. By way of the humanities, conservatives can introduce students of all educational levels to those values and traditions needed to safeguard our civilization. Students can read and discuss the books that dwell in the particulars of human existence but somehow manage to highlight the experiences, both good and bad, common to all. Neither deductive nor formalistic, the logic of the humanities is dialectical. It demonstrates that only through a continual interplay between the particular and the universal, between the concrete and the abstract, can a provisional synthesis be reached.

While Viereck believed that exposure to the humanities could make anyone a better human being, he maintained only that a select few could benefit from rigorous study at the college level. He opposed the trend toward universalizing higher education because it led to lower standards, dumbing down the curriculum. Once institutions of intellectual ferment and rigor, colleges were mired in mediocrity, focusing ever more on vocational studies instead of the humanities.[97] Viereck saw colleges as elite institutions of learning aimed at preparing the best and the brightest to serve as guardians of tradition, and he believed that a "humanistic, non-utilitarian education" does a far better job of making "aristocrats" out of students, instilling them with a strong sense of their civic and ethical responsibilities. Although they do not belong to an aristocratic class per se, these educated elites are infused with an "aristocratic spirit" which calls for "dutiful public service, insistence on quality and standards, the decorum and ethical inner-check of *noblesse oblige*."[98]

Viereck had a term for the person deserving of aristocratic status in the modern age—the "unadjusted man." Without title, power, or influence, the unadjusted man cuts a rather quixotic and eccentric figure in a democratic age. But his importance is immeasurable. Exercising the "only personal heroism left in a machine-era," the unadjusted man resists the forces of conformity—majority opinion, the latest trends and fashions, and technology.[99] He refuses to adjust or conform to "the ephemeral, stereotyped values of the moment" and instead reserves his reverence for "the ancient, lasting archetypal values shared by all creative cultures."[100] In other words, the unadjusted man only obeys archetypes, enduring values, and traditions that have "grown out of the soil of history: slowly, painfully, organically." But he defies stereotypes, short-lived and rootless values that have "been manufactured out of the mechanical processes of mass production: quickly, painlessly, artificially."[101] The unadjusted man, then, should not be confused with the cantankerous malcontent who opposes everything on principle. A selective non-conformist, the unadjusted man will readily "conform to the values he deems lastingly good."[102] His mantra is simple: "adjustment to the ages, non-adjustment to the age." In his ability to discriminate "between lasting roots and ephemeral surfaces,"[103] between the timeless and the momentary, the unadjusted man is a Viereckian conservative. The unadjusted man does not conform so much as he conserves.

Because of his ability to discriminate, the unadjusted man avoids the extremes of what Viereck called maladjustment and overadjustment. The maladjusted man sees himself as an island, completely insulated from society, and only wants to be left alone. An unreconstructed egoist, he values his privacy above all else and does not feel obligated to address public concerns. The overadjusted man, by contrast, finds himself landlocked on the mainland, conforming to majority opinion and to the passing whims of the age. Consumed with an "abnormal desire for normalcy," he sees conformity not just as a means to achieving certain goals but as an end in itself. His is a "public-relations personality of public smile, private blank." Devoid of any inner liberty, the overadjusted man succumbs to "robotization."[104]

In a democratic age, overadjustment is far more common than maladjustment and thus poses a greater threat. "Every overadjusted society swallows up the diversities of private bailiwicks, private eccentricities, private inner life, and the creativity inherent in concrete personal loyalties." While people in an overadjusted society may enjoy civil liberties and widespread prosperity, they do not have the psychological freedom to pursue a unique or eccentric path in life or to challenge conventional wisdom. Writing in the 1950s, Viereck already observed a world where people used their formal liberty to do little more than "commit television or go lusting after supermarkets."[105] In short, overadjusted society promotes consumerism, champions mediocrity, and appeals to the lowest common denominator. Anyone who deviates from that norm becomes a pariah in the eyes of the masses.

Drawing on Nietzsche's psychological insights, Viereck argued that the overadjusted man resents those who have distinguished themselves in any way. Although not fully aware of his status resentment, the overadjusted man longs to "cure" society of invidious differences by making everyone equal. He sublimates this psychological impulse in his support for political movements that ostensibly intend to safeguard traditions and liberty but actually serve a radical agenda of subverting social and political hierarchies and discrediting members of the establishment. Viereck understood McCarthyism in this way. While McCarthy and others of his ilk claimed they wanted to protect the American way of life by exposing communists, said Viereck, they were really motivated by a resentment of the East Coast establishment. "McCarthyism," he quipped, "was the revenge of the noses that for years were pressed against the outside windowpane while Marie Antoinette danced."[106]

Another important influence on Viereck's discussion of the overadjusted man was *The Revolt of the Masses* by Jose Ortega y Gasset. The overadjusted man has much in common with Ortega's "massman." But Viereck took issue with the class snobbery that pervaded Ortega's discussion of the massman. Unlike Ortega's massman, the overadjusted man does not necessarily belong to the working class.[107] "The rich," said Viereck, "are as susceptible to mass-man mentality as the poor."[108] The unadjusted man is just "[a]s likely to be a banker as a bricklayer."[109] This makes sense in light of his Nietzschean perspective. Many of McCarthy's supporters were bourgeois suburbanites content with their economic status but insecure in their social status. The children of working-class parents, they had escaped their origins but still felt inferior to the Ivy League elites who enjoyed a comparatively higher social status and dominated the most powerful institutions in the country. McCarthyism represented a sublimation of their status resentment.[110]

The popularity of McCarthy underscores the dangers of democracy, in which demagogues stir the darker passions of the people and promise to satisfy their desire for revenge. At its worst democracy reflects the desires of the overadjusted, who crave equality and sameness far more than liberty and diversity. Willing to sacrifice individual freedom if it serves their desired ends, the overadjusted are prone to a horrifying "barbarism."[111] Viereck believed that the unleashing of demotic energy fomented many revolutions throughout history, including those in France, Russia, and China. In these instances, the *demos* wanted to redress past injustices but, in its unwavering zeal, ended up committing far more heinous crimes. Indiscriminate in its savagery, an unrestrained *demos* will destroy all laws, traditions, and institutions associated with the past, even those proven to be effective at safeguarding individual freedom and social order. Unable to differentiate between that which deserves preservation and that which does not, the *demos* often throws out the baby with the bathwater. For this reason, democracy is not an unqualified good. Too much of it, what Viereck referred to as pure or direct democracy, can bring on disaster. "Direct democracy is government by direct, unfiltered mass pressure, government by referendum, mass petition, and popular recall of judges, government by Gallup poll and by the intimidating conformity of the lowest common denominator of public opinion," said Viereck; "direct democracy facilitates revolution, an unrestrained dictatorship by demagogues."[112] In short, direct democracy meant tyranny for Viereck.

His criticism of democracy notwithstanding, Viereck did not subscribe to authoritarianism. He believed that popular sovereignty represents a crucial check on the power of elites, but he saw an equal need for restraints on the power of the people. Viereck's views about democracy should sound pretty familiar, corresponding to those of the Founders, Tocqueville, Mill, and many others who feared tyranny from below (majority tyranny) as much as, or even more than, tyranny from above (minority tyranny). This was why Viereck, along with most Burkean conservatives, favored a political system that fights "both kinds of tyranny, the tyranny of kings and the tyranny of the conformist masses."[113] In his view, indirect democracy accomplishes this objective better than any other system, preventing "at one stroke the majority-tyranny of pure democracy and the minority-tyranny of an inflexible, unprunable aristocracy."[114] The virtue of indirect democracy is that it "fulfills the will of the people but by first filtering it through the people's representatives, through the parliamentary, judicial, and constitutional sieve, and through the ethical restraints of religion and tradition," said Viereck. Moreover, "indirect democracy facilitates evolution, a self-restrained leadership of *noblesse oblige*, and the judicial safeguarding of civil liberties."[115] Institutions such as the Constitution, the Supreme Court, the Senate, and the Electoral College—what Viereck saw as examples of "sublimated aristocracy"—militate against the excesses of popular will and protect traditional rights.

According to Viereck, the idea of traditional rights preceding democracy should be familiar to the conservative. Whereas liberals believe that democracy and liberty go hand-in-hand, conservatives are aware of the inherent tension between them, often pointing to the feudal origins of modern rights. "Parliamentary and civil liberties were created not by modern liberal democracy but by medieval feudalism, not by equality but by privilege," said Viereck. It was "medieval noblemen" who founded institutions that protected them from tyranny. "Modern democracy merely inherited from feudalism that sacredness of individual liberty and then, so to speak, mass-produced it. Democracy changed liberty from an individual privilege to a general right." With the Magna Carta of 1215, for example, the unadjusted man in medieval England—the so-called "Mad Squire"—earned the right to be "eccentric without apology," to speak his mind, to be an individual, to keep his property safe from rapacious kings. The privileges or rights enshrined in this historic document were born of courage and spilt blood. Over time, democracies extended these rights to everyone. But Viereck did not want his readers to forget that liberty is an aristocratic value to which pure democracy can pose a grave threat.[116]

The notion that liberty requires the maintenance of aristocratic values such as inequality and hierarchy may sound counterintuitive in a democratic age. It smacks of snobbery and contempt for the lower classes. But Viereck pointed out that hierarchy is inevitable. "Officially or unofficially, all government, without exceptions, is by elites," he said. "The distinction is: what kind of elites?"[117] His answer to this question was clear. He could not tolerate populists who flatter the people, telling them what they want to hear and promising to carry out their most intemperate demands. Instead, he supported leaders who act as trustees of the people and remain faithful to those traditions and standards that have served civilization in the past. They stand for "proportion and measure, self-expression through self-restraint, preservation through reform; humanism and classical balance; a fruitful nostalgia for the permanent beneath the flux."[118] In agreement with the Madisonian theory of representation, such leaders resist the temporary whims and passions of the people and make it their mission "to refine and enlarge the public views." They "discern the true interest of their country"—as Madison so aptly put it—and do what they believe is right, even if it is unpopular in the short term.[119] A country depends on such "aristocratic" leaders if it wants to remain free.

Viereck understood that in a democratic age there were few unadjusted men left. The proliferation of external pressures makes it increasingly difficult to have an authentic inner life. And it has become increasingly unlikely that the unadjusted few, who manage to remain independent of such powerful forces as consumerism, materialism, and technology, will wield power and influence. In the end, the "aristocracy" will no longer be an elite few enjoying fanfare and veneration but, rather, an unappreciated few who endure the pain and loneliness that an authentic life demands.

> What, then, is the test for telling the genuine from the synthetic? The test is pain. Not merely physical pain but the exultant, transcending pain of selfless sacrifice. The test is that holy pain, that brotherhood of sacrifice, that aristocracy of creative suffering of which Baudelaire wrote…In other words, in a free democracy the only justified aristocracy is that of the lonely creative bitterness, the artistically creative scars of the fight for the inner imagination against outer mechanization—the fight for the private life.[120]

We should not despair that there are only a few left who can take on this arduous task. "In any century," said Viereck, "what counts is not the quantity but the intensity of its unadjusted ones." Even if they do not enjoy reverence, the unadjusted can have a significant effect as long as they are never afraid of "speaking out—in creativity, in crisis—with a *personal* voice, unchainably unique."[121] When they make themselves heard, they become "the ethical Geiger counters of their society, the warning-signals of conscience."[122] Unfortunately, the masses may ignore the warnings of the unadjusted and accuse them of tilting at windmills. But modern aristocrats stay firm and never give up, regardless of the mounting pressures to conform to the age. "The last aristocracy possible in a mass age is neither money nor title but the aristocracy of being able to stand alone."[123]

Conclusion

The conservatism embraced by Peter Viereck certainly represents a road less traveled over the last half century. The road paved by William F. Buckley and his compatriots at *National Review* has led to such figures as Paul Ryan and Michele Bachmann. From Viereck's Burkean perspective, Ryan and Bachmann are reactionary Jacobins in their determination to turn back the clock to a pre-New Deal era and in their use of fear-mongering and demagoguery to discredit political enemies. As if channeling the spirit of Joseph McCarthy, Bachmann called for an "exposé" of anti-American members of Congress in 2008 and, more recently, alleged that there is a "deep penetration in the halls of our United States government by the Muslim Brotherhood."[124]

It is worth speculating what Viereck would have thought of Barack Obama, often the target of demagogic attacks from the right. When he was in the thick of his primary fight with Hillary Clinton, Pat Buchanan compared Obama to Adlai Stevenson on a number of occasions. Would Viereck have agreed with this comparison? Would Viereck have joined the so-called "Obamacons," conservative intellectuals who supported Obama in 2008? Obama has many of the qualities Viereck found praiseworthy. He is cerebral, pragmatic, deliberative, cool, and collected. His oratory gives hope and inspiration, appealing to the better angels of our nature, and he does not sink to the hard demagoguery typical of faux conservatives like Michele Bachmann and Donald Trump. Self-consciously literary, his writing reveals a remarkable sophistication. Echoes from the Western canon can be heard in the cadences of his language. Anyone who has read *Dreams from My Father* knows of his painful journey of self-discovery, fashioning a coherent identity out of a diverse heritage. Obama's personal dialectic brought about a synthesis in which he found not absolute certainty but an ethical tradition rooted in Western civilization, especially Christianity.[125]

As president, he has shown a commitment to conserving the best of our inherited values and institutions (e.g., charity and the New Deal but also capitalism and free enterprise) and to reforming that which experience tells us needs fixing (e.g., our health care and financial systems). "One definition of conservatism would be to conserve what is good and to devise solutions to problems as they arise," said Jeffrey Hart, one of the so-called "Obamacons," who does not regret his support for the president in 2008.[126] If Hart were to borrow Viereck's terminology, he would say that Obama reveres the archetypes but not the stereotypes. In defiance of the long odds, it just might be the case that one of Viereck's beloved unadjusted men found his way into the White House.

Though largely forgotten, Viereck remains an important figure for those who seek to recover a lost tradition in the history of conservative thought. This is hardly an empty intellectual exercise. The battle over the meaning of conservatism is the battle over its soul. The suggestion here is not that Viereck spoke for the one and only true meaning of conservatism or that his thought alone reflects the soul of conservatism. Viereck himself argued that conservatism is a diverse and multifaceted intellectual tradition. But to ignore the Burkean strain of conservatism that Viereck represented so well leaves us with a distorted picture. And it allows Paul Ryan, Michele Bachmann, and other prominent figures on the right to lay claim to the meaning of conservatism without challenge. The upshot is a conservatism that has more interest in dismantling than in conserving. Meanwhile, the Ryans and Bachmanns exploit the discourse of "conservatism" as they pursue an ever more radical agenda. Recovering the political thought of Peter Viereck can help the student of conservatism understand how we fell down the rabbit hole into a world where up is down and down is up. Understanding is the essential first step if we want to make our way out of Wonderland.

NOTES

1. Nash, *The Conservative Intellectual Movement in America Since 1945*, 68.
2. Bogus, *Buckley*, 137. These are Buckley's words.
3. Viereck quoted in Reiss, "The First Conservative," *The New Yorker*, October 24, 2005.
4. Viereck, *Conservatism Revisited*, 75.
5. Ibid., 153.
6. Miller, "Veering Off Course," *National Review*, October 26, 2005.
7. Frank Meyer quoted by Claes G. Ryn, "Peter Viereck and Conservatism," introductory essay to *Conservatism Revisited*, 6.
8. Nash, *The Conservative Intellectual Movement*, 136.
9. Ibid., 156.
10. Viereck, *Shame and Glory of the Intellectuals*, 11.
11. Viereck, *Unadjusted Man*, 235.
12. Ibid., 236.
13. Viereck, *Conservatism Revisited*, 153.
14. Viereck, *Unadjusted Man*, 247.
15. Adlai Stevenson quoted in Viereck, *Conservatism Revisited*, 154.

16. Viereck, *Shame and Glory of the Intellectuals*, 263.
17. Ibid., 252.
18. Viereck, *Unadjusted Man*, 331.
19. Viereck, *Shame and Glory*, 121–122.
20. Ibid., 122.
21. Peter Viereck Papers, Box 105, dated December 1964 (Rare Book and Manuscript Library at Columbia University).
22. Viereck, *Conservatism Revisited*, 60.
23. Ibid., 153.
24. Viereck, *Conservative Thinkers*, xii.
25. Viereck, *Conservatism Revisited*, 142.
26. Viereck, *Strict Wildness*, 91–92.
27. Viereck, *Conservatism Revisited*, 115–116.
28. Viereck, *Conservative Thinkers*, 59.
29. Reiss, "The First Conservative."
30. Peter Viereck Papers, Box 118. Recounted in a letter to Arthur Schlesinger, dated June 9, 1997 (Rare Book and Manuscript Library at Columbia University).
31. Reiss, "The First Conservative."
32. Viereck, "But—I'm a Conservative!" *The Atlantic Monthly*, April 1940.
33. Viereck, *Conservatism Revisited*, 71.
34. Orwell, *1984*, 267.
35. Viereck, *Conservatism Revisited*, 72.
36. Viereck, *Conservatism Revisited*, 81; *Conservative Thinkers*, 14.
37. Viereck, *Unadjusted Man*, 208.
38. Viereck, *Shame and Glory*, 56.
39. Viereck, *Shame and Glory*, 56; *Conservatism Revisited*, 65.
40. Viereck, *Unadjusted Man*, 208.
41. Viereck, *Unadjusted Man*, xii.
42. Ibid., 35.
43. Viereck, *Conservatism Revisited*, 155.
44. Viereck, *Shame and Glory*, 37–39.
45. Viereck, *Conservative Thinkers*, 15.
46. Viereck, *Conservatism Revisited*, 72.
47. Viereck, *Conservatism Revisited*, 72–73.
48. Viereck, *Conservatism Revisited*, 70; *Shame and Glory*, 201.
49. Viereck, *Shame and Glory*, 83; *Metapolitics*, 180.
50. Viereck, *Shame and Glory*, 46.
51. Viereck, *Metapolitics*, 179.
52. Viereck, *Shame and Glory*, 202.
53. Viereck, *Shame and Glory*, 249.
54. Viereck, *Conservatism Revisited*, 70.

55. Ibid., 134.
56. Viereck, *Shame and Glory*, 312; *Conservatism Revisited*, 134.
57. Viereck, *Conservatism Revisited*, 134.
58. Ibid., 135 & 147.
59. Viereck, *Shame and Glory*, 325.
60. Viereck, *Conservative Thinkers*, 101–102.
61. Benjamin Disraeli quoted in Viereck, *Unadjusted Man*, 80.
62. Burke, *Reflections*, 106.
63. Viereck, *Shame and Glory*, 150.
64. Viereck, *Unadjusted Man*, 91.
65. Ibid., 81. See also *Conservatism Revisited*, 75.
66. Viereck, *Strict Wildness*, 62.
67. Viereck, *Shame and Glory*, 78–79.
68. Viereck, *Unadjusted Man*, 80.
69. Viereck, *Conservatism Revisited*, 146.
70. Viereck, *Strict Wildness*, 73.
71. Viereck, *Shame and Glory*, 195.
72. Ibid., 43.
73. Viereck, *Metapolitics*, 202.
74. Viereck, *Shame and Glory*, 40–43.
75. Ibid., 46 & 48.
76. Viereck, *Conservative Thinkers*, 18.
77. Viereck, *Unadjusted Man*, 296–298.
78. Viereck, *Conservatism Revisited*, 17.
79. Viereck, *Conservative Thinkers*, 18, 53, 30.
80. Viereck, *Unadjusted Man*, 81.
81. Viereck, *Shame and Glory*, 201–202.
82. Viereck, *Unadjusted Man*, 299.
83. Viereck, *Shame and Glory*, 201.
84. Viereck, *Unadjusted Man*, 37.
85. Viereck, *Conservative Thinkers*, 11–12.
86. Viereck, *Shame and Glory*, 249.
87. Viereck, *Shame and Glory*, 165.
88. Viereck, *Shame and Glory*, 197 & 199.
89. Ibid., 38.
90. Viereck, *Conservative Thinkers*, 31.
91. Viereck, *Shame and Glory*, 260–261.
92. Viereck, *Conservatism Revisited*, 107.
93. Ibid., 71, quoting the 1948 report of the Commission on Liberal Education.
94. Ibid., 71.
95. Viereck, *Shame and Glory*, 48.

96. Ibid., 248.
97. Viereck, *Unadjusted Man*, 20.
98. Viereck, *Conservatism Revisited*, 72 & 74.
99. Viereck, *Unadjusted Man*, 5.
100. Ibid., 17.
101. Viereck, *Conservatism Revisited*, 137; *Unadjusted Man*, 17–18.
102. Viereck, *Unadjusted Man*, 12.
103. Ibid., 6.
104. Ibid., ix–x, 3–4; *Metapolitics*, xxxiv.
105. Viereck, *Unadjusted Man*, 18, 3.
106. Ibid., 216.
107. Ibid., 23–24.
108. Viereck, *Metapolitics*, 307.
109. Viereck, *Conservatism Revisited*, 82.
110. Viereck, *Unadjusted Man*, 113–117.
111. Viereck, *Conservatism Revisited*, 82.
112. Viereck, *Unadjusted Man*, 131.
113. Viereck, *Conservative Thinkers*, 26.
114. Viereck, *Unadjusted Man*, 245.
115. Ibid., 131.
116. Ibid., 28–30.
117. Ibid., 132.
118. Viereck, *Conservatism Revisited*, 70.
119. Madison, "No. 10," in the *Federalist Papers*.
120. Viereck, *Conservatism Revisited*, 138.
121. Viereck, *Unadjusted Man*, 53–54.
122. Viereck, *Shame and Glory*, 13.
123. Peter Viereck Papers, Box 66, Folder 36. This line comes from Viereck's lecture notes (Rare Book and Manuscript Library at Columbia University).
124. Linkins, "Michele Bachmann Points to Huma Abedin as Muslim Brotherhood Infiltrator," *The Huffington Post*.
125. See Remnick, *The Bridge: The Life and Rise of Barack Obama*.
126. See Dougherty, "Obama's Right Wing," *The American Conservative*.

CHAPTER 6

Conservatism Agonistes: Leaving the Stag Hunt

Celebrated historian and political thinker Garry Wills, yet another self-identified conservative whom most consider a liberal, witnessed firsthand the radical impulses of modern American conservatism when William F. Buckley excommunicated him from the *National Review* circle in 1970. While reflecting on this experience several years later, he pointed to the irony in the conservatives' reluctance to conserve—and eagerness to subvert the existing order. "The right wing in America," Wills said, "is stuck with the paradox of holding a philosophy of 'conserving' and an actual order it does not want to conserve. It keeps trying to create something new it might think worthy, someday, of conserving."[1]

Liberals have now found themselves in the awkward position of trying to conserve the traditions and institutions they helped build. They must in effect become "conservatives," even if many do not consider them credible bearers of that moniker. By reputation, liberals are still seen as the unreflective champions of change and progress, but they are the ones who have an actual interest in defending established institutions from the right-wing onslaught, making sure that the legacy of the New Deal and the Great Society will endure for generations to come. And, as will be seen in this chapter, liberals are also the ones who have assumed the mantle of preserving our intellectual inheritance.

Movement conservatives, on the other hand, have proven to be completely out of step with Western political thought, revealing their radicalism most profoundly in their refusal to acknowledge most collective action problems and the active role that government must often play

© The Author(s) 2016
R.J. Lacey, *Pragmatic Conservatism*,
DOI 10.1057/978-1-137-59295-8_6

to solve them. A collective action problem can be defined as a situation where individually rational behavior yields collectively irrational (less than optimal) outcomes. Political and social theorists have long recognized the tension between individual freedom and the general welfare. A society composed of individuals serving only their own interests, even if doing so within the law and without directly violating the rights of others, can produce general results from which everyone suffers. As most political thinkers in the Western tradition have recognized, the only solution to such problems is for the state to promote collective rationality by compelling—or at least creating strong incentives for—individuals to behave in accordance with the general welfare. Curiously, conservatives today talk and act as if this idea were a socialist innovation that can only spell doom for humanity.

"YOU SHOULD REGULATE MORE BECAUSE WE'RE ALL TOO GREEDY"

The Oscar-winning documentary *Inside Job*, a remarkably lucid explanation of the 2008 financial crisis, offers an excellent example of a collective action problem that the state failed to address. There is a crucial moment in the film when Dominique Strauss-Kahn, the former director of the International Monetary Fund, tells a story about a dinner party hosted in the fall of 2008 by Secretary of the Treasury Henry Paulson. In attendance were a number of officials and CEOs from the biggest financial institutions in the United States, and the economic crisis was the obvious topic of conversation. In a staggering moment of honesty, perhaps inspired by sheer panic, all of these men admitted that they were in part responsible for the calamity. Then, according to Strauss-Kahn, they turned to Paulson and said, "You should regulate more because we're all too greedy; we can't avoid it. The only way to avoid this is to have more regulation."[2]

Over a year after the initial fears of widespread economic implosion had subsided, President Obama tried to deliver on the suggestion made at Paulson's dinner party. As expected, Obama faced hostility from Wall Street and the Republicans when he championed and eventually passed the Consumer Financial Protection Act in 2010. But, in that unguarded moment at Paulson's party, the bank officials revealed not only their own culpability for the crisis but also their understanding of the system that allowed—even encouraged—their reckless behavior. A return to regulation, they conceded, was the only way to prevent banks and other institutions from acting in a way that was immensely profitable in the short term but disastrous for the financial system as a whole.

Viewers of *Inside Job* learn that deregulation led to the development of securitization, a system that allows lenders to sell trillions of dollars in mortgages and other loans to investors willing to buy them. Investment banks are the middlemen who facilitate this process, combining thousands of loans to create complex derivatives called collateralized debt obligations (CDOs) and then selling them to investors around the world. As Barney Frank explains in the film, the problem with securitization is that "the people who make the loan are no longer at risk if there is a failure to repay."[3] Because lenders did not bear the risk, they no longer had the incentive to be cautious. After all, if borrowers failed to make their payments on time and defaulted on their mortgages, the investors who purchased the loan were the ones stuck with the loss. Knowing that they could immediately sell loans to investors, lenders no longer cared whether a borrower could repay and had an incentive to make as many loans as possible, no matter how risky they may have been. The investment banks, whose profits were based on the number of CDOs they sold, had the same perverse incentive. Quantity had replaced quality in the real estate loan industry.

The tragedy of securitization is that it allowed lenders and investment banks to transfer risk to woefully uninformed investors. Of course, if the market had been working, investment banks would not have been able to sell CDOs so easily. Knowing that these complex bundles of risky loans were bad investments, most investors would have steered clear of them. But investors did not know, thanks to an unchecked conflict of interest. The rating agencies, paid by the investment banks, gave CDOs the highest investment grades, including even AAA ratings. The securitization food chain—linking borrowers, lenders, bankers, credit rating agencies, and investors—was infected with the blight of misinformation.

Now we all know that the crash was inevitable because the entire system rested on a fatal conceit—that real estate would forever increase in value, and thus was a safe bet for everyone involved, including both borrowers who were encouraged to take out sub-prime mortgages and investors who bought those mortgages in large bundles. In September 2008, the conceit was exposed as mass delusion when the economic bubble burst and nearly brought about the second Great Depression. The takeaway for viewers of the film is clear: the absence of government regulation or oversight of some kind made this crisis possible, if not inevitable. The title of the film notwithstanding, the many actors involved in the crisis—including borrowers, lenders, and bankers—were not villains pulling an "inside job" on the financial system; they were rational individuals who clearly saw the incentive structure before them and followed their own interests accordingly. The result of their individually rational behavior was a collective disaster.

It is hardly an exaggeration to suggest that the conflict between conservatives and liberals in America today arises in large part from their opposing views about collective action problems. Conservatives generally see a natural agreement between private and general interests to which government poses the gravest threat. In short, they believe that government is the *cause* of collective action problems. Liberals, on the other hand, find that government often represents the best chance at a *solution* to many collective action problems. The reason for this divergence is that conservatives fixate on a unique kind of collective action problem called moral hazard.

Moral hazard is the idea that individuals will behave more recklessly or wastefully when given some kind of insurance that covers the costs. Broadly construed, insurance can be understood as any form of protection or coverage that alters a person's behavior. For example, it has often been asserted, though never substantiated, that Volvo drivers are more likely to get in accidents. It may be the case that driving a Volvo, by reputation the safest and sturdiest car on the road, is a kind of insurance that creates a moral hazard, giving people a sense of security that makes them more careless behind the wheel. (But it is also possible that self-selection would explain such a finding—that is, people who buy Volvos are worse drivers.)

Supporters of the Tea Party have invoked moral hazard in their opposition to the bank bailouts in late 2008: knowing that the US government is there to help them should anything go wrong, the big financial institutions will continue to make the kinds of risky investments that led to the financial crisis in the first place.[4] The strong likelihood of another government bailout can be seen as a form of insurance that will encourage further reckless behavior on Wall Street.

In general, conservatives are quick to identify moral hazards created by government. They oppose a single-payer health care system, for example, because they believe it will encourage the frivolous use of health care services and drive up costs. Even though a surfeit of evidence shows that moral hazard is not a major cause of rising health care costs and that single-payer and other kinds of universal health care systems are actually more efficient, conservatives insist on seeing the issue through this particular lens. In their view, it just has to be the case that when government intervenes to make a service free or affordable, people will start using it far more frequently.

Meanwhile, the facts support what common sense tells us: receiving health care is so onerous to most people that, even if told the visits will be free, they will not start running to the doctor every time they get a sniffle.[5]

Empirical evidence notwithstanding, it should not come as a surprise when conservatives refuse to remove their moral hazard lens. Their opposition to big and intrusive government in the area of social policy has been informed by moral hazard for quite some time. As they see it, moral hazard can explain why people receiving any kind of government benefit— such as unemployment insurance, food stamps, or welfare—might be less motivated to return to the workforce and contribute fully to the free market economy. By ensuring that individuals will not suffer the consequences of their actions, the generous welfare state gives them the incentive to remain careless and lazy.

The conservative critique is not completely devoid of merit. In the wake of the Great Society, the welfare state had undoubtedly produced perverse incentives that discouraged work. The Personal Responsibility and Work Opportunity Reconciliation Act of 1996, though hardly an unmitigated success, was an attempt to reinvigorate the incentive to work among welfare recipients. For more than two decades, liberals have been mindful of the conservative concern about government-sponsored moral hazard. Lest we forget, it was a moderately liberal Democrat by the name of Bill Clinton who promised welfare reform during his presidential campaign and got it passed by the end of his first term.

The problem is that conservatives see moral hazard in every government activity related to social and economic policy. They simply refuse to discriminate between programs that work and those that do not. Because conservatives believe government almost always harms the general welfare, they propose reducing its size as much as possible, slashing and cutting with extreme prejudice. But, as President Obama and other liberals have suggested, a more sensible course of action for lawmakers with concerns about wasteful spending is not to butcher government with a machete, but to operate on it with a scalpel.

Liberals have a more balanced view of government intervention because they are also concerned with a type of collective action problem that conservatives completely ignore: problems of cooperation. As political thinkers in the Western tradition have understood for many centuries, collective action problems often arise when government is nowhere to be seen, allowing free and rational individuals to act in ways that, though not directly harmful to others, bring distress and suffering to their community.

For example, liberals tend to favor single-payer health insurance because they believe it will correct for the problems of cooperation in our current system. Even with the passage and implementation of the Affordable Care Act, over 30 million people still do not have health insurance.[6] Even if most of these people do not choose to go without health insurance but are priced out of the private market, they can be understood as free-riders. The problem with free-riders (or the uninsured) in a health care system is that they create inefficiencies. This is because they rarely get preventive care or routine treatment when they have minor illnesses. For most uninsured people, it is too expensive to pay for doctor visits and medicine out of pocket. This places the uninsured population at greater risk of becoming seriously ill, at which point they will be rushed to the emergency room and given expensive treatment to keep them alive. Because they are not able to pay their steep medical bills, the rest of us incur the cost with higher premiums or taxes. If everyone were insured, the system would be more efficient, and thus costs would not be as high. Unfortunately, because they cannot afford to act otherwise, it is still rational for millions of people to go without health insurance and avoid treatment until catastrophe strikes. The end result is the most costly and inefficient health care system in the world.[7]

Liberals can point to a number of other inefficiencies in the American health insurance model. While conservatives believe that the private sector is always more efficient than government could ever be, liberals know that administrative costs are much higher when private insurers expend so much time and energy competing for policy holders, especially healthy ones, and finding ways to deny policy holders coverage when they file a medical claim. It is eminently rational for each insurer to engage in these activities, but the significant costs imposed on the system are collectively irrational. Unsurprisingly, the administrative costs of health care are far higher in the United States than in any comparable country with universal coverage.[8]

There is a particular kind of cooperation problem to which liberals pay careful attention: externalities. An externality can be defined as the unintended consequences of a private transaction from which a third party suffers. John Dewey argued that this third party becomes a "public" if it suffers from a private transaction "to such an extent that it is deemed necessary to have those consequences systematically cared for" by the government.[9] Those of us who choke on the pollutants billowing from nearby factories, for example, constitute a "public" which asks for government regulation of the industries at fault. These industries do not want to contaminate our air; it is merely the unfortunate byproduct of doing business. Because of the costs involved, it is not rational for these industries to act in an environmentally responsible manner. As a result, government must step in to ensure that companies will do the *irrational* thing (i.e., eliminate or reduce their pollution output) and bring about a collectively *rational* outcome (i.e., a cleaner and healthier world).

"...THEY WILL STILL NOT VOLUNTARILY ACT TO ACHIEVE THAT COMMON OR GROUP INTEREST"

For many centuries, social theorists have been searching for ways to solve various collective action problems. Political science has focused on the constructive role that *government* can play to ensure cooperation among self-interested individuals who, left to their own devices, would never honor their agreements with others, even though they would benefit in the long run from doing so. Yet conservatives today act as if this idea never existed. For all their talk about preserving tradition and holding sacred the ideas and values inherited from our revered ancestors, modern conservatives have shown a surprising contempt for intellectual history. In their dismissal of problems of cooperation, conservatives ignore a central (and ubiquitous) concept in the Western tradition which political thinkers on both the right and the left have accepted for quite some time.

From the right side of the political spectrum, Thomas Hobbes argued in *Leviathan* that human beings living in the state of nature—that is, without stable government—are in a constant state of war. Without a strong government imposing law and order, human beings pursue their self-interest relentlessly, leading to a precarious existence of mutual mistrust and regular eruptions of violence. In a world where human beings are not guided or restrained by an innate sense of justice or morality, said Hobbes, it is quite rational—indeed, within one's rights—to initiate warfare against others for gain, security, or reputation. The problem is that, if each person exercises this right of nature, the collective result is a "nasty, brutish, and short" life for everyone.[10] For this reason, said Hobbes, the Law of Nature instructs us to seek peace whenever we can. But there is a catch: the sensible person knows that seeking peace in the state of nature is mere folly, for there is no reason to trust that others will lay down their arms as well. Only when an awe-inspiring sovereign makes people fear the consequences of not seeking peace more than they fear their fellow men will people heed the Law of Nature and cooperate with others. In other words, Hobbes saw the state of nature as a collective action problem that only a powerful autocrat could solve.

A very different thinker who also viewed politics through the lens of collective action was Jean-Jacques Rousseau, an enemy of autocracy and a supporter of direct democracy. Often credited for inspiring the French Revolution, Rousseau believed that only after people enter civilization do collective action problems emerge. In the state of nature, prior to the tragic fall of man into his corrupted state of civilization, human beings led solitary and peaceful lives that did not require working with others. But with the accoutrements of civilization—language, tools, property, and the division of labor—came problems of cooperation. In the *Discourse on the Origin of Inequality*, Rousseau famously drew on the parable of the stag hunt to highlight the perennial conflict between private and general interest. In his description, a successful stag hunt requires cooperation from everyone involved. The strategy is to form a circle around the stag. If any of the hunters abandons his assigned post, the deer will get away and the entire hunting party will go hungry. Unfortunately, it is quite likely that one of the hunters will abandon this mutual undertaking the moment he sees within his reach a hare—easier prey that a person can catch on his own. Aware that others in the group may undermine this fragile enterprise in the pursuit of self-interest, each hunter has a strong incentive to violate the agreement and search for smaller game when the opportunity arises. While cooperation would yield far better results for all, breaking from the group is the individually rational course of action.

Like Hobbes, Rousseau believed that government existed to ensure cooperation in such cases. But Rousseau did not think that cooperation required the concentration of power in the hands of a single sovereign. Instead, he argued that democracy could promote cooperation far more effectively. This is because democracies do a better job of producing laws that reflect the general interest. It is important to add that, despite the diffusion of power in a democracy, its government will never hesitate to use coercion when necessary. The citizen who insists on defying the general will, said Rousseau, must be "forced to be free."[11]

Though they differ greatly in their views about the distribution of power, Hobbes (the authoritarian) and Rousseau (the democrat) agree that government represents the answer to many collective action problems. In addition to these two thinkers, the canon of Western political thought includes countless others who accept the premise that government interference of some kind is often required to make recalcitrant individuals cooperate with others in their community. More recently, the study of collective action problems has become more systematic, even scientific. Rational choice theorists, for example, have used the prisoners' dilemma and other models to formalize in mathematical terms the rational basis for violating agreements. This is what the mathematicians and formal theorists have revealed: While it is true that everyone suffers from the lack of cooperation, it is often more rational for an individual to violate agreements than to risk the dire consequences of sticking to them.

Perhaps the most important thinker of recent memory to comment on the issue of collective action problems is Mancur Olson, an economist who taught for many years at the University of Maryland. His first and most influential book, *The Logic of Collective Action*, is required reading for every doctoral student in political science today—and for good reason. Olson made an essential contribution to the study of groups on which social scientists from many disciplines, particularly political scientists, have drawn. He challenged the conventional wisdom accepted by most American political scientists at the time that groups will necessarily act to further their goals or interests. Before Olson, political scientists assumed that, if members of a group stand to benefit from a particular collective outcome, each person in that group would voluntarily do what is necessary to achieve that objective. As a result, the group would do everything it could to advance its interests. After Olson, political scientists opened their eyes to the reality, illuminated both theoretically and empirically, that individual and collective rationality do not always converge. Even when all of the individuals in a large group "are rational and self-interested, and would gain if, as a group, they acted to achieve their common interest or objective," said Olson, "they will still not voluntarily act to achieve that common or group interest."[12]

Why is this so? Once again, the explanation is the free-rider problem. Rational individuals see all too well that they can still enjoy the benefits of collective action while they stay home and let everyone else in the group do the work. Even if someone stands to benefit immensely from a certain collective good, it is rational to take a free ride, to avoid paying the price. After all, some other suckers will ante up. The problem is that because most individuals make the same calculation, the group will never cohere and pursue its interests. Olson concludes that free and self-interested individuals will only pursue what is in their common interest if they are forced—or given strong incentives—to do so. Of course, Olson was not saying anything new. Readers of Hobbes and Rousseau were already familiar with his argument. He was merely updating an old idea and introducing it to his largely American audience, whose naïve understanding of democracy seemed to be derived from classical pluralism. James Madison, perhaps the original pluralist, simply assumed that people who share a common interest would form a well-organized group in order to influence government policy.[13]

"...LED BY AN INVISIBLE HAND TO PROMOTE AN END WHICH WAS NO PART OF HIS INTENTION"

Students of politics, if at all familiar with the history of Western political thought, are in no position to deny the prevalence of collective action problems arising from the relentless pursuit of self-interest. Nor can they deny the important role that governments play in solving these problems, reconciling private interests with the general welfare. Yet this is exactly what conservatives in the United States are doing today. Despite overwhelming evidence to the contrary, they operate under the assumption that private and general interests are naturally in harmony—that when individuals are free to pursue their own interests short of violating the rights of others, society as a whole automatically benefits.

The idea that the individual pursuit of happiness is always harmonious with collective outcomes does have intellectual roots and can be found most readily in the works of Friedrich Hayek, the Austrian-born philosopher and economist who won the Nobel Prize in 1974. Known for his defense of classical liberalism, Hayek has enjoyed a renaissance in recent years due to the great enthusiasm for his work among Tea Party activists. Recent champions of Hayek include conservative pundits Glenn Beck and John Stossel, both of whom have spoken at length on air about Hayekian principles. It is worth noting that Hayek has attracted supporters outside academia for quite some time. Attempts at popularizing his work date back to the 1940s when *Reader's Digest* published a condensed and more accessible version of his most famous book, *The Road to Serfdom*. In this landmark work, Hayek warned that central economic planning by the government will push society down a slippery slope at the bottom of which tyranny and misery await. Hayek was one of the first thinkers to understand that unrestrained government intrusion in private (especially economic) life is the essential characteristic of all totalitarian regimes, whether they fall on the ideological left or right. The Nazis and the Soviets may have hated each other, but they shared a terrifying enthusiasm for the omnipresent state.

The enduring popularity of *The Road to Serfdom* has turned Hayek into a poster child for the conservative denial of collective action problems, even though he disavowed the conservative label and always considered himself a part of the classical liberal tradition. Central to his classical liberal thought is "spontaneous order," the term Hayek used for "those unintended patterns and regularities, which we find to exist in human society." He saw spontaneous order as a system or aggregate structure that is "due to human action but not to human design."[14] This system or structure is the unintended consequence of free individuals acting solely out of self-interest. Drawing on his understanding of markets, Hayek claimed that such systems—again, neither planned nor engineered—are more complex, productive, and efficient than anything even the best and brightest human beings could devise intentionally. His is an anti-rationalist theory in the sense that he challenged the claim that a few smart people, using their knowledge, reason, and problem-solving skills, can design a system that serves the interests of all. Only out of the chaos of spontaneous individual actions can the best social order emerge. The primary role of government, then, is not to build a just social order but rather to safeguard the right to life, liberty, and property, which will allow individuals to unleash their creative and competitive energies and, albeit unintentionally and indirectly, promote the common good.

Hayek did not claim to be the originator of this idea. He cited a number of intellectual ancestors, including Scottish Enlightenment thinkers Adam Ferguson and Adam Smith. The idea of spontaneous order features prominently in Smith, who celebrated what he saw as the self-regulating capacity of markets. In *The Wealth of Nations*, Smith wrote famously (or infamously) that each person who is engaged in economic life

> intends only his own gain, and he is in this, as in many other cases, led by an invisible hand to promote an end which was no part of his intention. Nor is it always the worse for the society that it was no part of it. By pursuing his own interest he frequently promotes that of the society more effectually than when he really intends to promote it. I have never known much good done by those who affected to trade for the publick good.[15]

Without intending it at all, said Smith, self-interested individuals in the market often serve the "publick good"—and far more effectively than the do-gooders who act with all the best intentions. The reference to "an invisible hand" almost smacks of divine intervention, but Smith was using a metaphor to illustrate the point that the public interest is usually better served, no matter how counterintuitive or even magical it may seem, when each person cares for his own welfare.

It is crucial to note, however, that most of Hayek's intellectual ancestors, including Ferguson and Smith, did not believe that the individual pursuit of happiness automatically yields optimal collective results. For example, Smith feared the deleterious effects that unfettered markets and the division of labor would have on public virtue, making the working class stupid and ignorant—and thus more susceptible to poor moral judgment and unlawful behavior. To counteract this dangerous trend, he called for state-funded education.[16] Even Hayek acknowledged that government would be justified in providing "security against severe physical privation" and "a minimum sustenance for all." In a society that has achieved the level of wealth seen in developed countries, said Hayek, "there can be no doubt that some minimum of food, shelter, and clothing, sufficient to preserve health and the capacity to work, can be assured to everybody." He also saw the utility of a "comprehensive system of social insurance," arguing that "there is no incompatibility in principle between the state providing greater security in this way and the preservation of individual freedom."[17] These caveats suggest that the most important thinkers in the classical liberal tradition did not see spontaneous order as an absolute truth. On the whole—"frequently," as Smith said—free markets will promote the "publick good." But when they do not, both Smith and Hayek argued, the government has a legitimate interest in making judicious corrections.

But how could Hayek square his defense of government providing economic security with his famous slippery slope argument? Quite easily. The guiding principle of his political thought—and that of Milton Friedman's, for that matter—was equality under the law. Hayek opposed public policies aimed at promoting equality of ends because such efforts necessitate treating people unequally, giving perks and privileges to the less fortunate and punishing those at the top of the socio-economic ladder with higher tax rates and other undue burdens.[18] But he supported social insurance programs designed to manage risk, to guarantee some security in the event of catastrophic misfortune, because they do not violate the equality under the law principle. Everyone is covered by these programs and is entitled to their benefits should they find themselves in need of them. This explains why a true Hayekian could support universal health or unemployment insurance programs into which everyone paid equally but would disparage such policies as affirmative action and progressive taxation. According to Hayek, a welfare state that treats everyone the same will never fall prey to tyranny. By design it will exercise restraint for the simple reason that an oppressive measure that applied to everyone equally would never garner much support.

"…GOVERNMENTS CANNOT BE SUPPORTED WITHOUT GREAT CHARGE"

When they do not rely on the adherents of spontaneous order in their war against intrusive government, modern conservatives often invoke the political thought of John Locke to proclaim a natural—and absolute— right to property. They argue that Locke provides philosophical justification for *laissez faire*, a government so limited in scope that it does no more than protect people from force, theft, and fraud. But such a reading does not bear scrutiny.

It is certainly true that Locke believed that the law of nature confers on all human beings the right to life, liberty, and property. He said that the "law of nature" demands that "no one ought to harm another in his life, health, liberty, or possessions."[19] But, interestingly, he argued that the right to property in the state of nature is not absolute. It is limited to what a person can "enjoy" or "make use of to the advantage of life before it spoils." Indeed, "whatever is beyond this is more than his share, and belongs to others."[20] Just as much practical as it is ethical, this limit produces a rough equality of conditions in the state of nature. Of course, this egalitarian idyll disappears with the invention of money, whereupon a person can "make use of" large holdings of property with paid labor, or he can exchange unwanted property for money, saving as much as he wants without doing harm to others because metal coins and paper currency never spoil. The upshot is that once they participate in a monetary system of exchange, people give their "tacit and voluntary consent" to the "disproportionate and unequal possession of the earth."[21]

While Locke considered inequality an acceptable outcome in civilized society, he saw no reason to prevent government from mitigating its ill effects. In his view, raising revenue to serve the public good was a legitimate aim of government. Unlike economic libertarians today, he did not argue that the taxation of earnings is on moral par with slavery or theft. So long as the people give their express consent, government has every right to tax them to fund public enterprises. " 'Tis true governments cannot be supported without great charge, and 'tis fit every one who enjoys his share of the protection should pay out of his estate his proportion for the maintenance of it," said Locke. "But still it must be with his own consent, *i.e.*, the consent of the majority, giving it either by themselves or their representatives chosen by them."[22]

Not only did Locke claim that the government can tax with the consent of the governed; he also accepted that serving the commonweal may require rather high taxes. The only real caveat was that government should never "be absolutely arbitrary over the lives and fortunes of the people" or "assume to itself a power to rule by extemporary arbitrary degrees." For it is "bound to dispense justice and decide the rights of the subject by promulgated standing laws, and known authorized judges." In other words, government cannot deprive someone of life, liberty, or property without a just cause, and its actions must always follow due process and the law. But Locke made it clear that taxation approved by the majority can only be deemed unjust—that is, "absolutely arbitrary over the lives and fortunes of others"—when it fails to serve the public good and reduces people to a state of poverty. "[The legislative] power, in the utmost bounds of it, is limited to the public good of the society," said Locke. "It is a power that hath no other end but preservation, and therefore can never have a right to destroy, enslave, or *designedly to impoverish the subjects*."[23] (Italics added for emphasis.) Having established impoverishment as the line that government tax policy cannot cross, Locke made it clear that government should enjoy considerable latitude in its efforts to raise revenue for the commonweal. By doing so, he paved the way for the creation of a robust welfare state that serves the public good in a variety of ways, including redistributive measures that solve collective action problems. It would seem, then, that rumors of Locke's economic libertarianism are greatly exaggerated.

Despite the nuances in the political thought of Locke, Smith, and Hayek, modern conservatives recklessly appropriate these thinkers, along with others in the classical liberal tradition, to make the claim that property rights are absolute and spontaneous order is a universal principle. In a stunning display of intellectual dishonesty, they cling to a few thinkers in the classical liberal tradition to defend their position, misread them egregiously, and ignore the rest of Western political thought. On these flimsy intellectual grounds, they favor a radical agenda of dismantling the welfare state and deregulating nearly all industries (including those responsible for the recent financial crisis).

While conservatives fail to identify any major thinkers in the Western canon who actually provide philosophical justification for *laissez faire*, they cleverly deflect attention from their own radicalism by casting liberals in this light. They often build a straw man in suggesting that proponents of reasonable government intervention in the market favor a command economy—as if there is no difference between Lenin and Obama, between communism and liberalism. In truth, liberals do not dispute the obvious: that free markets work far better than central economic planning ever could. They merely argue that the market is a complex and occasionally flawed system. Sometimes the market fails to produce goods that society needs (e.g., affordable health care for all), while at other times it produces outcomes that society finds undesirable (e.g., pollution). In support of their modest attempts to solve collective action problems liberals can claim a rich and diverse intellectual ancestry in the Western intellectual tradition. Modern conservatives do not have such a distinguished lineage.

"...CHARACTER IS ALL AND CIRCUMSTANCES NOTHING"

If the usual suspects—including Burke, Locke, Smith, and Hayek—fail to qualify as their intellectual ancestors, where do modern conservatives get their ideas? Does their ethos descend from a rich intellectual tradition hitherto not mentioned? Or is modern conservatism simply a crass ideology fabricated by those who stand to benefit from its uncompromising position on economic freedom? Although self-interest may play a role, modern conservatism does rest on a set of ideas inherited from two rather dubious traditions, Calvinism and Social Darwinism.

"I think I can see the whole destiny of America contained in the first Puritan," said Alexis de Tocqueville in *Democracy in America*.[24] He suggested in this famous passage that the Puritans were instrumental in shaping the American character. But just how the Puritans sealed the fate of a nation became clearer in the works of Max Weber and R. H. Tawney. These early twentieth-century thinkers gave us a deeper understanding of how Puritan theology, largely Calvinist in its orientation, invigorated the capitalist spirit. Thanks to their insights, it is easy to see why America has embraced the capitalist spirit with such gusto, for so many of its early settlers, especially in New England, were Puritans.

As Tawney pointed out, human beings have always had a capitalist spirit, a desire to make a business enterprise increasingly profitable, but Puritanism "braced its energies and fortified its already vigorous temper."[25]

As adherents of the doctrine of predestination, Puritans did not believe that anyone could earn grace—that is, God's merciful love and a spot in heaven—through good works or observing sacraments. For reasons that remain unknown God awarded this gift to a select few, and no one could change His plan for each person. But the Puritan could prepare for the gift of grace by opening his heart to God. This was an intensely "lonely" endeavor that required "an immense effort of concentration and abnegation." Ultimately this profoundly individualistic theological outlook fostered "the moral self-sufficiency of the Puritan," but it also "corroded his sense of solidarity." After all, "if each individual's destiny hangs on a private transaction between himself and his Maker, what room is left for human intervention?"[26]

Eventually, the spiritual individualism of the Puritan spilled into his material life. Besides preparing for grace, each Puritan looked incessantly for signs indicating whether God had given him, or anyone else, this gift. Because they saw worldly success as a sign of divine grace, Puritans worked without rest not only to satisfy their desire for material gain but also—and mainly—to prove that they were among God's chosen few. Puritans generally agreed that economic success was the most important sign because they considered it the inevitable outcome of Christian virtue. As Calvin put it, "There is no question that riches should be the portion of the godly rather than the wicked, for godliness hath the promise in this life as well as the life to come."[27] They believed that "the requirements of business and the claims of religion" were aligned. "By a fortunate dispensation," said Tawney, "the virtues enjoined on Christians—diligence, moderation, sobriety, thrift—are the very qualities most conducive to commercial success."[28] Over time the connection between economic success and religious virtue became engrained in the Puritan mind. "Convinced that his character is all and circumstances nothing, [the Puritan] sees in the poverty of those who fall by the way, not a misfortune to be pitied and relieved, but a moral failing to be condemned," said Tawney. When someone enjoyed "riches," the Puritan saw "the blessing which rewards the triumph of energy and will."[29]

Even as the Calvinist notion of predestination fell out of favor with the American people, the emphasis on work ethic continued to hold sway, producing a radically individualistic ethos where the character of a person determines his fate. Many Americans came to believe that good people will always succeed in the end, while the bad will fail. Horatio Alger's popular "rags-to-riches" novels for young boys, published in the late nineteenth century, capture this idea perfectly. Every book has the same narrative arc: Unfailingly industrious and upright, a young boy rises above his modest origins to become a business tycoon, a Senator, or some other paragon of success. The myth of the self-made man, often celebrated by rich businessmen, has unmistakable Puritan origins. "Few tricks of the unsophisticated intellect are more curious than the naïve psychology of the business man, who ascribes his achievements to his own unaided efforts," said Tawney. "That individualist complex owes part of its self-assurance to the suggestion of Puritan moralists, that practical success is at once the sign and the reward of ethical superiority."[30] The Puritan mindset created the widespread belief that people who work hard and play by the rules will always thrive in a free enterprise system, while the poor and dispossessed deserve what they get.

In the late nineteenth century, Social Darwinism emerged as a secular version of the Puritan creed. Espoused by such thinkers as Herbert Spencer and William Graham Sumner, Social Darwinism reinforced the Puritan view that character is destiny and that each individual must take sole responsibility for his success or failure in life, but it deployed scientific (or pseudo-scientific) rather than theological arguments. Simply substituting heredity for grace, the rich and successful could now attribute their good fortune to natural selection rather than God. Those who rise to the top of the socio-economic ladder have prevailed because of their biological superiority, proving themselves to be the fittest in the struggle for survival. "The millionaires," said Sumner, "are a product of natural selection, acting on the whole body of men to pick out those who can meet the requirement of certain work to be done."[31]

It is not a stretch to suggest that Americans were particularly attracted to this idea because of their Puritan heritage. Social Darwinism continued to uphold the Protestant work ethic as an unassailable virtue without which no one could achieve worldly success. As the intellectual historian Richard Hofstadter argued, the English philosopher and sociologist Herbert Spencer "bridged the gap" between Calvinism and Social Darwinism by asserting "that the industrious, temperate, and frugal man of the Protestant ideal was the equivalent of the 'strong' or the 'fittest' in the struggle for existence." His was a philosophy that supported "the Ricardian principles of inevitability and *laissez faire* with a hard-bitten determinism that seemed to be at once Calvinistic and scientific." Likewise, Hofstadter described Yale sociologist William Graham Sumner, probably the most influential Social Darwinist in America, as a "latter-day Calvin," who "came to preach the predestination of the social order and the salvation of the economically elect through the survival of the fittest."[32]

Given its Puritan heritage, there is little wonder why Spencer, the pioneer of Social Darwinism, received more fanfare in America than he did in his native country and why so many champions of his theory sprouted up on American soil. The many supporters of individualism and *laissez faire* in the United States finally found in Social Darwinism a philosophical and scientific foundation for their beliefs, an ultra-conservative ethos that blamed the least fortunate in society for their own woes and defended the savage inequalities of the Gilded Age.

Spencer and his followers came to these conclusions because they believed that Darwinian evolution applies just as much to society as it does to nature. In their view, if government refrains from interfering in economic life and helping those in need, natural selection will play itself out in society, weeding out the unfit and ultimately creating a stronger human species. Interested primarily in long-term aggregate outcomes, or in what is best for the species as a whole, Social Darwinists often showed a chilling indifference toward the wretched of the earth. "If they are not sufficiently complete to live, they die; and it is best they should die," said Spencer of the poor and unfortunate. "The whole effort of nature is to get rid of such, to clear the world of them, and make room for better."[33] Sumner could be equally heartless. "A drunkard in the gutter is just where he ought to be," he said. "Nature has set up on him the process of decline and dissolution by which she removes things which have survived their usefulness."[34] Social Darwinists envisioned a future in which humanity could achieve perfection because the inferior stock, including the lazy, the weak, the dumb, and the sick, died off before they could procreate.

Spencer insisted that realizing such a future required strictly limiting the role of government in society and holding individuals accountable for their own fates. To this end, he called for a government that was confined to safeguarding negative liberties, administering justice, enforcing contracts, and providing for the national defense. He subscribed to what Robert Nozick would later call a "night-watchman state." In his ideal society, government would not be involved in regulating industry, assisting the poor and infirm, providing public education, or even delivering mail. He thought that any such interference brings aid to the unfit, those who have failed in the competition of life for not adapting to their environment, and thus hampers social progress.

Sumner shared this radically libertarian outlook. "At bottom there are two chief things with which government has to deal," he said. "They are the property of men and the honor of women. These it has to defend against crime."[35] Sumner expressed contempt for—and defined as "socialism"—any state intervention that tries to "save individuals from any of the difficulties or hardships of the struggle for existence."[36] The primary victim of such schemes, according to Sumner, was the average American, a paragon of diligence, honesty, thrift, and temperance, who managed to support himself and his family without receiving handouts from anyone else. Through no fault of his own this "Forgotten Man" suffers at the hands of intellectuals and reformers who raise his taxes, crushingly so, in order to fund programs aimed at helping the unfit, an assortment of idlers, rogues, profligates, and imbeciles.

Despite the good intentions behind such efforts, the results were dire for the fit—and for society as a whole. "If we do not like [the struggle for existence], and if we try to amend it, there is only one way in which we can do it," he said.

> We can take from the better and give to the worse. We can deflect the penalties of those who have done ill and throw them on those who have done better. We can take the rewards of those who have done better and give them to those who have done worse. We shall thus lessen the inequalities. We shall favor the survival of the unfittest, and we shall accomplish this by destroying liberty. Let it be understood that we cannot get outside this alternative: liberty, inequality, survival of the fittest; non-liberty, equality, survival of the unfittest. The former carries society forward and favors all its best members; the latter carriers society downwards and favors all its worst members.[37]

According to Sumner, when the state acts as a benefactor for the unfit, which requires the redistribution of wealth from the haves to the have-nots, it unfairly punishes those who have "done better" in life by "destroying [their] liberty" and, in the process, "carries society downwards." He saw this as a losing proposition for both the forgotten men and the general welfare. The only people who prosper in this scenario are the "worst members" of society. They are rewarded for failing to accomplish anything of value and relying on the generosity of others.

By the early twentieth century, with the Progressive movement making significant headway in the corridors of power, the vogue of Social Darwinism had faded. Decrying the rise of what he considered to be socialist thinking and policies not long before his death in 1903, Spencer saw that the tide of history had turned against his political doctrines. "Herbert Spencer was a name to conjure with twenty-five years ago. But how the mighty are fallen! How little interest is shown in Herbert Spencer at the present time!" exclaimed a religious observer in 1917. "A generation ago he was quoted confidently, and by many his opinion on a question was accepted as final. Occasionally a man now far beyond middle life still quotes him, but the quotation is received with a shrug of the shoulders and a conviction that an old fogy is speaking."[38] The reputation of Social Darwinism was tarnished further with the rise of racially motivated eugenics and nationalism in the 1920s and 1930s, especially in Nazi Germany. Given its unsavory track record, Social Darwinism should have become nothing more than a curious intellectual artifact that, while influential over totalitarian ideologies of the past, has no resonance today.

If only that were so. The fact is, Social Darwinism has proven remarkably resilient. Though its advocates have had to work under more respectable names, the Social Darwinist worldview has continued to exercise considerable influence. Over the last few decades, conservatives are the ones who have kept this idea alive, arguing that class and race differences are largely a function of variations in individual talent, particularly innate intelligence as measured by IQ, but also in other character traits, such as work ethic and sobriety. This argument supports their belief that people must take responsibility for, and accept, their lot in life, and never expect government to reward their failure with generous social programs.

A fine example of this kind of crypto-Social Darwinism operating today is *The Bell Curve* by Richard J. Herrnstein and Charles Murray, which caused quite a stir upon its release in 1994. In an intimidating tome that runs over 800 pages and includes countless graphs and tables reporting the results of seemingly sophisticated statistical analyses, the authors make a highly controversial claim: the class structure in American life largely reflects the variations in genetically inherited intelligence, and no amount of government intervention on behalf of those at the bottom of the socio-economic ladder will significantly alter the class structure or racial disparities in America. Regardless of the investments that government makes in assisting those from disadvantaged backgrounds, the most intelligent will always rise to the top of the socio-economic ladder, while the less intelligent will sink to the bottom. Categorically rejecting the mainstream argument among social scientists today that members of underperforming groups have been denied opportunities to reach their full potential, the authors attribute all group differences to immutable genetic factors. Just like their Spencerian forebears in the late nineteenth century, Herrnstein and Murray dismiss structural forces, positing that American society erects no significant impediments to individuals hoping to make their way in the world. Each individual will succeed or fail by virtue of inborn character traits.

What awaits the patient reader who manages to get to the end of *The Bell Curve* is a harrowing vision of the future in which a growing underclass occupies city centers, continues to have illegitimate children, and relies completely on the "custodial state" for subsistence. "In short, by *custodial* state, we have in mind a high-tech and more lavish version of the Indian reservation for some substantial minority of the nation's population, while the rest of America tries to go about its business."[39] Then, Herrnstein and Murray lay out a pastoral alternative to the custodial state, in which each person must find ways to contribute something of value to his small community. Though their vision appears heartwarming and quaint, the chilling subtext is clear: Without support from the custodial state, the genetically inferior will depend on family and private charity, and thus their numbers will remain respectably low, never exceeding that which a small community can support ad hoc.[40] Like their Social Darwinist predecessors, Herrnstein and Murray believe that the generosity of the welfare state is misplaced and find hope in what they see as a benign neglect of the least fortunate, including the poor, blacks, Hispanics, and other groups.

To support such bold claims about class, race, and public policy, Herrnstein and Murray rely on theories and results that have the veneer of scientific rigor but in fact do not meet accepted scholarly standards. In his famous and devastating takedown of *The Bell Curve*, the late Stephen Jay Gould exposed the fallacious premises on which the authors' arguments ultimately rest. To start with, if their argument is to have any worth, they must be able to demonstrate the validity of four premises. "Intelligence," said Gould, "must be depictable as a single number, capable of ranking people in linear order, genetically based, and effectively immutable. If any of these premises are false, their entire argument collapses."[41] As Gould makes quite clear, most of the premises are clearly invalid or dubious at best. Murray and Herrnstein try to make these inconvenient truths go away by engaging in flagrant intellectual dishonesty. For example, while Gould cites several experts who challenge the first premise, that general intelligence or cognitive ability can be measured with a single number, Murray and Herrnstein assure the reader that the use of IQ is unassailable. "Among the experts," they claim, "it is by now beyond much technical dispute that there is such a thing as a general factor of cognitive ability on which human beings differ and that this general factor is measured reasonably well by a variety of standardized tests, best of all by IQ tests."[42] This kind of deception is par for the course. In an effort to maintain their ruse and sell their argument to an unwitting audience, the "authors omit facts, misuse statistical methods, and seem unwilling to admit the consequences of their own words."[43] In the end, their entire project rests on unpersuasive theory, shoddy scholarship, and inconclusive empirical findings.

Championed by luminaries on the right, who seek arguments that support *laissez faire* and the dismantling of the welfare state, *The Bell Curve* is ultimately a piece of advocacy dressed up in scholarly garb. As Gould put it, *The Bell Curve* amounts to no more than a "manifesto of conservative ideology" which

> evokes the dreary and scary drumbeat of claims associated with conservative think tanks: reduction or elimination of welfare, ending or sharply curtailing affirmative action in schools and workplaces, cutting back Head Start and other forms of preschool education, trimming programs for the slowest learners and applying those funds to the gifted.[44]

While it purports to make an original contribution to social science, Gould is spot on when he says that this manifesto, "with its claims and supposed documentation that race and class differences are largely caused by genetic factors and are therefore essentially immutable, contains no new arguments and presents no compelling data to support its anachronistic social Darwinism." That the book has garnered so much attention, he suggests, is a reflection of "the depressing temper of our time—a historical moment of unprecedented ungenerosity, when a mood for slashing social programs can be powerfully abetted by an argument that beneficiaries cannot be helped, owing to inborn cognitive limits expressed as low IQ scores."[45] It is because we live in a time when modern conservative ideology has become mainstream that such "anachronistic social Darwinism" can rear its ugly head and yet appear reasonably attractive, if not downright beautiful, to so many.

The link between modern conservatism and crypto-Social Darwinism becomes clearer when one considers the fact that *The Bell Curve* is a sequel of sorts to Charles Murray's earlier book, *Losing Ground*, which upon its release in 1984 not only received rave reviews from conservatives but also helped them frame the welfare reform debate over the next decade. Much to the chagrin of progressives, he concludes in this book that the War on Poverty not only failed to help the people mired in the underclass but also exacerbated their condition by creating a culture of dependence on government handouts and a perverse incentive to break up families. The central argument of the book, which clearly draws from the concept of moral hazard, is that government efforts to solve the problem of poverty will always make matters worse, for there are plenty of capable people on the dole who would prove their mettle and escape the culture of poverty if forced to pull themselves up by their bootstraps. His policy prescription is simple and familiar: dismantle the welfare system entirely, if possible, or at least make deep cuts in social spending. We will be doing the poor a favor by liberating them from the shackles of welfare dependence and giving them the motivation to succeed. One can see why the book quickly achieved canonical status in the Reagan administration.

If *Losing Ground* purports to show how the welfare state encourages laziness and poor life choices among those who have the ability to succeed in life, *The Bell Curve* explains why the welfare state has no chance of helping those who are inherently inferior. In other words, government either creates problems by holding back the capable or throws its money away by trying to improve the life prospects of the incapable. The arguments of these complementary books rest on the Social Darwinist premise that government should refrain from interfering with the competition of life. Failing to do so, says Murray, deprives many people of the opportunity to rise to the occasion—to be the best that they can be—and harms the general welfare by wastefully redistributing wealth from the productive to the unproductive, from the smart and hard working to the dumb and lazy.

While the rhetoric may be less egregious, the message does not differ all that much from what Herbert Spencer and William Graham Sumner argued a century earlier. Both Social Darwinists then and conservatives today have argued that people who have native ability, work hard, and play by the rules will thrive in a free enterprise system and those who do not will get their just deserts. Somehow they find it inconceivable that the slings and arrows of misfortune do not discriminate between the ostensibly capable and incapable. No one is invulnerable to the savageries of life, especially when markets reign without restraints.

"The legitimate object of government"

Perhaps no group has a better understanding of the vicissitudes of markets than the working class. Accordingly, workers around the world have found it beneficial to organize unions and bargain collectively with their employers for higher wages, better benefits, and safer working conditions. Union membership in the United States exploded after the passage of the Wagner Act in 1935. Among other things, this law protected workers' right to organize unions, gave the newly created National Labor Relations Board the authority to hold elections that would decide whether workers in a particular place of employment would be represented by a union, and allowed for the creation of "closed shops" in which all employees in a unionized workplace are required to join the union (including those who did not vote for it and do not want to be members). By 1954, about 35% of wage and salary workers in the United States were union members, thanks in large part to the Wagner Act.[46] It was a time of unprecedented economic prosperity and an expanding middle class.

Much to the dismay of many liberals, unions represent only about 12% of wage and salary workers in America today.[47] This decline stems in large part from the conservative onslaught against unions over the last thirty or more years. The recent hostility to public sector unions in Wisconsin, Indiana, and other states is just the latest chapter in this story. Conservatives attack unions for a whole host of reasons—allegedly, they hurt businesses, impede economic growth, and create fiscal crises at all levels of government. But, as the recent debate illustrates, the main reason for the conservative opposition to unions rests on principle: they see mandatory membership as an infringement on economic freedom. Tim Pawlenty made this point in New Hampshire during a Republican presidential debate in June of 2011. He expressed his support for a federal right-to-work law, which would weaken unions nationwide by making "closed shops" illegal. "We live in the United States of America," he said, "and people shouldn't be forced to belong or be a member in any organization. And the government has no business telling people what group you have to be a member of or not."[48]

Even if they draw the wrong conclusions from it, conservatives have a point. As Mancur Olson argues in his classic work, the survival of unions requires an element of coercion. He wrote: "By far the most important single factor enabling large, national unions to survive was that membership in those unions, and support of the strikes they called, was to a great degree compulsory."[49] Requiring workers to be dues-paying members of a union, to accept the terms of a collectively bargained contract, and not to cross a picket line during a strike may have bolstered unions, but it certainly restricts the individual freedom to choose.

That said, Olson urges his readers to view the issue through the lens of collective action. Conservatives refuse to accept that the benefits of these coercive measures—higher wages, better benefits, and safer working conditions for the middle class—far outweigh the costs. The truth of the matter is that the vast majority of workers want these collective benefits, but if you make it easier for them to stop paying membership dues and to cross picket lines (that is, to take a free ride), unions have a much harder time staying alive. Their survival and effectiveness require coercion, argued Olson, and this is no different from any other form of coercion that societies deem necessary for the common good. For example, governments collect taxes to finance fire departments and enforce speed limits to keep highways safe. No one expects citizens to pay taxes or observe speed limits voluntarily if they oppose these measures and there are no consequences for disobeying them. We recognize that government must use force—or the looming threat of force—to ensure widespread cooperation.

Generally speaking, democracies conform to what Abraham Lincoln called "the majority principle" in his First Inaugural Address. The minority cannot nullify a law simply because they do not like it. Similarly, workers in a place of employment can vote in a democratic election to decide whether they want to be represented by a union. If the majority supports a union, the matter is settled. Everyone is a member and must accept the costs and benefits of what comes with this association. Rousseau believed that the best way to resolve collective action problems, such as the proverbial stag hunt, was to put it to a vote. Let the people decide whether coercive measures are necessary to ensure cooperation. The hunters in his example could have passed a law that somehow sanctioned those who abandoned their posts, thereby ensuring that the hunt would be successful and everyone would enjoy a healthy portion of venison. For the same reasons, some form of punishment awaits tax evaders, speeders, and others who fail to cooperate with laws passed by democratic majorities.

The conservative denial of collective action problems in such policy areas as consumer financial protection, health care, environmental regulation, and labor usually rests on empty appeals to "principle" and ad hominem attacks on those who call on the power of government to enforce cooperation. In January of 2011, for example, Michele Bachmann made a speech on the House floor calling Obama's health care reform law "the crown jewel of socialism."[50] Even though Obamacare is hardly the equivalent of socialized medicine (which, incidentally, already exists in the United States for military personnel and veterans), Bachmann would rather score easy political points through old-fashioned red-baiting than debate the program on its practical merits.

Unfortunately, high-brow conservatives are not immune to hollow invocations of principle either. About a month before the reform was passed, political philosopher Harvey Mansfield accused Obama in *The Weekly Standard* of trying to avert questions of "principle" and pretending that health care policy is "beyond political dispute." The "principle" at stake in Mansfield's view is the following: "Should the government take over health care or should it be left to the private sphere?"[51] This is a grotesque distortion and oversimplification of the issue. The reform does not turn health care providers into government employees or restrict consumer choice of providers in the private market. And, despite what Mansfield asserts, Obama and the Democrats were always motivated by higher principle. They believe that health care is a right to which everyone is entitled.[52] Beyond that, they also point to the collective benefits of universal coverage, including lower per capita costs and better overall outcomes, to which the health care systems in the rest of the developed world can attest. Mansfield refused to address the fact that the status quo, a largely for-profit private insurance system, was unsustainable. While over 46 million people lived without insurance and health care costs soared at an alarming rate, Mansfield decided to sidestep substantive matters.

Seemingly oblivious to the problem of collective action, Mansfield tried to deflect attention from these inconvenient truths by engaging in shameless demagoguery, peppering his essay with ominous terms—such as "government takeover," "Big Government," and "rational administration"—that made health care reform look like a socialist enterprise. This kind of coded language is used to end rather than to promote discussion.[53]

It is distressing to see that "principle" has become the tool of the political obstructionist, of the apologist for the status quo. Mansfield charged Obama with affecting "the cool of a nonpartisan" and eschewing politics in his attempt to marshal the resources of the administrative state to make policy.[54] He seems to have forgotten how many political compromises were made by Obama and the Democrats in order to get the law passed. The final result was a moderate—and what many on the left deem a woefully watered down—reform that comes nowhere close to socialized medicine or single-payer insurance, the two most common models in the industrialized world. President Obama and the Democrats did not get what they wanted; they did what was politically feasible. Fearful of even a moderate policy solution, Republicans were uncompromising in their refusal to meet the Democrats halfway, trying to derail reform completely on so-called principled grounds.

The only way conservatives can deny the reality of collective action problems is to dwell in a world of meaningless principle. "It is your inalienable right to leave the stag hunt should you desire," say conservatives. Never mind that most of us will go hungry as a result.

Perhaps conservatives should recall what Abraham Lincoln wrote in 1854: "The legitimate object of government, is to do for a community of people whatever they need to have done, but can not do, *at all*, or can not, *so well do*, for themselves—in their separate, and individual capacities."[55] People cannot catch stags, pay for health care, or bargain with their employers so well on their own. But they do these things remarkably well together.

NOTES

1. Wills, *Confessions of a Conservative*, 211.
2. Ferguson, *Inside Job* (Sony Pictures Classics, 2010).
3. Ibid.
4. Tea Party darling Michele Bachmann wrote the following about the bank bailouts: "The moral hazard this bill creates will ripple through the entire financial marketplace. Providing banks with a bailout guarantee will perpetuate a cycle of irresponsibility, shielding creditors from taking the fall for making risky decisions and forcing taxpayers to ante up again and again." See Bachmann, "Giving More Power Where Power Is Not Due," in the *Star Tribune* (December 10, 2009).
5. See Gladwell, "The Moral-Hazard Myth," in *The New Yorker* (October 29, 2005).
6. 2015 Current Population Survey, March Supplement.
7. The US spent more on health care per capita in 2008 ($7164) than any other country in the world, and its health care costs as a percentage of GDP in 2008 (15.2) were also the highest in the world. See World Health Organization, *World Health Statistics 2011*, <http://www.who.int/whosis/whostat/2011/en/index.html>. Also see Krugman, *The Conscience of a Liberal*, 214–243.
8. In 1999, for example, the US spent $1059 per capita on health administration expenditures, while Canada spent only $307. Administration accounted for 31.0% of health care costs in the US and 16.7% in Canada. See Woolhandler, Campbell, and Himmelstein, "Costs of Health Care Administration in the United States and Canada," in *The New England Journal of Medicine* 349:8 (August 21, 2003). The authors conclude that the US would save significantly on administrative costs if it adopted a single-payer system.
9. Dewey, *The Public and Its Problems*, 15–16.

10. Hobbes, *Leviathan*, 186.
11. Rousseau, *The Basic Political Writings*, 150.
12. Olson, *The Logic of Collective Action*, 2.
13. See Madison, "No. 10," in the *Federalist Papers*.
14. Hayek, *Studies in Philosophy, Politics and Economics*, 97.
15. Smith, *An Inquiry into the Nature and Causes of the Wealth of Nations*, 456.
16. Ibid., 787–788.
17. Hayek, *The Road to Serfdom*, 89–90.
18. See Hayek, *The Constitution of Liberty*, 85–102.
19. Locke, *Second Treatise*, chapter 2, section 6.
20. Ibid., chapter 5, section 31.
21. Ibid., chapter 5, section 50.
22. Ibid., chapter 11, section 140.
23. Ibid., chapter 11, sections 135–136.
24. Tocqueville, *Democracy in America*, 279.
25. Tawney, *Religion and the Rise of Capitalism*, 226.
26. Ibid., 228–229.
27. John Calvin quoted in Lipton, ed., *Reinhold Niebuhr: Major Works of Religion and Politics*, 501.
28. Tawney, *Religion and the Rise of Capitalism*, 245.
29. Ibid., 230.
30. Ibid., 266–267.
31. Sumner, *The Challenge of Facts and Other Essays*, 90.
32. Hofstadter, *Social Darwinism in American Thought*, 51, 66.
33. Spencer, *Social Statics*, 380.
34. Sumner, *What Social Classes Owe to Each Other*, 131.
35. Ibid., 101.
36. Sumner, *The Forgotten Man*, 79.
37. Sumner, *The Challenge of Facts and Other Essays*, 25.
38. Walsh, "Herbert Spencer: A Fallen Idol," in *Catholic World*, Vol. 105, 632.
39. Herrnstein and Murray, *The Bell Curve*, 526.
40. Ibid., 527–552.
41. Gould, "Curveball," in *The Bell Curve Wars*, 12.
42. Murray and Herrnstein, "Race, Genes and I.Q.—An Apologia," in *The New Republic* (October 31, 1994), 27.
43. Gould, "Curveball," *The Bell Curve Wars*, 13.
44. Ibid., 20–21.
45. Ibid., 11.
46. Mayer, "Union Membership Trends in the United States," in *Federal Publications*, Paper 174 (August 31, 2004), 12, <http://digitalcommons.ilr.cornell.edu/key_workplace/174/>.

47. Ibid.
48. The Republican presidential debate originally aired on CNN on June 13, 2011.
49. Olson, op cit., 68.
50. Montopoli, "Michele Bachmann: Health Care Law 'Crown Jewel of Socialism,'" in *cbsnews.com* (January 19, 2011).
51. Mansfield, "What Obama Isn't Saying," in *The Weekly Standard* 15:20 (February 8, 2010), <http://www.weeklystandard.com/articles/what-obama-isnt-saying>.
52. Mansfield did not bother to read the 2008 Democratic Party Platform, which says the following in its Preamble: "We believe that quality and affordable health care is a basic right."
53. Mansfield, "What Obama Isn't Saying."
54. Ibid.
55. Lincoln, "Fragment on Government," in *Selected Speeches and Writings*, 91.

CHAPTER 7

Conclusion

After the attacks on September 11, 2001, the British government loaned George W. Bush a bust of Winston Churchill which was prominently displayed in the Oval Office for the remainder of his presidency. It was not only a gesture of unity between the two countries in the aftermath of tragedy but also a reminder of their special relationship, forged in the struggle against fascism during World War II. No doubt the president hoped to draw inspiration from the visage of Churchill, who led his country through its darkest hours, most notably during the Battle of Britain.

What the president probably did not know was that his hero, the iconic Prime Minister and leader of the Conservative Party, played a significant role in the expansion of the British welfare state and, in particular, championed the creation of a universal health care system.[1] A Burkean conservative who always sought a balance between tradition and change, Churchill understood the necessity of using state power to solve collective action problems—that is, to do for the community what its people cannot do so well, if at all, on their own.

Churchill first recognized the advantages of the welfare state when he served as a cabinet minister under Prime Minister Herbert Henry Asquith. In 1908, he traveled to Germany, where he studied the workings and benefits of various government programs, and the following year, he published a collection of speeches, *Liberalism and the Social Problem*, in which he argued that state welfare was an essential corrective to the excesses of capitalism. Then, just two years later, Churchill worked alongside his peers in the Liberal Party, including Lloyd George, to pass the National Insurance

© The Author(s) 2016
R.J. Lacey, *Pragmatic Conservatism*,
DOI 10.1057/978-1-137-59295-8_7

Act of 1911. In particular, Churchill was responsible for spearheading the provision on unemployment insurance, but he also embraced with equal enthusiasm the section in the Act that created National Health Insurance for British workers. In a letter to George V, Churchill praised the Act as a vital instrument for political and social stability, calling it "far more important to the prosperity contentment & security of Your Majesty's Kingdom, than any other measure of our times."[2] Ardent in his belief that the National Insurance Act bolstered the market economy in his country and helped safeguard against the dreaded socialist alternative, Churchill would continue to support modest expansions of the welfare state during the inter-war period, pushing for laws that funded family allowances, school milk, public education, and pensions for widows and orphans.

Although these legislative achievements were worthy of celebration, Churchill understood that the British system of social insurance remained incomplete when he became Prime Minister in May of 1940. Most striking were the huge gaps in the health insurance scheme. Mainly covering male workers, National Health Insurance excluded most women and children, and even eligible beneficiaries of the scheme did not receive coverage for more costly medical treatments, including consultations with specialists, complicated diagnostic procedures, hospital stays, and major surgeries.[3] In 1942, the Coalition Government asked Sir William Beveridge to write a report that reviewed the existing systems of social insurance in the United Kingdom and that made recommendations for post-war reform. A Liberal economist who had worked for Churchill during the creation of the National Insurance Act of 1911, Beveridge called for a dramatic expansion of national insurance which would offer every single British citizen comprehensive protection from the vagaries of life, including poverty, unemployment, and illness. Published in December of 1942, the report enjoyed widespread support from the British people, who hoped to be repaid for their wartime sacrifices.

The report would also eventually receive the endorsement of the Prime Minister. "I personally am very keen that a scheme for the amalgamation and extension of our present incomparable insurance system should have a leading place in our Four Years' Plan," said Churchill in a radio broadcast on March 21, 1943. "[Y]ou must rank me and my colleagues as strong partisans of national compulsory insurance for all classes for all purposes from the cradle to the grave." In the same address, Churchill paid special attention to the issue of health care. "We must establish on broad and solid foundations a National Health Service," he declared. "Here let me say that there is no finer investment for any community than putting milk into babies. Healthy citizens are the greatest asset any country can have."[4]

In March of the following year, Churchill expressed his support for universal health insurance in more explicit terms. "The discoveries of healing science must be the inheritance of all. That is clear. Disease must be attacked, whether it occurs in the poorest or the richest man or woman, simply on the ground that it is the enemy," he said in an address to the Royal College of Physicians. "Our policy is to create a national health service in order to ensure that everybody in the country, irrespective of means, age, sex, or occupation, shall have equal opportunities to benefit from the best and most up-to-date medical and allied services available." He went on to praise his Government for proposing "a very large-scale plan" which only failed to garner "the attention of the whole country" because of everyone's understandable preoccupations with the war effort.[5] While the war remained the highest priority in the short term, Churchill clearly intended to place comprehensive health care reform at the top of the post-war policy agenda.

The underlying principle that inspired Churchill's call for an expanded welfare state was equality of opportunity. His discussion of education makes this abundantly clear. Churchill saw a "broader and more liberal" system of education as the linchpin to promoting social mobility, ensuring that class origins do not determine one's prospects in life. Although he dismissed as woefully misguided any efforts to create equality of ends, he exhibited a deep commitment to equality of opportunity. "Human beings are endowed with infinitely varying qualities and dispositions, and each one is different from the others. We cannot make them all the same," he said. "It is in our power, however, to secure equal opportunities for all." This was especially true in the realm of education.

> The facilities for advanced education must be evened out and multiplied. No one who can take advantage of a higher education should be denied this chance... We must make sure that the path to the higher functions throughout our society and Empire is really open to the children of every family. Whether they can tread that path will depend upon their qualities tested by fair competition. All cannot reach the same level, but all must have their chance. I look forward to a Britain so big that she will need to draw her leaders from every type of school and wearing every kind of tie.

Churchill evoked here an image of a future in which fairness would prevail and the elite would hail not just from a particular class but from all walks of life. Although turning this vision into reality would require significant investments in education, Churchill considered it an achievable and necessary goal in the modern era. After all, the future would belong to those "highly-educated races who alone can handle the scientific apparatus necessary for pre-eminence in peace or survival in war." Maintaining the traditional practices of exclusion, not only in education but also in other areas of life, would leave Britain behind the rest of the world.[6]

Although in principle he supported a generous welfare state that provided comprehensive social insurance and guaranteed equality of opportunity, Churchill cautioned against promising too much too fast. In a note written to the members of his cabinet in January of 1943, he warned of a "dangerous optimism" about what could be accomplished in the years after the war. "Unemployment and low wages are to be abolished, education greatly improved and prolonged; great developments in housing and health *will* be undertaken," he said. "The Beveridge plan of social insurance, or something like it, is to abolish want." Although Churchill supported the expansion of national insurance, providing coverage from the cradle to the grave for all British citizens, he believed that visions of the post-war future, especially those propagated by socialists in the Labour Party, were becoming downright utopian. He thought it prudent to manage expectations about the future by reminding people of the many challenges that lay ahead. In the years immediately after the war, he said, the United Kingdom would likely have to finance and maintain a large military, occupy the countries of its defeated enemies, improve conditions in its remaining colonies, and endure a lengthy period of rationing.[7]

These challenges did not foreclose the possibility of making significant post-war improvements, but they cast doubt on the "false hopes and airy visions of Utopia and Eldorado" with which the British people were being regaled. Churchill believed that responsible leadership required striking a balance between pessimism and optimism, between despair and fantasy. "While not disheartening our people by dwelling on the dark side of things," he said, "I have refrained so far from making false promises about the future." Churchill did not wish to dash the post-war hopes of the British people; he only wanted to make sure that they remained tethered to reality.[8]

But the results of the 1945 general election suggest that the British people were not interested in the realism dished out by the Tories. Now finding himself the leader of the opposition, Churchill spent the next six years attacking the economic policies of the Labour Party. He accused Labour of subscribing to "doctrinaire Socialism," which, in his view, hampered economic growth and created a fiscal crisis for the government. As his wartime speeches and memos demonstrate, Churchill favored a more active state that would provide cradle-to-grave social insurance and equality of opportunity. But he stood firm against the socialist impulse to nationalize significant portions of the economy. "We reject entirely the Socialist doctrine that the State should own and manage all the industry and commerce of the country," he said at a Conservative Party fete in 1948. While he acknowledged that the state had an important role to play in the economy, he castigated Labour for failing to see the benefits of a market economy. "[W]e hold that the mainspring of our industrial life must still be that free competition upon which our commercial greatness has been founded."[9]

Unfortunately, he said, the single-minded approach of the Labour Party brought about disastrous economic results. "Only one single new idea has been contributed by the false guides who have led us astray," he declared. "Only one. You know the one I have in mind. Nationalization. What an awful flop! Show me the nationalized industry which has not become a burden on the public either as taxpayers or consumers or both."[10] Having dramatically expanded the size and scope of government, the Labour Party found it necessary to raise revenue by way of "crushing taxation," which not only led the British government down the road to "financial bankruptcy" but also undermined individual initiative and enterprise.

For the most part, however, Churchill did not oppose the social policies for which the Labour Government received so much popular acclaim throughout Britain. He may have quibbled with the scale of the new programs passed by Labour, but he supported, at least in principle, much of what they accomplished. In fact, he bitterly resented the credit given to Labour for policy achievements that had been conceived by the Coalition Government over which he presided during the war years. "When we turn to the field of social legislation, we are confronted with ridiculous boastings. The Socialists dilate upon the National Insurance Scheme, Family Allowances, improved education, welfare foods, food subsidies, and so forth," he complained before more than one audience in 1948. But it was important to remember, he said, that "these schemes were devised and set in motion in days before the Socialists came into power" and that they "date from the National Coalition Government" of which he was the head. In order to drive home the point that an expanded welfare state did not originate with the Labour Party, he resorted to a little boasting. "I have worked at National insurance schemes almost all my life and am responsible for some of the largest measures ever passed," he said proudly.[11] This was no lie. For much of his career, Churchill supported social insurance schemes which "bring the magic of averages to the rescue of millions"—that is, use the tools of statistics to ensure that those in need receive help in times of need.[12]

It was actually because of his commitment to social insurance that Churchill opposed the National Health Service (NHS) Act of 1946 and rallied his party to vote against it. The Tories came out against it because it involved state control and ownership of the medical industry, turning doctors, nurses, and other health care workers into civil servants. Instead of socialized medicine, Churchill and many of his fellow Tories favored expanding the existent National Health Insurance program to bring about universal coverage—that is, creating what we would now call a single-payer system. That said, it should be noted that the Tories' resistance was tepid, certainly never reaching the heated level of Republican opposition to the Affordable Care Act. For one, they knew that a full-scale onslaught against a bill that enjoyed so much popular support was imprudent politically.[13] But it was also the case that many Tories, as Churchill put it, "supported in principle" what the NHS was trying to accomplish.[14]

So it should not come as a surprise that, after its passage, Churchill liked to claim credit for the creation of the NHS, insisting that the "main principles of the new Health Schemes were hammered out in the days of the Coalition Government." But he was also quick to blame the Labour Government, especially Minister of Health Aneurin Bevan, for having "plunged health policy into its present confusion."[15] The NHS suffered from cost overruns, according to Churchill, because of poor planning and administration.[16] This was certainly shrewd political maneuvering on Churchill's part—to take credit for the successes of the NHS but to place blame elsewhere for its failures—but it was not merely a Machiavellian ruse. Churchill was on record as a supporter of universal health care; he just had reservations about the NHS as it came to be under the Labour Government. Furthermore, he had a legitimate interest in reminding the British people that, despite Conservative opposition to the NHS and other schemes passed after the war, Labour did not have a monopoly on compassion for the working and middle classes, and that the recent achievements of the Labour Government had a lineage that could be traced back to the policy agendas of both Conservatives and Liberals.

When the Tories returned to power in 1951, Churchill was given the opportunity to prove that his rhetoric was more than just cheap political opportunism. Restored as prime minister, he now led a government controlled by the Conservatives outright. Without having to work directly with leaders of the other parties, as he had done under the Coalition Government, Churchill could have slashed or even repealed many of the programs for which Labour had worked so hard, including its crown jewel, the NHS. Only three years old when Churchill resumed control of the government, the NHS could have met an early death. Along with the British Medical Association (BMA), many Conservatives were eager to make that happen. But Churchill was not interested in answering to self-serving interest groups, especially the BMA, to which he was already quite hostile because of its resistance to the National Insurance Act of 1911. Nor did he succumb to the ideological rigidity to which many Conservatives were prone. It was clear even before the election that Churchill was not interested in killing the NHS. "I trust however that no one will in any way relax his or her efforts to make a success of the new Health scheme," he said at a constituency meeting in July of 1948. "It may be that there has been great carelessness and lack of foresight in its preparation…but no one should allow a great national scheme to suffer through the misbehavior of the Minister in charge."[17] To Churchill, the NHS was a "great national scheme" whose failures—including poor planning and wretched leadership—necessitated not its demise but reform.

It should come as no surprise, then, that Churchill returned to 10 Downing Street with the view that the NHS needed to be studied. He asked Cambridge economist Claude Guillebaud to head a committee that would assess the effectiveness of the NHS. The committee concluded that the NHS was very successful overall but needed more funding to ensure that it would remain so in the future. A pragmatist at heart, Churchill acknowledged the obvious merits of the program and decided to work with what he inherited. So, instead of threatening to dismantle the program because it did not agree with their policy preferences, the Tories under Churchill made their peace with the NHS and, per the recommendations of the Guillebaud committee, increased funding to build more clinics and hospitals. Under his watch Parliament also passed the National Insurance Act of 1954, which increased pensions for retirees and veterans and social insurance benefits by 23% across the board. These generous increases benefited roughly six million people.[18] In the end, Winston Churchill can be remembered for bolstering the NHS and, more generally, helping create and expand the modern welfare state in the United Kingdom.

Modern conservatives in the United States might not want to face this irrefutable truth about the hero whose bust graced the Oval Office of

George W. Bush. After all, Obama has done far less for the social welfare of Americans, yet it is conventional wisdom among conservative pundits and politicians in this country that he is a socialist. A logical mind would have to conclude that if Obama is a socialist, then Churchill was a Bolshevik. But, of course, he was nothing of the sort. Seeking a balance between tradition and reform throughout his distinguished career, Churchill was a descendant of Edmund Burke. In his address to the Royal College of Physicians, he located his call for universal health care in the context of tradition. "As between the old and the new, you have undoubtedly the advantage of antiquity," he said.

> This College must play its part in keeping alive the historic tradition of the medical profession, and must ever foster those high standards of professional behavior which distinguish a profession from a trade. This is what you have tried to do as an institution, for nearly 400 years. I confess myself to be a great admirer of tradition. The longer you can look back, the farther you can look forward. This is not a philosophical or political argument—any oculist will tell you this is true. The wider the span, the longer the continuity, the greater is the sense of duty in individual men and women, each contributing their brief life's work to the preservation and progress of the land in which they live, the society of which they are members, and the world of which they are the servants.[19]

He saw a direct link between the traditional calling of the medical profession and universal health care. Those who could look back and appreciate the storied career of medical care throughout the ages could also look forward and imagine a future with better health for all.

Ultimately, Churchill was interested in looking at the facts to determine what would produce the desired outcomes, but he also believed that, on the whole, change must be informed by tradition. The two had to work in tandem; one without the other would invite disaster. In a speech to the Royal Academy of Art, Churchill made the case for a balance between tradition and innovation. "Without tradition art is a flock of sheep without a shepherd," he said. "Without innovation it is a corpse."[20] As he made clear later in his address, he was not just talking about art. Whether they are doctors, artists, or statesmen, people must steer a middle course between the lessons of the past and the demands of the present. To reiterate what he said to the Royal College of Physicians, it was crucial that people devote themselves "to the preservation and progress of the land in which they live, the society of which they are members, and the world of which they are the servants."

Like Edmund Burke and his American heirs, Winston Churchill recognized that policy must be guided by experience, both past and present. He eschewed abstract doctrine and fought ideological extremism throughout his life. Nowhere can one find in his words or actions the tropes of modern American conservatism, such as small government, low taxes, and absolute property rights. As the leader of the opposition in the years after the war, he expressed his dismay about bloated government and excessive taxation and regulation, but only on practical grounds. He believed that these measures, while necessary in time of war, had outlived their usefulness. But he never turned his practical recommendations into absolute principle. In the years after the war, for example, Churchill certainly wanted to shrink the size and scope of government, but he never insisted that small government is always better.

Churchill's conservatism had little in common with that of William F. Buckley and his followers. While Churchill sought a delicate balance between preservation and progress, Buckley was a self-confessed radical, eager to overturn the established order. In an interview with political theorist Corey Robin, Buckley made a startling admission that revealed the revolutionary temperament behind his political commitments. When Robin asked him to imagine the "kind of politics" he might "embrace" if he were a young man fresh out of college at the turn of the twenty-first century, Buckley said, "I'd be a socialist. A Michael Harrington socialist... I'd even say a communist." Buckley could see a younger version of himself dedicated to various left-wing causes such as "global poverty" and "death from AIDS."[21]

Buckley's candid response suggests that by disposition he was a contrarian who opposed the status quo and hoped to undermine it. When he came of age in the early 1950s, he set his sights on the established liberal order. It stands to reason that, if he had come of age in our time, the Reagan legacy would have been his most likely target. Of course, only the gullible would accept Buckley's words at face value. One can imagine Buckley saying them with a gleam in his eyes, trying not so much to bear his soul as to provoke in a playful manner. But, even if glib or ironic, his comments still reveal a larger truth about the character of Buckley's brand of conservatism. It rests on a strong desire to overturn what had come before, to subvert established norms and institutions, and to impose a particular ideological blueprint on the political order.

Buckley's early career captures perfectly the hubris and recklessness of movement conservatism. Fresh out of college the young upstart first earned a reputation as an *enfant terrible* with the publication of *God and Man at Yale*, in which he called the tradition of academic freedom a sham that allowed professors to teach the evils of atheism and collectivism with impunity. He argued that the board of trustees at Yale, representing the values of most alumni, should fire any faculty member who failed to show his support for Christian values and capitalism. In *McCarthy and His Enemies*, Buckley and his co-author, L. Brent Bozell, praised the senator from Wisconsin for starting a popular movement that fought communist infiltration and made the elimination of all security risks in government a top priority. In their view, it hardly mattered that his demagoguery and false accusations might ruin the lives of innocent people and harm the very institutions he ostensibly tried to save, for the ever-present threat of communism made his unsavory methods necessary.

Buckley and Bozell acknowledged that McCarthyism was "in many respects as revolutionary as the Communist movement itself," but it did not concern them.[22] Indeed this is exactly how Buckley came to see himself—as a revolutionary. In 1957, Buckley appeared on a television show hosted by Mike Wallace and described himself as a "revolutionary against the present liberal order." When Wallace asked what he would specifically like to overthrow, Buckley replied, "Well, a revolution in the U.S.—or a counterrevolution—would aim at overturning the revised view of society pretty well brought in by FDR."[23] Buckley made it clear that he sought to subvert the political order created by the New Deal. He showed so little respect for tradition, those time-honored practices that grew out of the lessons of the past, that he expressed a revolutionary desire to uproot institutions created in response to the Great Depression simply because they disagreed with his abstract and uncompromising vision of justice.

Buckley has cast a long shadow over the history of American conservatism, stretching for more than half a century. His radical temperament and ideological rigidity have come to define conservatism as we know it. But, in this world of terminological confusion, the conservatives who have drawn inspiration from Buckley and his crowd actually have far more in common with the Jacobins, who stirred so much fear and loathing in the heart of Edmund Burke. A deeper appreciation for those American thinkers who have sustained the legacy of Burke and offered a more intellectually sophisticated and mature brand of conservatism might not only expose these Jacobins for what they truly are but also enrich the ongoing discussion about what it means to be a conservative. The failure to recognize the contributions of such thinkers as Walter Lippmann, Reinhold

Niebuhr, and Peter Viereck impoverishes our understanding of conservatism and, more generally, leaves out an important tradition in American political thought. In its modest way, this book has tried to restore this underappreciated tradition to its rightful place—and to help bring back a measure of sanity to our political discourse.

NOTES

1. For an overview of Churchill's support for the welfare state, see Watson, "The Forgotten Churchill," in *The American Scholar*.
2. Rintala, *Creating the National Health Service*, 19.
3. Ibid., 21.
4. Churchill, "Postwar Planning," in James, ed., *Winston S. Churchill: His Complete Speeches* (vol. 7), 6759–6761.
5. Ibid., "The Royal College of Physicians," 6895–6896.
6. Ibid., "Postwar Planning," 6761–6762.
7. Churchill, *The Hinge of Fate*, 838.
8. Ibid., 838–839.
9. Churchill, "Britain 'Floundering and Sinking,'" in James, ed., *Winston S. Churchill: His Complete Speeches* (vol. 7), 7675–7676.
10. Churchill, "Socialist Blunders," in James, ed., *Winston S. Churchill: His Complete Speeches* (vol. 8), 8227.
11. Churchill, "Conservative Women's Conference" and "Britain 'Floundering and Sinking,'" in James, ed., *Winston S. Churchill: His Complete Speeches* (vol. 7), 7628–7629, 7674.
12. Churchill liked this phrase and used it often. See, for example, Churchill, "Postwar Planning" and "A New Parliament," in James, ed., *Winston S. Churchill: His Complete Speeches* (vol. 7), 6760, 7679.
13. Rintala, *Creating the National Health Service*, 8–9, 132; Triggle, "The NHS—An Easy Birth?" in *BBC News*.
14. Churchill, "Perils Abroad and at Home," in James, ed., *Winston S. Churchill: His Complete Speeches* (vol. 7), 7715.
15. Ibid., "Conservative Women's Conference," 7629.
16. Ibid., "Conservative Women's Conference," "A New Parliament," and "Perils Abroad and at Home," 7628–7629, 7679–7680, 7715.
17. Ibid., "A New Parliament," 7679–7680.
18. Gilbert, *Winston S. Churchill: Never Despair, 1945–1965*, 1044, n. 2.
19. Churchill, "The Royal College of Physicians," in James, ed., *Winston S. Churchill: His Complete Speeches* (vol. 7), 6897.
20. Churchill, "Art," in James, ed., *Winston S. Churchill: His Complete Speeches* (vol. 8), 8474.

21. Buckley quoted in Robin, *The Reactionary Mind*, 129.
22. Buckley and Bozell, *McCarthy and His Enemies*, 281.
23. Buckley quoted in Judis, *William F. Buckley, Jr.*, 162. See also Bogus, *Buckley*, especially 100–104. Bogus does a wonderful job of capturing Buckley's radical temperament throughout his book.

BIBLIOGRAPHY

Bachmann, Michele. 2009. Giving more power where power is not due. *The Star Tribune*, December 10. http://www.startribune.com/opinion/79012857.html

Bell, Daniel. 1960. *The end of ideology*. Cambridge: Harvard University Press.

Bodein, Vernon P. 1944. *The social gospel of Walter Rauschenbusch*. New Haven: Yale University Press.

Bogus, Carl T. 2011. *Buckley: William F. Buckley Jr. and the rise of American conservatism*. New York: Bloomsbury.

Brooks, David. 2007. Obama, Gospel, and verse. *New York Times*, April 26.

Brown, Charles C. 1992. *Niebuhr and his age: Reinhold Niebuhr's prophetic role in the twentieth century*. Philadelphia: Trinity Press.

Brown, Stuart Gerry. 1955. Democracy, the new conservatism, and the liberal tradition in America. *Ethics* 66(1): 1–9.

Buckley, William F. 2002 [1951]. *God and man at Yale*. Washington, DC: Regnery Publishing.

Buckley, William F., and L. Brent Bozell. 1954. *McCarthy and his enemies*. Chicago: Henry Regnery.

Burke, Edmund. 1844. *Correspondence of the right honourable Edmund Burke*, 4 vols, ed. Charles William and Richard Bourke. London: Francis & John Rivington.

Burke, Edmund. 1981–2000. *The writings and speeches of Edmund Burke*, 8 vols, ed. Paul Langford. Oxford: Clarendon Press.

Burke, Edmund. 1985–1871. *The works of the right honorable Edmund Burke*, 12 vols. Boston: Little, Brown, & Company.

Burke, Edmund. 1986 [1790]. *Reflections on the revolution in France*. New York: Penguin Books.

© The Author(s) 2016
R.J. Lacey, *Pragmatic Conservatism*,
DOI 10.1057/978-1-137-59295-8

Burke, Edmund. 1998 [1777]. *A philosophical inquiry into the sublime and beautiful and other pre-revolutionary writings*. New York: Penguin Books.

Byrne, William F. 2011. *Edmund Burke for our time: Moral imagination, meaning, and politics*. DeKalb: Northern Illinois University Press.

Canavan, Francis P. 1987. *Edmund Burke: Prescription and providence*. Durham: Carolina Academic Press.

Chesterton, G. K. 1909. *Orthodoxy*. New York: John Lane Company.

Childs, Marquis, and James Reston (eds.). 1959. *Walter Lippmann and his times*. New York: Harcourt, Brace.

Churchill, Winston S. 1962 [1950]. *The hinge of fate* (volume 4 of the *The Second World War*). New York: Bantam Books.

Cobban, Alfred. 1960 [1929]. *Edmund Burke and the revolt against the eighteenth century*. London: Allen & Unwin.

Cogley, John. 1966. An interview with Reinhold Niebuhr. *McCall's Magazine* 93: 5.

Cone, Carl B. 1957/1964. *Burke and the nature of politics*, 2 vols. Lexington: University of Kentucky Press.

Conniff, James. 1994. *The useful cobbler: Edmund Burke and the politics of progress*. Albany: State University of New York Press.

Dam, Hari N. 1973. *The intellectual odyssey of Walter Lippmann*. New York: Gordon Press.

de Tocqueville, Alexis. 1988. *Democracy in America*. New York: Harper Perennial.

Dewey, John. 1927. *The public and its problems*. New York: Henry Holt and Company.

Diggins, John Patrick. 1994. *The promise of pragmatism*. Chicago: University of Chicago Press.

Diggins, John Patrick. 2011. *Why Niebuhr now?* Chicago: University of Chicago Press.

Dougherty, Michael Brendan. 2012. Obama's right wing. *The American Conservative*, July 23. http://www.theamericanconservative.com/articles/obamas-right-wing/

Eulau, Heinz. 1951. Mover and shaker: Walter Lippmann as a young man. *The Antioch Review* 11(3): 291–312.

Eulau, Heinz. 1952. Man against himself: Walter Lippmann's years of doubt. *American Quarterly* 4(4): 291–304.

Eulau, Heinz. 1954. Wilsonian idealist: Walter Lippmann goes to war. *The Antioch Review* 14(1): 87–108.

Eulau, Heinz. 1956. From public opinion to public philosophy: Walter Lippmann's classic reexamined. *American Journal of Economics and Sociology* 15(4): 439–451.

Ferguson, Charles. 2010. *Inside job*. New York: Sony Pictures Classics.

Forcey, Charles. 1961. *The crossroads of liberalism: Croly, Weyl, Lippmann, and the progressive era, 1900–1925*. New York: Oxford University Press.

Fox, Richard. 1985. *Reinhold Niebuhr: A biography.* New York: Pantheon Books.

Freeman, Michael. 1980. *Edmund Burke and the critique of political radicalism.* Chicago: University of Chicago Press.

Frohnen, Bruce. 1993. *Virtue and the promise of conservatism: The legacy of Burke and Tocqueville.* Lawrence: University Press of Kansas.

Gilbert, Martin. 1988. *Winston S. Churchill: Never despair, 1945–1965.* Boston: Houghton Mifflin.

Gladwell, Malcolm. 2005. The moral-hazard myth. *The New Yorker,* August 29. http://www.newyorker.com/archive/2005/08/29/050829fa_fact

Gould, Stephen Jay. 1995. Curveball. In *The bell curve wars,* ed. Steven Fraser. New York: Basic Books.

Guroian, Vigen. 1981. The possibilities and limits of politics: A comparative study of the thought of Reinhold Niebuhr and Edmund Burke. *Union Seminary Quarterly Review* 36(4): 189–203.

Guroian, Vigen. 1984. On revolution and ideology: Convergence in the political legacies of Niebuhr and Burke. *Union Seminary Quarterly Review* 39(1–2): 25–40.

Guroian, Vigen. 1985. The conservatism of Reinhold Niebuhr: The Burkean connection. *Modern Age* 29: 224–232.

Hamilton, Clive. 2009. Bush, God, Iraq and Gog. *Counterpunch,* May 22.

Hartz, Louis. 1955. *The liberal tradition in America.* New York: Harvest.

Hayek, Friedrich. 1960. *The constitution of liberty.* Chicago: University of Chicago Press.

Hayek, Friedrich. 1967. *Studies in philosophy, politics and economics.* Chicago: University of Chicago Press.

Hayek, Friedrich. 1971. *The road to serfdom.* London: Routledge.

Heimann, Eduard. 1956. Niebuhr's pragmatic conservatism. *Union Seminary Quarterly Review* 11(1): 7–8.

Herberg, Will. 1955. The three dialogues of man. *The New Republic,* May 16.

Herberg, Will. 1956. Christian apologist to the secular world. *Union Seminary Quarterly Review* 11(1): 11–16.

Herberg, Will. 1961. Reinhold Niebuhr: A Burkean conservative. *National Review,* December 2.

Herrnstein, Richard J., and Charles Murray. 1994. *The bell curve.* New York: Free Press.

Hobbes, Thomas. 1985. *Leviathan.* New York: Penguin Classics.

Hofstadter, Richard. 1955 [1944]. *Social Darwinism in American thought.* Boston: Beacon Press.

James, Robert Rhodes (ed.). 1974. *Winston S. Churchill: His complete speeches.* New York: Chelsea House Publishers.

Judis, John B. 1988. *William F. Buckley, Jr.: Patron saint of the conservatives.* New York: Simon & Schuster.

Kegley, Charles W., and Robert W. Bretall (eds.). 1956. *Reinhold Niebuhr: His religious, social, and political thought.* New York: Macmillan.

Kirk, Russell. 1967. *Edmund Burke: A genius reconsidered.* New Rochelle: Arlington House.

Kirk, Russell. 1985 [1953]. *The conservative mind from Burke to Eliot.* Washington, DC: Regnery Publishing.

Kramnick, Issac. 1977. *The rage of Edmund Burke: Portrait of an ambivalent conservative.* New York: BasicBooks.

Kramnick, Issac (ed.). 1999. *The portable Edmund Burke.* New York: Penguin Books.

Krugman, Paul. 2007. *The conscience of a liberal.* New York: W. W. Norton & Co.

Lasch, Christopher. 1965. *The new radicalism in America, 1889–1963: The intellectual as a social type.* New York: Knopf.

Lasch, Christopher. 1991. *The true and only heaven: Progress and its critics.* New York: W. W. Norton & Co.

Laski, Harold J. 1950 [1920]. *Political thought in England: Locke to Bentham.* London: Oxford University Press.

Lawler, Peter Augustine. 2002. Conservative postmodernism, postmodern conservatism. *Intercollegiate Review* 38(1): 16–25

Lester, Emile. 2014. British conservatism and American liberalism in midtwentieth century: Burkean themes in Niebuhr and Schlesinger. *Polity* 46(2): 182–210.

Lincoln, Abraham. 2009. *Selected speeches and writings.* New York: Library of America.

Linkins, Jason. 2012. Michele Bachmann points to Huma Abedin as Muslim Brotherhood infiltrator. *The Huffington Post,* July 17. http://www.huffingtonpost.com/2012/07/17/michele-bachmann-huma-abedin-muslim_n_1680083.html

Lippmann, Walter. 1910. An open mind: William James. *Everybody's Magazine* 23: 800–801.

Lippmann, Walter. 1913. *A preface to politics.* New York: Mitchell Kennerley.

Lippmann, Walter. 1914. *Drift and mastery.* New York: Mitchell Kennerley.

Lippmann, Walter. 1929. *A preface to morals.* New York: Macmillan.

Lippmann, Walter. 1934. *The method of freedom.* New York: Macmillan.

Lippmann, Walter. 1937. *The good society.* Boston: Little, Brown and Co.

Lippmann, Walter. 1944. *U.S. war aims.* Boston: Little, Brown and Co.

Lippmann, Walter. 1955. *Essays in the public philosophy.* Boston: Little, Brown and Co.

Lippmann, Walter. 1993 [1927]. *The phantom public.* New Brunswick: Transaction Publishers.

Lippmann, Walter. 1993 [1928]. *American inquisitors.* New Brunswick: Transaction Publishers.

Lippmann, Walter. 1997 [1922]. *Public opinion*. New York: Free Press.

Lock, F.P. 1998. *Edmund Burke*, vol. 1, 1730–1784. New York: Clarendon Press.

Lock, F.P. 2006. *Edmund Burke*, vol. 2, 1784–1797. New York: Clarendon Press.

Locke, John. 2002. *The second treatise of government and a letter concerning toleration*. New York: Dover Publications.

Lovin, Robin W. 1995. *Reinhold Niebuhr and Christian realism*. New York: Cambridge University Press.

MacAskill, Ewen. 2005. George Bush: 'God told me to end the tyranny in Iraq.' *The Guardian*, October 7.

Machiavelli, Niccolo. 2003 [1513]. *The Prince*. New York: Bantam Classics.

Madison, James. 2003. No. 10. In the *Federalist papers*. New York: Signet Classics.

Mansfield, Harvey. 2010. What Obama isn't saying. *The Weekly Standard* 15: 20, February 8. http://www.weeklystandard.com/articles/what-obama-isnt-saying

Mattson, Kevin. 2008. *Rebels all!* New Brunswick: Rutgers University Press.

Mayer, Gerald. 2004. Union membership trends in the United States. *Federal Publications*, Paper 174 (31 August 2004). http://digitalcommons.ilr.cornell.edu/key_workplace/174/

Mill, John Stuart. 1859. *On liberty*. London: John W. Parker and Son.

Miller, John J. 2005. Veering off course. *National Review*, October 26. http://www.nationalreview.com/articles/215772/veering-course/john-j-miller#

Montopoli, Brian. 2011. Michele Bachmann: Health care law 'crown jewel of socialism,' *cbsnews.com*.http://www.cbsnews.com/8301-503544_162-20028978-503544.html.

Morley, John. 1879. *Burke*. New York: Harper and Brothers.

Murray, Charles, and Richard J. Herrnstein. 1994. Race, genes and I.Q.—An apologia. *The New Republic*, October 31.

Nash, George H. 1976. *The conservative intellectual movement in America since 1945*. New York: Basic Books.

Niebuhr, Reinhold. 1927. *Does civilization need religion?* New York: Macmillan.

Niebuhr, Reinhold. 1933. After capitalism—What? *World Tomorrow* 16: 203–205, March.

Niebuhr, Reinhold. 1949a. *Faith and history*. London: Nisbet & Co.

Niebuhr, Reinhold. 1949b. *The nature and destiny of man, I & II*. New York: Charles Scribner's Sons.

Niebuhr, Reinhold. 1951. We need an Edmund Burke. *Christianity and Society* 16: 3.

Niebuhr, Reinhold. 1953a. *Christian realism and political problems*. New York: Charles Scribner's Sons.

Niebuhr, Reinhold. 1953b. Coronation afterthoughts. *Christian Century* 70: 771–772, July.

Niebuhr, Reinhold. 1954–1955. Liberalism and conservatism. *Christianity and Society* 20: 3–4.

Niebuhr, Reinhold. 1955a. *The self and the dramas of history*. New York: Charles Scribner's Sons.

Niebuhr, Reinhold. 1955b. Liberalism: Illusions and realities. *The New Republic*, July 4.

Niebuhr, Reinhold. 1958. *Pious and secular America*. New York: Charles Scribner's Sons.

Niebuhr, Reinhold. 1959a. The democratic elite and American foreign policy. In *Walter Lippmann and his times*, ed. Marquis William Childs and James Reston. New York: Harcourt, Brace.

Niebuhr, Reinhold. 1959b. *The structure of nations and empires*. New York: Charles Scribner's Sons.

Niebuhr, Reinhold. 1961. Unintended virtues of an open society. *Christianity and Crisis* 21: 137–138, July.

Niebuhr, Reinhold. 1965a. *Beyond tragedy*. New York: Charles Scribner's Sons.

Niebuhr, Reinhold. 1965b. *Man's nature and his communities*. New York: Charles Scribner's Sons.

Niebuhr, Reinhold. 1968. *Faith and politics*. New York: George Braziller.

Niebuhr, Reinhold. 2013 [1935]. *An interpretation of Christian ethics*. Louisville: Westminster John Knox Press.

Nietzsche, Friedrich. 1989 [1967]. *On the genealogy of morals and Ecce Homo*. Trans. Walter Kaufmann. New York: Vintage.

Obama, Barack. 2004 [1995]. *Dreams from my father*. New York: Random House.

Olson, Mancur. 1965. *The logic of collective action*. Cambridge, MA: Harvard University Press.

Orwell, George. 1950 [1949]. *1984*. New York: Signet Classics.

Paine, Thomas. 1995. *Collected writings*. New York: Library of America.

Pappin III, Joseph L. 1993. *The metaphysics of Edmund Burke*. New York: Fordham University Press.

Parkin, Charles. 1956. *The moral basis of Burke's political thought*. Cambridge: Cambridge University Press.

Reiss, Tom. 2005. The first conservative. *The New Yorker*, October 24.

Remnick, David. 2010. *The bridge: The life and rise of Barack Obama*. New York: Alfred A. Knopf.

Riccio, Barry D. 1994. *Walter Lippmann: Odyssey of a liberal*. New Brunswick: Transaction Publishers.

Rice, Daniel F. 2015. The fiction of Reinhold Niebuhr as a political conservative. *Soundings* 98(1): 59–83.

Rintala, Marvin. 2003. *Creating the National Health Service*. London: Frank Cass.

Robin, Corey. 2011. *The reactionary mind*. New York: Oxford University Press.

Rousseau, Jean-Jacques. 1987. *The basic political writings*. Indianapolis: Hackett Publishing Company.

Ryn, Claes G. 2003. *A common human ground: Universality and particularity in a multicultural world*. Columbia: University of Missouri Press.

Ryn, Claes G. 2005. "Peter Viereck and conservatism," introductory essay to *Conservatism revisited*. New Brunswick: Transaction Publishers.

Santayana, George. 1906. *The life of reason*, vol. 1 (*Reason in common sense*). New York: Charles Scribner's Sons.

Schlesinger, Jr., Arthur. 1953. The new conservatism in America: A liberal comment. *Confluence* 2: 61–71, December.

Schlesinger Jr., Arthur. 2000. *A life in the twentieth century: Innocent beginnings, 1917–1950*. New York: Houghton Mifflin.

Sifton, Elisabeth. 2005. *The serenity prayer: Faith and politics in times of peace and war*. New York: W. W. Norton & Co.

Sifton, Elisabeth (ed.). 2015. *Reinhold Niebuhr: Major works on religion and politics*. New York: Library of America.

Smith, Adam. 1976. *An inquiry into the nature and causes of the wealth of nations*. Oxford: Oxford University Press.

Spencer, Herbert. 1851. *Social statics*. London: John Chapman.

Stanlis, Peter J. 1958. *Edmund Burke and the natural law*. Ann Arbor: University of Michigan Press.

Stanlis, Peter J. 1991. *Edmund Burke: The enlightenment and revolution*. New Brunswick: Transaction Publishers.

Steel, Ronald. 1973. The world we're in. *The New Republic*, April 14.

Steel, Ronald. 1980. *Walter Lippmann and the American century*. Boston: Little, Brown and Company.

Strauss, Leo. 1971 [1953]. *Natural right and history*. Chicago: University of Chicago Press.

Sullivan, Andrew. 2006. *The conservative soul*. New York: HarperCollins.

Sumner, William Graham. 1884. *What social classes owe to each other*. New York: Harper and Brothers.

Sumner, William Graham. 1914. *The challenge of facts and other essays*. New Haven: Yale University Press.

Sumner, William Graham. 1919. *The forgotten man*. New Haven: Yale University Press.

Tanenhaus, Sam. 2009. *The death of conservatism*. New York: Random House.

Tawney, R.H. 1952 [1926]. *Religion and the rise of capitalism*. New York: Harcourt, Brace and Co.

Triggle, Nick. 2008. The NHS—An easy birth? *BBC News*, June 25. http://news.bbc.co.uk/2/hi/health/7405526.stm

Trilling, Lionel. 1950. *The liberal imagination*. New York: Viking.

Viereck, Peter. 1940. But—I'm a conservative! *The Atlantic Monthly*, April. http://www.theatlantic.com/magazine/archive/1940/04/but-im-a-conservative/304434/?single_page=true

Viereck, Peter. 1956. Niebuhr in the conformists' den. *The Christian Scholar* 39(3): 224–227.

Viereck, Peter. 2003. *Metapolitics*. New Brunswick: Transaction Publishers.

Viereck, Peter. 2004. *Unadjusted man*. New Brunswick: Transaction Publishers.

Viereck, Peter. 2005. *Conservatism revisited*. New Brunswick: Transaction Publishers.

Viereck, Peter. 2006. *Conservative thinkers*. New Brunswick: Transaction Publishers.

Viereck, Peter. 2007. *Shame and glory of the intellectuals*. New Brunswick: Transaction Publishers.

Viereck, Peter. 2008. *Strict wildness*. New Brunswick: Transaction Publishers.

Viereck Papers. 2006. (Rare Book and Manuscript Library at Columbia University).

Walsh, James J. 1917. Herbert Spencer: A fallen idol. *Catholic World* 105: 632–636.

Watson, George. 2011. The forgotten Churchill. *The American Scholar* 80 (Summer): 66–70.

Weingast, David Elliott. 1949. *Walter Lippmann: A study in personal journalism*. New Brunswick: Rutgers University Press.

West, Cornel. 1989. *The American evasion of philosophy*. Madison: University of Wisconsin Press.

White, Morton. 1957. *Social thought in America: The revolt against formalism*. Boston: Beacon Press.

White, Stephen K. 1994. *Edmund Burke: Modernity, politics, and aesthetics*. Thousand Oaks: Sage Publications.

Wills, Garry. 1979. *Confessions of a conservative*. Garden City: Doubleday.

Wolin, Sheldon. 2004. *Politics and vision*, expanded ed. Princeton: Princeton University Press.

Woolhandler, Steffie, Terry Campbell, and David Himmelstein. 2003. Costs of health care administration in the United States and Canada. *The New England Journal of Medicine* 349(8): 768–775.

World Health Organization. 2011. *World health statistics 2011*. http://www.who.int/whosis/whostat/2011/en/index.html

Wright, Benjamin F. 1973. *Five public philosophies of Walter Lippmann*. Austin: University of Texas Press.

INDEX

© The Author(s) 2016
R.J. Lacey, *Pragmatic Conservatism*,
DOI 10.1057/978-1-137-59295-8

Printed by Books on Demand, Germany